The Case For Coaching

Making evidence-based decisions

Jessica Jarvis is the CIPD Adviser on Learning, Training and Development.

David A. Lane is a coach and academic. He is visiting Professor to the School of Education at Middlesex University and has been an executive coach for twenty years. David is Research Director at the International Centre for the Study of Coaching at Middlesex University and Director of the Professional Development Foundation. He Chairs the BPS Register of Psychotherapy and is convenor of the EFPA Psychotherapy Group.

Annette Fillery-Travis is Senior Research Fellow at Middlesex University. Annette is Programme Director and research supervisor at the Professional Development Foundation. Her research career has spanned the clinical, natural and social sciences and she has over 70 publications in these literatures.

The Chartered Institute of Personnel and Development is the leading publisher of books and reports for personnel and training professionals, students, and all those concerned with the effective management and development of people at work. For details of all our titles, please contact the publishing department:

tel: 020–8612 6204
email: publish@cipd.co.uk
The catalogue of all CIPD titles can be viewed on the CIPD website:
www.cipd.co.uk/bookstore

The Case for Coaching

Making evidence-based decisions

Jessica Jarvis, David A. Lane and Annette Fillery-Travis

Chartered Institute of Personnel and Development

Published by the Chartered Institute of Personnel and Development,
151 The Broadway, London, SW19 1JQ

First published 2006

Typeset by Curran Publishing Services, Norwich, Norfolk

Printed in Great Britain by Cromwell Press, Trowbridge, Wiltshire

British Library Cataloguing in Publication Data
A catalogue of this publication is available from the British Library

ISBN 1 84398 134 3

ISBN-13 978 1 84398 134 3

Chartered Institute of Personnel and Development
151 The Broadway, Wimbledon, London SW19 1JQ
Tel: 020–8612 6200
Email: cipd@cipd.co.uk   Website: www.cipd.co.uk
Incorporated by Royal Charter.   Registered Charity No. 1079797

Contents

Part 2: Reviewing the evidence

Chapter 4: Does coaching work? An organisational perspective

Part 3: Evaluating the results and building the case for coaching

List of Case studies

List of Figures

List of Tables

Acknowledgements

The research for this book includes research that was commissioned by CIPD from the International Centre for the Study of Coaching, Middlesex University, together with independent research undertaken by the ICSC and its associates.

We would like to thank all the individuals and organisations who have participated in the research for this book. In particular we would like to thank:

- Paul Fisher, Full Potential Group
- Richard Uglow, Enrichyou Ltd
- David Anderson, BPB Paperboard
- Karen Boanas, Canada Life
- Gareth Jones, Courtenay HR
- Camilla Aitchison, Dixons Group
- Lynn Davidson, Everest
- Morag Mathieson, Glenmorangie Plc
- Angela Goldberg, formerly at the Greater London Authority
- Eunice Aquilina, BBC
- Nicky Hillier, High & Mighty
- Tracey Smith, Kwik-Fit Financial Services
- Jackie Hoare and Chris Wakerley, Boxwood
- Ross Gorbert, Bovis Lend Lease
- Ola Adams and Pamela Tilt, Nationwide
- Sara Ireland, formerly at Norfolk, Suffolk and Cambridgeshire Strategic Health Authority.
- Nigel Briers, Perkins Shibaura Engines Ltd
- Katrine Smith and Anjna Rughani, Panasonic Europe
- Stuart Haden, formerly at Selfridges & Co.
- Lester Desmond, Shell
- Jonathan Harding, Surrey and Sussex Strategic Health Authority
- Colin Coombs, Tate Museums
- Michael White, The Children's Society
- Roger Williams, United Utilities
- Isobel Aitchison, Glasgow Housing Association

- Steve Williamson, Pertemps Recruitment Partnership
- Donna Baddeley, Midland Area Housing Association
- Jackie Kernaghan, London School of Economics
- Clare Gardner, Rugby Cement
- Ellie Casey, Loughborough University
- Sharon Green, Stephenson Harwood
- Janet Tabor, Regal Fish Supplies
- John Turner, Blackrock International
- Nigel Hawke, T J International
- Peter Weller and Tony Pascoe, Castle Cement
- Ian Walker, Exeter County Council
- Neil Hounslow, Lloyds TSB
- Mike Chubb,
- Gerber Food Soft Drinks

We would also like to thank the following coaches and researchers who gave their time for the purposes of this research: Margaret Chapman, Anji Marychurch, Kate Cowie, Helen Pitcher, John O'Brien, Carol Braddick, Alison Williamson, Philip Pirie, Karen Izod, Graham Jones, Noreen Tehrani, James Marlar, Anthony Grant, David Megginson, David Clutterbuck, Robin Linecarr, Stephen Palmer, Paul Brankin, Jamie McDonald, and Alison Hardingham.

Introduction

We can now safely say that coaching isn't just another HR fad, despite its explosive growth in the last few years. It seems that coaching has arrived and is set to stay. CIPD research certainly suggests that coaching is a growing trend rather than a passing fashion. It is slowly but steadily diffusing through UK organisations and becoming an essential and valuable feature of their learning and development strategies. However, few organisations today, if any, would claim they have already successfully embedded coaching, but clearly many are investing heavily in order to head in that direction. What are their expectations about what coaching will deliver? And what are those expectations based on? Is there reliable evidence to support the belief in the effectiveness of coaching and to encourage organisations to invest?

A number of significant questions remain unanswered about the contribution of coaching to individual and organisational performance, the most significant one being whether any hard evidence exists that coaching actually works. With pressure to prove the value of coaching coming from all sides, a number of different stakeholders are now strongly committed to exploring how, and to what extent, coaching impacts on individual and business performance. They know that the extent to which coaching becomes a mainstream component of organisational practice is dependent on the degree to which coaching can be shown to improve business performance.

This is the starting point for this book. What does the research evidence that exists today tell us about the impact and power of coaching in organisational settings? Unfortunately, although worldwide interest in coaching has been high, research into the practice and impact of coaching in business settings appears to be lagging behind the practice itself. Rigorous research data is surprisingly hard to find, the specific literature on coaching in organisational settings being particularly sparse.

Examining the current research base offers far greater opportunities than just attempting to assess effectiveness or calculate a figure for return on investment. It allows us to examine the factors and processes involved in understanding 'how coaching works'. What are the features inherent in the design of coaching interventions that help to create and sustain real behaviour change, and how can this be mined to result in positive benefits for individuals and organisations as a whole? The answers that we obtain to this important question can help us determine what effective coaching practices look like, or at least give us some pointers in terms of what factors are likely to support or hinder the impact and effectiveness of coaching initiatives.

A step in the right direction

This book gathers together UK-based evidence on coaching to assess what it tells us about the impact and effectiveness of coaching in organisational settings. The chapters in Part 1 aim to set the scene by describing the current coaching landscape, the larger context for coaching within the wider field of learning and development, and the role of HR in coaching activities. Part 2 contains the central chapters of the book and reviews research available on four main themes:

- Coaching delivered by executive coaches
- Coaching delivered by managers
- Coaching delivered by internal coaches
- Organisational conditions for effective coaching.

Two further chapters present the findings of two original pieces of research – an analysis of questionnaires completed by our case study organisations about the results they have experienced from implementing coaching activities, and an analysis of responses from a sample of coaches about their views on the effective management and delivery of coaching in organisational settings. Throughout these central chapters we quote the experiences of our case study respondents (approximately 30 organisations) to support and fill in the gaps in the literature. Full versions of these case studies may be found in the Appendix at the very back of this book.

Towards the end of the book, in Part 3, we pull together the themes from the research and case studies and offer advice in evaluating coaching activities and making the case for coaching. Hopefully, by making a strong case you can create enthusiasm, support and buy-in to coaching from all your stakeholders and thus smooth the way for effective coaching practices.

When planning and writing this book, the main questions we wanted to address were:

- Does coaching work?
- Is there any hard evidence that it impacts on individual and organisational performance?
- How does coaching work?
- What helps or hinders the success of coaching initiatives?
- What are the lessons learned so far from those who have been involved in the delivery and management of coaching in organisational settings?
- How can we use the available research evidence to make the case for coaching?

Answering these questions is a tough remit for this book. But although we can only report on the evidence base that exists today, it should at least provide an initial framework of information that can be used when making the case for coaching in your organisation, and should help you evaluate your success and improve your practices. It would be impossible to report the full findings of all the research studies that have been reviewed for this book (unless it was extremely long!), but we have tried to select studies that are representative of the research available.

This book will therefore be useful reading for practitioners trying to make the case for introducing coaching in their organisations, as well as for those currently using coaching but who want to manage their coaching activities more effectively and learn from the experiences of others. It will also be of interest to coaches themselves who want to be able to make an evidence-based and business-focused case when they are trying to sell their services to HR buyers. We hope you all find it useful.

Part 1

Setting the scene

1

Setting the scene for coaching: the current landscape

Coaching has received a great deal of attention in recent years because it offers organisations a win/win solution to the development of their workforce. It has the scope to help individuals reach their potential while also improving the productivity and competitiveness of the business as a whole. Although the popularity and heightened visibility of coaching has certainly been fuelled by the media, this is not wholly the reason for its success. Many characteristics of contemporary organisational life have contributed to the burgeoning attractiveness of coaching, including the rapid pace of change, which means that employees have continually to adjust and adapt their skill sets, and flatter organisational structures that require individuals to make large step-changes in performance when promoted or making other job moves (see Figure 1).

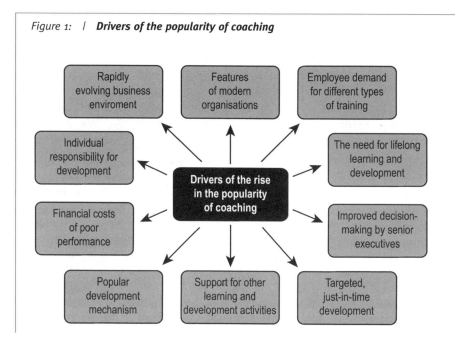

Figure 1: | *Drivers of the popularity of coaching*

It's an exciting time to be involved in coaching. The industry has reached a crossroads and is at a new stage in its maturation. There has been considerable progress in our understanding of how to effectively manage and deliver coaching. And people are starting to accept that coaching is not just a 'nice to have' learning initiative – it is something that has the potential to make a significant contribution to their business.

Now that the initial hype and excitement is dying down, we must ensure that coaching does not become another flash-in-the-pan HR activity that fails to fulfil its potential. Most notably, we need to demonstrate that coaching is having a significant impact both on individual and organisational performance.

THE METEORIC RISE OF COACHING

Before we take a closer look at organisations' use of coaching today, let's remind ourselves of its progress to date. Those of us who have been monitoring the rise of coaching over the last few years are well aware of the hype and self-promotion that has frequently surrounded it. And we have seen the problems caused by people entering the market calling themselves coaches but lacking the necessary training, experience and knowledge base. Both of these issues have marred the reputation of coaching and have led to a degree of wariness and cynicism from the business community. There has also been a degree of in-fighting between related professional bodies and associations as they vie for status and position. Without a leading industry body and a clear voice of authority, there are few objective sources of information, guidance and advice for practitioners.

HR practitioners have been on the receiving end of this, trying to make sense of it all. Because of the relatively recent emergence of coaching, few HR professionals have in-depth expertise of managing coaching activities and few understand how to make the best use of it. The CIPD surveyed its members and found that they were finding it an uphill struggle (CIPD, 2004). The vast majority report that finding high-quality coaches is 'a difficult task', the lack of regulation 'worrying', and the terminology confusing and off-putting (CIPD, 2004). All in all, HR practitioners are battling with a variety of issues that stop them gaining full value from their coaching activities. Also among the problems reported are a lack of agreement about what a good coach is, engaging different stakeholders in coaching relationships, and evaluating the impact of activities. All of these are significant challenges for HR professionals as they work to draw up a framework to ensure value for money and alignment with their organisation's strategic objectives. Many feel that the complexity of the coaching marketplace and its rapid pace of development is a nightmare for HR practitioners navigating through it.

The problem has never really been with the idea or concept of coaching itself. Few people would deny the value of one-to-one consultation and support for an individual's development. This approach has a long and successful history in organisational training and development, being a key feature of a wide array of activities including personal effectiveness programmes, 360-degree feedback, career counselling and, more recently, mentoring schemes. The scepticism that has plagued coaching has probably come about because of its rapid rise and the resulting flurry of excitement. Coaching has become the largest growth area in HR development activity and sceptics are still waiting for it to falter.

But, gradually, coaching has started to shake off some of its negative press. Those within the industry have been doing their bit. Coaches are keen to raise the reputation of their industry and weed out practitioners who operate unethically. And professional bodies and associations have been working enthusiastically on codes of practice, ethics, guidelines and standards to raise levels of practice. From the demand side, organisations have realised they need a more discerning and educated approach to managing their coaching activities and in dealing with the still fragmented and confusing coaching industry. By setting themselves high standards – of practice, expectations and outcomes – at procurement, they have helped to improve levels of practice. A lot has been learned and progress has been made, but there is still a long way to go.

THE CURRENT SNAPSHOT

So what is the picture today? Because the pace of coaching has moved so rapidly, it has been a challenge to keep track of its progress and use in organisational settings. In the last few years, the CIPD's annual learning, training and development surveys have given us a rich source of information about the coaching marketplace, the 2006, 2005 and 2004 survey reports providing significant evidence about current trends and issues. The research from the 2004 survey was reported in the CIPD Guide *Coaching and Buying Coaching Services* (Jarvis, 2004), but this information has now been updated and extended for this book, taking in the latest 2006 and 2005 findings. The evidence paints an unequivocal picture of the progress of coaching in UK organisations and identifies a number of underlying issues.

The use of coaching now and in the future

The survey findings highlight the undeniable growth of coaching and illustrate its growing role in contemporary learning and development strategies. Coaching is no longer the preserve of a small minority of organisations. Table 1 shows that coaching by line managers is used by almost nine in ten respondent organisations, and that coaching by external practitioners is used by almost two in every three.

Table 1: | *The percentage of organisations using coaching*

Type of coaching	Percentage of respondents reporting using it
Coaching by line managers	88
Coaching by external practitioners	64

Source: CIPD (2005)

And the use of coaching is not yet at its peak. Respondents to the 2005 CIPD survey indicated that coaching activities, with e-learning, represent the largest growth areas in training and development activities. Coaching by line managers looks set to increase significantly over the next few years, almost three-quarters of respondents reporting that they expect to increase their use of these activities, and only 1 per cent expecting to reduce their efforts in this area (Table 2).

Table 2: | ***Expected change in use of coaching over the next few years (per cent)***

Type of coaching	Increase	Decrease	Stay the same
Coaching by line managers	74	1	25
Coaching by external practitioners	36	13	51

Source: CIPD (2005)

Interestingly, there are some signs of a slowing in demand for external coaching. Thirteen per cent anticipate some decrease in activity and only a third expect an increase. External coaches will always be an important resource for organisations because few managers have the same level of expertise and breadth of experience that external coaches offer (as well as their perceived greater neutrality and confidentiality), but it seems that the major focus for the next few years is building internal coaching expertise by developing the skills of managers and internal coaches.

A major area of current focus for UK organisations appears to be developing a coaching culture. This trend was tracked in the 2006 CIPD survey and the results indicated that there is a buzz of activity in this at the moment. Eighty per cent of respondents using coaching claim that their organisation aspires to develop a coaching culture, and 75 per cent report investing time, resources and effort into achieving this aim (CIPD, 2006).

Strategy and objectives: what is driving organisations to use coaching?

Although use of coaching is widespread in UK organisations, we have not yet reached a stage at which the majority of organisations have fully integrated and successfully organised their coaching activities. Two-thirds of organisations report that they do not have a formal strategy for their coaching activities, and only 6 per cent claim to have one that covers all their staff (CIPD, 2004).

Although every organisation will have its own motives for introducing and using coaching, CIPD research, through respondents' most commonly reported reasons, provides us with a strong flavour of what these are. By far the three most frequently cited objectives of coaching activities are to improve individual performance, productivity and skills. The research helps us put some of the coaching sales propaganda into perspective. For example, other reported organisational benefits of coaching such as improving staff retention, reducing the costs of training, and helping employees achieve work–life balance, hardly register at all as objectives for using coaching (Table 3).

*Table 3: | **Objectives for organisations' use of coaching***

	Percentage of respondents reporting this as a main objective
Improving individual performance	78
Dealing with underperformance	30
Improving productivity	28
Career planning/personal development	27
Growing future senior staff	26
Fostering a culture of learning and development	24
Motivating staff	21
Accelerating change in the organisation	16
Demonstrating the organisation's commitment to staff	16
Improving staff retention	10
Reducing the cost of sending staff to external courses	9
Helping staff to achieve better work–life balance	5
Satisfying demand for coaching from employees	2

Source: Training and Development 2004 (CIPD, 2004)

The 2006 CIPD survey evidence provides further insights into the rationale for investing in coaching, but in specific reference to developing a coaching culture. It seems likely that organisations are seeking to develop organisational cultures characterised by coaching because they believe it will aid their performance. This is confirmed by the survey findings – 93 per cent of respondents using coaching believe that a coaching culture is either 'very important' or 'important' to the success of their organisation (CIPD, 2006). And the results show that improving individual and business performance are again the main objectives for developing a coaching culture (72 per cent).

Looking forward, coaching is likely to play a major role in leadership development activities for UK organisations. Although coaching is not the most frequently used activity for developing leaders (about one-third report using internal and external executive coaches as part of leadership development activities), it is considered to be among the most effective. External executive coaching is considered to be the third most effective means of developing leaders, 84 per cent of respondents rating it as effective. Internal executive coaching is not far behind, 80 per cent considering it to be an effective means of development for senior executives (CIPD, 2005). With two-thirds of organisations reporting a shortage of effective leaders, it seems likely that executive coaching may continue to be an area of growth in the next few years.

Who is involved in the delivery of coaching?

There are numerous types and contexts for coaching, including 'corridor coaching', manager coaching, executive coaching, team coaching, and so on. Organisations are therefore using a combination of internal and external practitioners to deliver the coaching that is required.

This includes external coaches, specialist internal coaches, line managers and peers, as well as members of the HR department (see Figure 2).

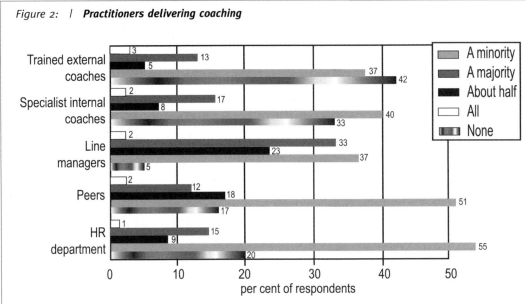

Figure 2: | *Practitioners delivering coaching*

Source: CIPD Training and Development 2004

Organisations are increasingly prepared to develop coaching skills within the organisation in order to build capacity and internal expertise. The majority of coaching is provided for middle and junior managers and is delivered by internal resources, primarily by line managers. Executive coaching, although heavily promoted and discussed in the media, is actually only a minority activity on the spectrum of corporate coaching. Use of external coaches tends to be reserved for coaching senior-level or high-potential employees or to help organisations build coaching capabilities within the organisation via the design and delivery of internal coaching skills programmes.

With regard to developing a coaching culture, it seems that organisations are taking a variety of different approaches to advancing their internal expertise. Forty-seven per cent indicated that they are training line managers to act as coaches, while 18 per cent said they are providing coaching via a network of internal and external coaches. Thirty-five per cent reported that they are taking a dual approach and implementing both coach-training for managers and coaching via internal and external coaches (CIPD, 2006).

Does coaching work?

When asked about effectiveness, 84 per cent regard coaching by line managers as 'effective' or 'very effective', while 92 per cent judge coaching by external practitioners to be effective. Interestingly, although coaching by line managers is more widespread, coaching by external coaches is considered to be more effective as a means of learning (Table 4).

*Table 4: | **The perceived effectiveness of different training methods***

	Very effective	Effective	Not very effective	Not effective at all
Coaching by line managers	19	65	16	0
Coaching by external practitioners	23	69	8	0

Source: CIPD (2005)

The 2005 survey evidence supports the high level of belief in coaching reported by the HR community in the previous year's survey. As Table 5 demonstrates, HR practitioners strongly believe that coaching is an effective way of promoting learning and can have an impact on the organisation's bottom line. If managed effectively, coaching is believed to have the ability to deliver tangible benefits to individuals and the organisations they work for.

*Table 5: | **The benefits of coaching***

	Percentage of respondents who agree
Coaching can deliver tangible benefits to both individuals and organisations	99
Coaching is an effective way to promote learning in organisations	96
Coaching and mentoring are key mechanisms for transferring learning from training courses back to the workplace	93
When coaching is managed effectively it can have a positive impact on an organisation's bottom line	92

Source: CIPD (2004)

The impact of coaching on organisational culture is also believed to be very beneficial – 93 per cent of respondents using coaching believe that a coaching culture is either 'very important' or 'important' to the success of their organisation (CIPD, 2006).

Altogether, these results form a very positive endorsement by the HR community of coaching as a means of learning. However, despite the widespread use of and belief in coaching, there is still a lot of work to be done if the positive beliefs about the potential contribution of coaching are to be realised. Few organisations have a strategy for their activities – only 5 per cent of respondents claim to have 'all' their line managers trained to coach their team members – and, worryingly, very little evaluation is taking place. Unless coaching is managed and designed effectively, the results may not measure up to expectations. If we let this happen, coaching could become increasingly bedevilled by accusations of hype and false claims of success.

LOOKING FOR ANSWERS: DOES COACHING WORK?

Coaching is not a cheap option. There are significant costs involved in implementing coaching initiatives, not least in terms of the time and effort of the people who get involved.

However, if we have substantial evidence to suggest that the gains from coaching far outweigh the costs, organisations will not be deterred from investing in coaching. But this is a big 'if'. Is there reliable evidence to support the belief in the effectiveness of coaching and to encourage organisations to invest?

Until coaching can answer its critics by revealing evidence of the value it delivers to organisations, such questions are unlikely to go away. The continuing success and belief in coaching is likely to be determined by its ability to deliver demonstrable value. As Neil Offley, Programme Director at the NHS Leadership Centre, commented in the CIPD guide (Jarvis, 2004):

> *We hope that evaluation and research will help show how coaching can deliver real benefits, and overcome a perception of it being the latest fad.*

To counter criticisms and avoid being labelled 'cowboy coaches', coaching professionals are increasingly asking searching questions about the theoretical foundation of their services. Consumers of coaching services have grown progressively more sophisticated and have started to use more rigorous coach assessment and selection processes. They are also requesting facts and data about the effectiveness of coaching. As a result, there has been a significant push for coaches to ground their services in evidence-based approaches and a call for more research on the impact of coaching in a variety of organisational settings.

This is the core purpose of this book. What does the research evidence that exists today tell us about the impact and power of coaching in organisational settings? We want to know how organisational coaching affects the lives of individuals. What do individuals who have been coached say about the impact of coaching on their work, relationships and personal development? And what evidence is there that any success at the individual level filters down to produce positive benefits at an organisational level that can be seen to alter performance and results?

REVIEWING THE EVIDENCE

Coaching-specific research is the core and lifeblood of an emerging profession.

Grant (2004)

There are many unresolved issues facing practitioners trying to implement and support coaching in their organisations. We know that expecting unprepared, untrained and unsupported managers to coach their teams does not work. But how exactly should managers be trained in order to be effective coaches, and what are the best means of gaining their buy-in and support? We know that choosing and managing coaches requires forethought and expertise on the part of the HR buyer, but what are the criteria that really matter when choosing coaches? Research tells us that many people have a strong belief in the power of coaching, but what are the actual means by which coaches facilitate and support change? And what does this tell us about how to design processes and systems for building coaching capability within an organisation?

Although worldwide interest in coaching has been high, research into the practice and impact of coaching in business settings appears to be lagging behind the practice itself. There is a broad base of research about coaching more generally, particularly from the sports world and in educational settings, and this does tend to suggest that coaching is effective in improving aspects of an individual's behaviour. There is also a wealth of research relating to specific elements of coaching, such as the use of specific techniques/tools (eg goal-setting). But much less is known about the impact of coaching in business settings. Rigorous research data is surprisingly hard to find, the specific literature on coaching in organisational settings being particularly sparse. Many researchers have experienced and expressed these difficulties. For example, Horner (2002) comments:

> *There was surprisingly little empirical research on the efficacy of executive coaching in the practice of management and leadership. This is particularly so for the practice of coaching by external coaches, although this lack of empirical foundation has not inhibited practitioners or authors from advocating their approaches or publishing their views.*

If coaching is to be taken seriously, it is essential that it is based in sound research evidence and theory. This is not just something for 'ivory tower' academics working in universities. It should concern everyone who is involved in coaching because it is crucial to their credibility. As Anthony Grant argues (Grant, 2004):

> *Evidence-based coaching is not complex or ethereal. At its simplest it involves the intelligent and conscientious use of best current knowledge in making decisions about how to design, implement and deliver coaching interventions to clients and in designing and teaching coach training programmes.*

We hope that the information contained in this book will be a step forward in arming HR practitioners with current knowledge about the impact of coaching in organisational settings, and building their understanding about what factors can help and hinder effectiveness. This information can then be used as an input for decisions about the design and implementation of effective coaching interventions.

2

Making the wider case for learning and development

Before we start to consider the case for coaching it is important to position it firmly within the wider field of learning and development. Identifying, developing and retaining talent are now pervasive issues for all organisations. It is widely accepted that organisations' intangible assets (ie their human capital) are crucial for building long-term value and building a flexible and agile base to support future growth. Employee and organisational learning have stepped forward into the limelight in recent years as organisations have realised that the ability of an organisation to respond quickly and flexibly to change is largely dependent on the capability of its employees to learn, adapt and evolve.

The global and competitive nature of the business world has increased the drive for productivity and performance in the UK. As a result, organisations are closely examining the different facets of the puzzle of productivity and performance. An area receiving a great deal of attention is how well workforces are being managed with these goals in mind. HR practices, including learning and development activities, are being scrutinised because of their contribution to the support and motivation of employees to deliver high performance.

As a range of growing competitive pressures mount, organisations are realising that to succeed, they require managers and leaders who can hold the organisation together and maintain staff morale through times of change. In addition, they need employees at all levels who are willing and flexible enough to embrace change and quickly adapt and develop their skills. As a result, the question of how to deliver effective and swift employee development has taken centre stage.

PROOF AT LAST: HR PRACTICES DO HAVE AN IMPACT ON ORGANISATIONAL PERFORMANCE

Evidence has been stacking up in recent years to support the belief that HR practices such as learning and development activities can impact on organisational performance. One such example is the research agenda focused on high-performance work practices – a subject the CIPD has been monitoring for the last few years, and one that is steadily gaining popularity. High-performance working involves implementing a range of HR practices and policies to engage, involve and motivate employees in order to heighten their contribution and raise levels of productivity and performance across the organisation as a whole.

Although a range of HR practices and policies are regarded as high-performance work practices, most commentators would agree that flexibility and continuous learning lie at the heart of the performance impact of the high-performance working approach. Studies undertaken all over the world have shown that investment in high-performance work practices and the skills associated with them improves productivity and impacts on the bottom line (EEF and CIPD, 2003). This has given the HR community a firm basis for believing in the contribution of HR practices to organisational performance.

So how do learning and development practices actually improve business performance?

Despite the emergence of a significant body of research that demonstrates a relationship between people management and company performance, it still was not clear, until quite recently, how that relationship worked. Then a ground-breaking research study by the CIPD was published in 2003. *Understanding the People and Performance Link: Unlocking the black box* (Purcell *et al*, 2003) examined the mechanisms by which HR practices lead to improved organisational performance. Its findings help us understand why HR practices, and particularly learning and development activities, are vital for maximising employee skills and contribution.

The research found that employees' job performance is a result of their *ability*, their *motivation* to engage with their work, and the *opportunity* to deploy their ideas, abilities and knowledge effectively. Learning and development activities contribute to enhanced employee performance by creating opportunities to improve the motivation and skill levels of employees (Figure 3). Furthermore, if employees are satisfied with the training and development opportunities they receive, their commitment, motivation and job satisfaction are likely to be significantly higher. Motivation is seen to be absolutely critical. As Reynolds (2004) states in the CIPD research text *Helping People Learn*:

Even skilled employees provided with superb information will not contribute to organisational success if they are not motivated to act in the best interests of the organisation.

Figure 3: | *How learning and development activities can impact on business performance*

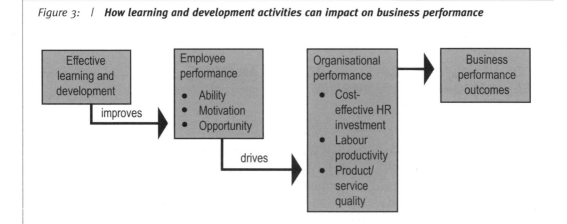

But alongside this, the crucial factor linking HR practices to organisational performance identified in the research was the way that HR practices build employee commitment and encourage employees to undertake 'discretionary' behaviour This is when committed employees seek to excel in their work and put considerable effort into helping achieve the goals of the organisation.

Discretionary behaviour defined

Making the sort of choices that often define a job, such as the way the job is done – the speed, care, innovation and style of job delivery. This behaviour is at the heart of the employment relationship because it is hard for the employer to define, monitor and control the amount of effort, innovation and productive behaviour required.

Purcell et al (2003)

This is where some commentators argue that learning and development practices have such an important role to play. Learning and development is not just another input to the people and performance model. Instead, it pervades the whole model by helping to create the conditions in which employees are more likely to engage in discretionary behaviour. The box below describes how learning and development initiatives such as coaching can contribute to the model.

How development activities such as coaching can help to build commitment and promote discretionary behaviour
- They develop employee skills in line with organisational objectives.
- They engage employees with their work, make them feel valued and foster commitment to the organisation.
- They promote self-responsibility and initiative.
- They facilitate adaptation to new challenges and change.
- They accommodate and support employees' obligations to their home lives so that they are productive and effective while they are at work.

In addition to creating a suitable climate for discretionary behaviour, one of the most important forms of discretionary behaviour for contemporary organisations is 'discretionary learning'. This is when individuals proactively seek to learn and develop their skills and abilities to enhance their capacity to do their job. This is at the heart of organisations' competitive advantage through people and is something that all organisations should be aiming to achieve.

Learning and training are vitally important in influencing employee attitudes and motivation, helping to create discretionary behaviour and improving performance. By collectively improving the performance of many employees, learning and development activities can enable the organisation to achieve superior performance in terms of workforce productivity, quality, innovation and customer satisfaction. The good news is that gaining buy-in and support for learning and development is no longer such an uphill struggle. There is a growing recognition of the importance of effective learning and development to business success.

A CHANGING LANDSCAPE FOR LEARNING AND DEVELOPMENT

Given the fast pace of change, employees must be encouraged and supported to continually update their skills and gain knowledge. How to do this – how to help people learn – has been the focus of a long-term research programme at the CIPD. Encouraging employees to learn and develop helps an organisation remain flexible in the face of uncertain future conditions. We have observed a shift in learning and development philosophy and thinking from an approach based on the delivery of training to one based on support and encouragement for individual learning. Reynolds (2004) describes this as a 'shift from training to learning' (Figure 4).

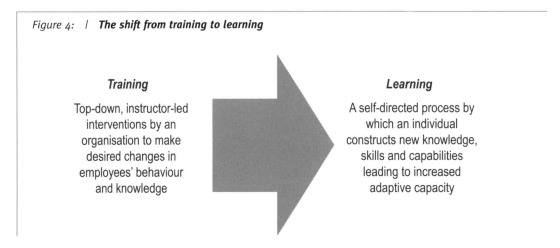

Figure 4: | *The shift from training to learning*

Training

Top-down, instructor-led interventions by an organisation to make desired changes in employees' behaviour and knowledge

Learning

A self-directed process by which an individual constructs new knowledge, skills and capabilities leading to increased adaptive capacity

Learning can be understood as the process by which an individual constructs new knowledge, skills and capabilities, whereas training is one of several responses an organisation can undertake to promote learning.

By its very nature, learning is an individual process – no one but the learner can learn. But it is possible to put in place interventions that encourage people to learn and develop. In the shift from training to learning, we are seeing learning and development interventions and activities that increasingly focus on supporting the learner. Too often in the past organisations have attempted to develop their workforces without developing the learning skills of staff, or motivating them to learn through consideration of their perspective – the 'what's in it for me' factor. Individual responsibility for learning (with assistance from the organisation in supporting learners) is now being promoted to address the balance. Significant efforts are also being made to support and encourage effective individual learning. Ninety-six per cent of respondents to the CIPD's 2004 training and development survey agreed that individuals need advice and support if they are to take more responsibility for their own learning. Such interventions and activities are part of an integrated approach to creating competitive advantage through the people in the organisation.

Evidence from the CIPD's annual training and development surveys supports this trend and indicates that we are in the middle of a profound shift in attitude and practice relating to organisational learning and development. The traditional response to learning in organisations has been to send employees on training courses. However, several limitations of this approach are now becoming apparent and a total reliance on formal classroom-based training is now a rarity. Learning and development professionals are using a much larger kitbag full of different activities and techniques. There has been a huge increase in the use of coaching, mentoring and e-learning in the last few years (see Figure 5).

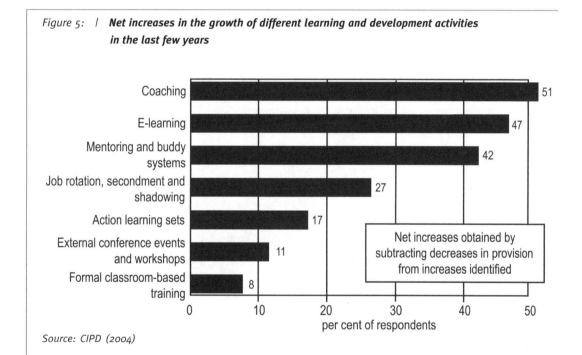

Figure 5: / **Net increases in the growth of different learning and development activities in the last few years**

Source: CIPD (2004)

Moreover, the popularity of concepts like blended learning and learning styles signifies the growing acceptance of the need for tailored approaches to employee development. All in all, a more developmental and individual-centred approach appears to be coming to the fore.

Organisations are also placing enormous importance on creating cultures that support learning and development. In fact, more than 70 per cent of organisations rate this among the three most important factors in supporting effective learning. And when asked to identify the single most important thing an organisation can do to promote learning, the overwhelming theme that emerged was the need for an organisational culture that supports learning. Other responses to this question are shown in the box overleaf.

Example responses to the question 'What is the single most important thing an organisation can do to promote learning?' (CIPD 2004)

Views from the front line

A learning culture:
A committed and supportive learning environment – without this nothing happens.
Promote an organisational culture in which individuals take responsibility for their learning and see it as an essential part of their day-to-day work.

The role of managers:
Clear understanding by managers of their role in developing their staff.
Develop line managers to have the skills and motivation to encourage and support learning.
Make 'developing others' part of a line manager's annual performance objectives.
Ensure that line managers are committed and rewarded for learning and development activities.

Adequate resources:
Ensure adequate resources are available for development.
Give employees time during the working day to 'learn'.

Encouragement for learning:
Make it an enjoyable and worthwhile experience.
Encourage employees to see their career and learning as their own responsibility.
Make it interesting so the value is communicated by word of mouth.
Sell the benefits of learning: What's in it for the learner? What's in it for the company?
Encourage individuals to discuss training needs and to keep an up-to-date personal development plan.

Understanding employee preferences:
Offer learning that will benefit the employees in their current role as well as providing opportunities to acquire skills for their continuing professional development.
Be open to learners' ideas of what works best for them – throw away the 'one-size-fits-all' attitude and think outside the box.
Recognise that different people 'prefer' to learn in different ways – providing different pathways to learning is crucial to developing self-motivation to learn.

Senior management commitment:
Acceptance at a senior level that learning is important – this should be widely communicated.
Commitment from senior management to provide time, resources and funding for learning.
Commitment to learning must be backed up by action: it's easy to say an organisation supports learning, but what practical steps has it taken?
Learning and development should be seen as an 'investment' not a 'cost'.

Clear strategic intent:
Have a clear strategy for the learning needs of the organisation that matches its strategic direction.

Deliver on promises – if your organisation claims 'people are our most important asset', put in place tangible evidence/actions.

Supporting learning:
Ensure that consultation takes place with employees to determine true training needs.
Ensure that learning can easily be applied back in the workplace and give people time to practise new skills after training.

Many factors intervene between the commitment to learn and the impact of learning in practice: the culture of the organisation, the quality of individual learning skills, support for transfer of learning back to the workplace. Companies are experimenting with more innovative ways to address these factors and motivate employees to learn and develop their skills.

WHY IS THE TIME NOW RIGHT FOR COACHING?

The shift towards a learner-centred approach has contributed to the growing attractiveness of coaching. This is because it offers one-to-one personalised support for development that can be aligned with the organisation's strategy and goals. However, many commentators also think coaching is popular because it fits the complexity and fast pace of modern organisational life. For example, Janice Caplan (2003) writes:

> *I believe the reason for the massive increase in the use of coaching is that it is a process and a solution that suits our times. It is an effective mechanism for enabling an organisation to meet competitive pressures, plan for succession and bring about change.*

In truth, a combination of factors have collided to lead to the growth of coaching in contemporary organisations (see Figure 6 on page 24).

Factors include:

- *a rapidly evolving business environment* – The fast pace of business as well as significant time pressures mean that dealing with change is becoming an everyday challenge. The ability to learn and adapt is quickly becoming an essential skill.

- *the social nature of the workplace* – Much of organisational life occurs through groups of people working together in a series of group and individual relationships. Organisational success ultimately results from the productive functioning of people working with others in teams, departments, and ultimately as a whole organisation. How well people work together largely depends on the quality of their interpersonal skills, including communication skills, emotional intelligence and self-awareness. Coaching offers a mechanism to help employees improve this range of interpersonal skills so they can have more productive working relationships.

Figure 6: | *Factors contributing to the growth of coaching*

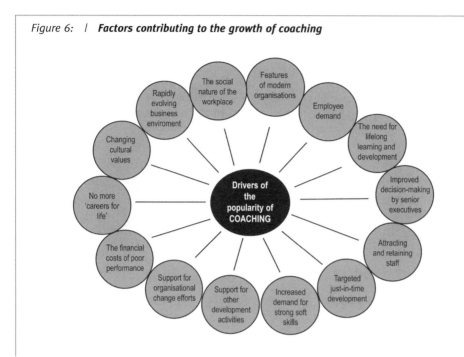

- *supporting organisational change efforts* – Research has shown that many change efforts fail because of the inability of individuals to effectively learn and adapt. Targeted development interventions such as coaching have become popular in helping individuals adjust to major changes in the workplace.

- *features of modern organisations* – Flatter organisational structures, broader management roles, complex career paths and lower job security have all been contributing factors to the growth of coaching. Organisational downsizing and the resulting flatter structures mean that newly promoted individuals often have to make large step-changes in performance because of the higher requirements of their new roles. Coaching can help these individuals quickly overcome gaps in their knowledge, skills, behaviour and ability.

- *attracting and retaining staff* – Today organisations are competing as fiercely for talented staff as for customers. Career progression and personal development are high on the wish-list of talented employees, and coaching can form part of a package of activities to attract and retain the best staff.

- *lifelong learning* – The importance of learning throughout a person's life is increasingly recognised and accepted. This has parallelled the requirement for organisations and individuals to develop their skills in order to keep up with a fast-paced, turbulent world market.

- *the need for targeted, individualised, just-in-time development* – The development needs of individuals can be diverse, and in smaller organisations there are often too few individuals with specific development needs to warrant the design of a formal training programme. This usually makes the 'one-size-fits-all' training programme that takes place every few months inappropriate. Coaching offers a flexible, responsive approach to development that can be delivered 'just in time' to turn around deficiencies in current performance or to strengthen underdeveloped skills.

- *the financial costs of the poor performance of senior managers/executives* – There is a growing acceptance of the costs associated with poorly-performing senior managers/executives. Coaching provides organisations with an opportunity to undertake pre-emptive and proactive interventions to improve their performance (Greco, 2001; Kilburg, 1996).

- *increasing demand for managers and leaders with better 'soft skills'* – Coaching, with its emphasis on self-awareness, feedback and practice, is considered a highly effective way of developing 'people skills' such as communicating and influencing, gaining trust and using feedback.

- *improved decision-making by senior employees* – For senior-level managers/executives it can be 'lonely at the top' because they have few people they can confide in and develop ideas and discuss decisions and concerns. A coach can be used as a 'safe and objective haven' to discuss issues and provide support (Masciarelli, 1999). This can be valuable when the return on the improvement in skill level and decision-making is considered.

- *no more 'careers for life'* – There is an increasing trend for individuals to take greater responsibility for their personal and professional development. With the decline of 'jobs for life', employees can no longer rely on employers to provide them with all of their career development needs. If individuals are to take responsibility for their development and ongoing career progression, they need support and advice in taking this forward. Coaching can help individuals identify development needs, plan activities and support personal problem-solving.

- *changing cultural values* – Many organisations are trying to move from a 'command-and-control' leadership approach to one where the contribution and development of employees at all levels in the organisation is facilitated and supported. Coaching can act as a bridge between old and new cultures by offering a framework and mindset for managers and leaders to use when making this shift.

- *employee demand* – The best learning is not done in a training room or at a conference but at work. People enjoy participating in coaching because it focuses on immediate work issues and is therefore highly relevant and applicable to their jobs. Participants receive direct one-to-one assistance and attention from an expert. This can fit in with their own timeframes and schedules and there is the potential for quick results if the individual is dedicated.

- *support for other learning and development activities* – Much of the money spent on training development activities is wasted if the personal development momentum is allowed to dissipate after the event. Ninety-three per cent of respondents in the CIPD's 2004 training and development survey agreed that coaching is a key mechanism for transferring learning from training courses back to the workplace. Coaching helps by creating the conditions for learning and behavioural change – security, support, feedback and opportunities to practise over time.

CIPD research has revealed that coaching is considered to be one of the most effective ways that people learn. So although training courses continue to have an important role in learning and development, they are no longer regarded as the only, or even the most effective, solutions to an individual's development needs. Other more contemporary approaches to learning such as coaching, mentoring and e-learning are now receiving much more attention as organisations look for innovative ways to develop their workforce.

WHAT DOES COACHING OFFER THAT OTHER LEARNING AND DEVELOPMENT ACTIVITIES DON'T?

Part of the rise in the popularity of coaching has resulted from the problems inherent in traditional training approaches. An alarming amount of training doesn't work, in terms of promoting changed behaviour back in the workplace. In fact, Baldwin and Ford (1988) reported that the rate of transfer of learning from the conventional classroom environment to the workplace can be as low as 10 per cent. The box below shows a variety of reasons why this can happen – but for the most part it seems that training courses fail to embed suitable feedback and support for the transfer of learning into the workplace.

Problems with traditional training
- It is hard to make training courses situationally relevant and applicable to each delegate.
- Traditional training approaches assume that each person has the same starting knowledge base.
- Content quickly goes out of date.
- Traditional training takes little account of people's different learning styles and preferences.
- Traditional training can sometimes be detached from the context in which work is produced.
- Traditional training lacks the supporting processes to follow up and make sure new ideas and skills are put into practice.

One-shot training courses can provide knowledge, but behaviour change usually requires a process of ongoing practice and feedback. This is exactly what coaching can offer. We learn best when we apply newly learned concepts and ideas to an immediate situation of personal relevance to us. Coaching provides the means for supporting other development activities by helping people apply new learning in 'real' work situations.

Coaching has many more distinctive characteristics:

- It provides people with feedback on both their strengths and weaknesses.
- It supports changes in attitudes and behaviour that can translate into more effective performance at work.
- It enables people to refocus and take a critical look at their approaches and style at work.
- It helps people identify barriers that are preventing them from being more effective in their jobs.
- It helps people commit to new performance goals.
- It gives people someone to listen/talk to without judgement.
- It helps to promote individual self-awareness and self-management.
- It offers a flexible and tailored approach to development.
- It demands individual responsibility for performance and development.
- It is a challenging and demanding experience, but this can help to accelerate learning.

Overall, coaching offers a number of advantages over other development interventions that fail to provide the means for people to actually make lasting changes. It seems that 'knowing what you need to change' is only one piece of the jigsaw – not enough to bring about actual changes in a person's style or work habits. Coaching's unique offer is its change orientation, flexibility and support for ongoing development.

WHEN IS IT RIGHT TO USE COACHING?

Although coaching is being used by a huge number of organisations, it is still only one mechanism for learning. Coaching is not a solution for all learning needs. It must be positioned carefully as one element in an organisation's total learning and development strategy. And it is important not to over-hype coaching and make excessive claims about its potential and use. In terms of overall trends in training and development, although use of coaching is increasing, it is not the most widely-used development tool or even considered to be the most effective (see Figure 7 and Table 6 on page 28).

On-the-job training remains the most widely-used type of employee development. It is considered to be highly effective and employees themselves say it is their favourite way of learning. So although coaching certainly has a lot to offer, it is important to understand that it sits within a raft of other learning activities that can all be effective in the right situation.

Figure 7: | **The percentage of organisations that use different development activities**

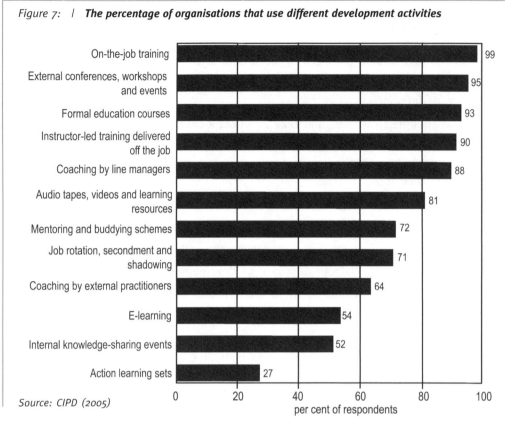

Source: CIPD (2005)

Table 6: | **The perceived effectiveness of different development activities**

	Percentage of respondents indicating 'effective' or 'very effective'
On-the-job training	96
Instructor-led training delivered off the job	94
Formal education courses	93
Coaching by external practitioners	92
Job rotation, secondment and shadowing	87
Mentoring and buddying schemes	85
External conferences, workshops and events	84
Coaching by line managers	83
Internal knowledge-sharing events	82
Action learning sets	77
Audio tapes, videos and learning resources	71

Source: CIPD (2005)

The challenge facing learning and development practitioners today is to understand what is the best and most cost-effective use of each learning method, whether it is coaching, training courses, e-learning or any other learning activity. The maximum benefit from learning and development activities can be achieved by finding the best fit for your organisation – ie the combination of activities best suited to your particular environment and strategy.

Making decisions about when to use coaching will depend on a variety of factors including the preferences of the individual learners, the nature of their development needs, the organisational conditions and whether an individual has the right attitude and approach to coaching.

There are some specific organisational situations in which coaching can be particularly helpful. Some examples of these are outlined below.

Coaching is particularly helpful in certain organisational situations
- People who initially set up *small businesses* do not necessarily have the skills to manage larger businesses and the fast-growing number of people they need to employ. It is also unlikely that they can be away from work for extended periods of time for development activities. In this situation, coaching can offer targeted, timely development on identified issues/areas that can be fitted into the individual's busy schedule.
- Organisations should only invest in coaching when there is *a belief that it can deliver significant and long-term improvements* in individuals' performance – ie when future performance will greatly exceed current performance and this can be translated into business benefits.
- Coaching can offer *support for expatriates* who have to adjust to a new culture and country. These people often have very specific requirements and they need immediate support when issues arise.
- When organisations are suffering from significant *skills shortages*, money may be better spent developing the skills of current employees through interventions like coaching, rather than spending a great deal of money recruiting external candidates.
- Where certain employees have high levels of specific skills and experience (or critical relationships with contractors/suppliers etc), the organisation might have difficulty replacing its human capital. In this situation, it may be more appropriate to provide these valued technical experts with coaching *to improve or develop some of their other skills* (interpersonal/managerial) so that their careers can progress within the organisation.
- *Periods of major organisational change* can require significant shifts in the behaviour and attitudes of some employees in order to fit in with new structures or cultures. Coaching can help individuals make these necessary changes.
- Coaching can help *individuals who are changing their job role* and require different skills and abilities. Coaching can be a valuable short-term intervention to help people adapt and cope with their role change.

The case for investing in coaching is different in each organisation. It is strongest in organisations that rely on the loyalty and efficacy of their people, and in organisations that experience a lot of change.

Determining if an individual needs coaching

A major part of HR's role in coaching is working out when coaching should be used – and, more importantly, when it shouldn't. The enthusiasm for coaching at the moment means that there is a danger that it can be seen as a panacea for all kinds of development needs. However, coaching should only be used when it is genuinely seen as the best way of helping an individual learn and develop. Coaching is just one of a range of training and development activities that organisations can use to develop their employees. It can also be an expensive proposition, the costs, time and resources involved quickly mounting up, even if the coaching initiative only lasts a few months. It is therefore important to fully consider the merits of coaching alongside other types of development interventions, such as training courses, mentoring or on-the-job training. Employee preferences should also be borne in mind. Although coaching can be a very effective development tool, as with any learning intervention it will only be effective when a genuine need for it is identified and when it is the best development tool for a specific purpose. Decisions on whether coaching is an appropriate approach are illustrated in Figure 8.

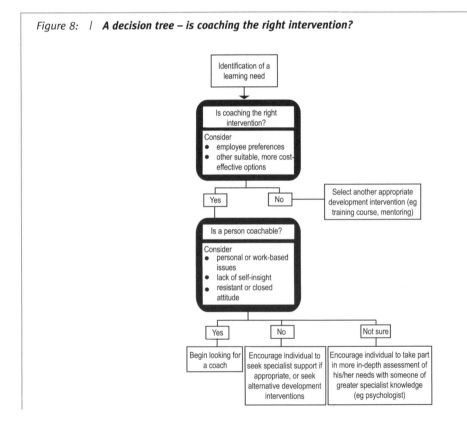

Figure 8: | *A decision tree – is coaching the right intervention?*

Recognising that someone could benefit from some coaching can happen in a variety of organisational settings. The first step will be the identification of a learning or development need. This is most frequently pointed out by the individuals themselves, by their line managers or by a member of the HR department (eg during a developmental centre). Once a learning need has been identified, the next step is for the manager and the individual to decide how best the need can be met and whether that involves coaching or some other form of development. The box below illustrates some examples of situations in which coaching is an appropriate approach.

When coaching can help most

- Sometimes an individual can be performing perfectly well, but could be *even more successful with some assistance*. In this situation, the coach is not helping the individual to 'fix' any particular problem, but instead will try to help motivate the individual to consider his or her future plans and the next steps in his or her job or career.
- Some individuals in the workplace are highly competent, technical experts. However, they can have *poor interpersonal skills* that make them appear arrogant or stubborn to those they work with. Coaches can help managers to better 'read' interpersonal situations and be more effective in their interactions with colleagues.
- In some cases, managers may *handle conflict situations in an aggressive and non-compromising way* that antagonises their colleagues. This may be quite intimidating to peers and team members. Coaching can help these individuals to develop the skills of negotiation and compromise so that conflict is resolved more effectively.
- Some managers have *difficulty supporting the development of their team members*. Coaching can help managers develop junior colleagues more effectively by learning some coaching skills themselves.
- As managers move from management or front-line positions to more senior levels, they often need *assistance in gaining a more strategic perspective*. This involves making decisions based on the best interests of the organisation as a whole, rather than their specific area of the business. Coaches can help managers to become more sensitive to wider organisational concerns and understand opportunities and problems occurring across multiple business units.

Is a person ready for coaching?

Some people may not respond well to coaching. There is a whole host of reasons why this may be the case, as shown in the box below.

When coaching is unlikely to help

- *When a person has psychological problems*, he or she should be offered referral to appropriate specialist support, not coaching. Coaches do not generally have the depth of psychological training to deal with these issues nor the medical training to address any physiological components that may also be part of the problem (eg addiction, depression).

- *When a person lacks self-insight or is not able to modify his or her behaviour from situation to situation*, coaching will not be effective because a coach will not be able to overcome such strong resistance to change.
- *When a person has a common developmental need*, the individual may not require an intervention as costly or as intensive as coaching. A course or development programme may be an equally effective and more cost-effective solution.
- *When a person is resistant or closed to coaching*, especially if the person believes he or she is being forced into it, it is unlikely to be effective. Coaching works best when there is a receptive audience. Attempts should be made to understand why the person feels this way.
- *When a person sees coaching as a 'quick fix' and does not take responsibility for changing his or her behaviour*, learning is unlikely to occur at all. Long-term successful behavioural change requires a great deal of effort and hard work for it to really happen.
- *When a person engages in socially inappropriate behaviour* – eg sexual harassment – the person will need long-term intensive counselling and may be subject to formal disciplinary processes. Because coaches cannot exclude themselves from testifying against clients in legal proceedings, it is also in the best interests of employees to have professional counsellors with more experience of the boundary issues.
- *When a person is leaving the company or retiring*, it is unlikely that in such a short timeframe the organisation will see any benefits in terms of improved performance. Outplacement or career counselling may be a more appropriate solution.

In all these cases the problems are best dealt with by interventions other than coaching, either because the individual's attitude will interfere with the effectiveness of coaching or because he or she needs alternative specialist support. In many of these situations we are looking at the boundaries between coaching and therapy. Sometimes a clinical intervention will provide more appropriate support for the individual. The HR practitioner should try to identify these issues as early as possible.

Think through the following questions when considering if someone is ready for coaching:
- Is the issue personal or work-based?
- Is the individual a willing participant in the coaching? Is he or she receptive to coaching?
- Does the issue require more in-depth psychological expertise?
- Does the individual accept that the coaching requires considerable effort from him or her for it to be successful? Is he or she resistant to change?
- Is there another equally effective development option that may be more cost-effective?

In this chapter we have considered the case for coaching against the wider backdrop of learning and development. We are seeing growing acceptance of the value of learning and development more generally as organisations struggle with continually changing competitive pressures, and this has aided positive attitudes towards coaching. However, coaching itself also has specific characteristics which are driving its popularity and respect. It is a highly suitable intervention in particular organisational situations, and for the development of certain individuals. But it is not a miracle cure and HR must take care that coaching is not used simply because it is the latest trend: it is to be considered alongside other development options and applied only when it really is believed to constitute the best solution to the issue being faced.

3

HR's role in managing coaching

When we first think about coaching, we tend to focus on the relationship between the coach and the individual. However, another extremely important stakeholder who is often overlooked is the person representing the organisation's interests in coaching – most often the HR professional. Given that the organisation is investing in coaching, it understandably has a keen interest in ensuring that its efforts result in improved individual performance and contribution towards its goals. This is the crux of the role of those in HR.

HR is accountable for guiding business investments in 'people' across a range of HR activities. In this way, taking responsibility for managing coaching activities fits very naturally with its remit. HR's role in coaching is varied and demanding. In a nutshell, it involves effectively overseeing, managing and monitoring the full range of coaching activities that take place. Depending on the organisation, this can include formal and informal activities, coaching by internal and external practitioners and coaching taking place at all levels in the organisation. Underpinning these activities is the management of a series of stakeholders who have an interest in the success of coaching (see Figure 9). A major part of HR's role is managing the expectations of these parties and exerting influence to encourage them to commit time, resources and support to coaching.

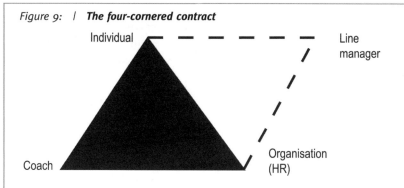

Figure 9: | *The four-cornered contract*

Source: Hay (1995)

Although HR professionals are usually responsible for managing coaching activities, in some organisations others may sponsor or lead coaching activities. In this chapter we consider the role of HR, and, equally, others who hold these responsibilities, in managing and overseeing coaching activities.

WHY HR MUST MAKE THE CASE FOR COACHING

In the past, the success of training and development functions (or professionals) was judged by the number of days' training delivered annually. And the value of different training courses was rated by their popularity. Thankfully, those days no longer exist. Now, however, HR is increasingly asked to justify its contribution and demonstrate how its activities benefit the organisation. If HR wants to become a credible, business-oriented department, it must be able to respond to requests for information on the value that coaching is delivering to individuals and to the organisation as a whole.

Changes in organisational life have resulted in a number of new challenges for HR practitioners. These include continuously equipping employees with new skills and know-ledge to keep up with the pace of change, enabling people to take charge of their own learning, supporting learning among a dispersed workforce, and capturing employees' attention in increasingly time-pressurised and stressful working environments. All of this has resulted in a more demanding role for HR, but it also offers a significant opportunity. Now is the time to prove HR's value in supporting organisations' strategic activities. By linking coaching firmly to the needs of the business and illustrating how it can help goals be achieved, the door is open for HR to build its credibility as a strategic partner and show how it can add value.

Unfortunately, not everyone (or even the majority of people) in an organisation will believe that coaching is worthwhile. Some financially-focused senior managers remain unconvinced by the return-on-investment evidence to date, and this makes building the case for coaching a challenge. HR activities are always competing for attention with other operational business activities. As an HR professional, it is your job to make a strong case and convince your senior managers that investing in coaching is worthwhile. HR practitioners have to focus on demonstrating the impact of coaching in order to win over sceptical or doubtful groups of staff. If attitudes to coaching are hostile or indifferent, the chances of obtaining a concerted effort to help make coaching a success are low.

Even if senior managers are initially supportive, coaching must be kept firmly on the day-to-day business agenda. Embedding coaching into an organisation's culture is likely to take a number of years and will therefore require an ongoing commitment and investment in terms of time, energy and resources. Clutterbuck and Megginson (2005) argue:

> *One of the most common mistakes we observe in HR's approach is to assume that the case only has to be made and accepted once. Support for coaching may fall away over time as other pressing business issues come to the fore.*

Because of this, HR must find different ways over time to remake the business case, reminding managers of why the organisation is seeking to develop coaching capability and how this links with the objectives of the business.

HR practitioners could of course just get on with coaching activities and wait until questions are asked about the value they are creating. But they would be missing a trick. If they want managers and employees to understand and support coaching initiatives, they need to explain what benefits coaching can provide and how it can support individual and organisational goals. The good news is that we are making progress. There is a growing recognition and acceptance of the importance of effective training and learning to organisational success. But we are not out of the woods yet. HR practitioners must take every opportunity to make the case for coaching to keep it at the heart of organisational learning and to keep resources channelled in its direction.

IF YOU CAN'T MEASURE IT, YOU CAN'T MANAGE IT

There has never been greater pressure to measure the impact of HR activities, and coaching is no different. Eighty per cent of respondents to the CIPD's 2004 training and development survey felt that 'HR has a crucial role to play in selecting and evaluating the impact of coaching initiatives.' Tough economic circumstances mean that frivolous spending on 'nice to have' activities that do not produce benefits is no longer tolerated. If an activity is not having an impact on organisational or employee effectiveness, its use is likely to be reviewed or stopped completely. Making good decisions about which activities to invest in requires reliable information about effectiveness, satisfaction and impact. And this requires evaluation and measurement.

At first glance, the idea of measurement and evaluation seems daunting because it brings greater accountability and pressure to achieve it. And for many HR professionals, dealing with 'numbers' and evaluation is not a favoured skill set. Making informal judgements on whether activities are valuable and important is a far more comfortable activity than the discipline involved in systematic evaluation. However, to build credibility and build its influence, HR must be competent in understanding and assessing costs and results. As Andrew Mayo (2004) argues,

> *In business and even in most public sector organisations today, numbers speak louder than words.*

The process of evaluating does not improve the benefits of coaching, it just helps to put a number and description on them. At the most basic level it is a process to establish the worth or value of something – in this case, coaching. By gathering information about the performance and results of coaching activities, HR can make sound decisions and report on progress to the rest of the business. If spend on coaching is not being tracked and results are not monitored, proving the value of coaching will be extremely difficult.

Information gained from evaluation activities can make a major contribution to the organisation and the effective management and delivery of coaching. Feedback to coaches will help them develop and hone their skills, and individual achievements via coaching can be identified and celebrated. But it is important to accept that evaluating coaching activities will not always provide you with good news. Negative feedback is equally important because it can help to identify 'hot spots' and improve future activities. Learning from mistakes is just as crucial for credibility as evidencing successes.

It is not enough to argue that the business is benefiting from coaching because people say they enjoy it, and because we assume that time spent learning is beneficial. Coaching should not be given a blank cheque. HR must confirm that it is delivering its primary function of improving both individual and organisational effectiveness. Otherwise there is no reason to keep investing – a win/win situation is a must!

HR should not be afraid of evaluation. In fact, for effective practitioners it can help to raise their credibility and standing. By aligning their activities with the business and demonstrating results, HR can truly say that it is acting as a business partner. Evaluation is also a way of getting stakeholders (and sceptics) more closely involved and buying into coaching as an initiative. It opens up an opportunity to talk about how coaching can play a role in improving performance and gives HR a chance to build relationships and credibility with people across the business. The upshot of effective measurement, evaluation and reporting will be a range of benefits such as increased job satisfaction, greater influence and respect.

WHAT ARE THE MAIN COMPONENTS OF HR'S ROLE?

Alongside HR's role in making the case for coaching, there is a whole host of areas in which HR can add value through its involvement. As much involvement as possible is desirable, but the extent to which HR can achieve it will doubtless depend on how much time it is able to dedicate to it. The extent of HR's role in managing coaching activities will depend hugely on the scope of coaching activities and how formal an approach is being taken. Figure 10 shows that there are four main areas of activity for HR involvement. (If you are planning a small or fairly low-key coaching initiative, HR may not need to consider or get involved with all these issues.)

Figure 10: | *Possible roles for HR in the management of coaching*

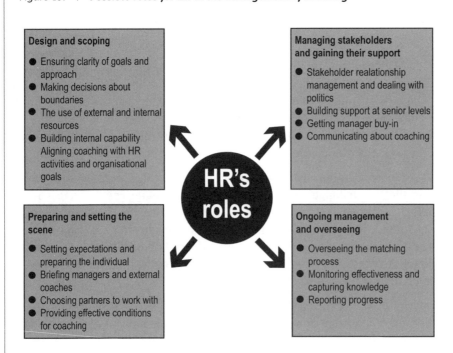

Design and scoping
- Ensuring clarity of goals and approach
- Making decisions about boundaries
- The use of external and internal resources
- Building internal capability Aligning coaching with HR activities and organisational goals

Managing stakeholders and gaining their support
- Stakeholder realationship management and dealing with politics
- Building support at senior levels
- Getting manager buy-in
- Communicating about coaching

Preparing and setting the scene
- Setting expectations and preparing the individual
- Briefing managers and external coaches
- Choosing partners to work with
- Providing effective conditions for coaching

HR's roles

Ongoing management and overseeing
- Overseeing the matching process
- Monitoring effectiveness and capturing knowledge
- Reporting progress

Figure 10 demonstrates just how much time and effort can be required to formally manage coaching activities, particularly in large organisations where coaching is being offered to a high number of people or where multiple coaching initiatives are in progress. For the remainder of this chapter, we briefly discuss HR's responsibilities in the areas illustrated in Figure 10 as well as offering some initial questions to prompt your thinking.

DESIGN AND SCOPING

Ensuring clarity of goals and approach

Considerable money, time and energy must be invested to make coaching work effectively, and it is important to be clear about exactly what you are trying to achieve via your coaching initiatives. The box below provides some starter-for-ten questions for you to think through your goals and approach to coaching. Many of your answers to these questions will also be useful in the evaluation, so they are well worth spending time on.

Clarifying your goals for coaching initiatives

Questions you should think through with other stakeholders:
- What performance improvements are desired?
- What are the organisational goals for the coaching intervention?
- Are the organisational conditions conducive to the type of coaching you are planning to introduce?
- Will employees readily accept the idea of coaching? Do they understand what it is?
- Will certain employee populations/individuals understand and accept why they have been offered coaching?
- Are managers supportive of coaching? Do they understand their role?
- What is the budget for the programme?
- What resources (internal and external) do you need to get an initiative off the ground?
- Who will be eligible for coaching?
- Would a pilot be helpful?

Making decisions about boundaries

How far do you want to take coaching in your organisation? Some organisations may want to introduce a few coaching programmes targeted at specific employee populations, while others may want coaching to help them change the culture in the organisation and create a shift in the way people interrelate and lead teams. There is little doubt that the majority of people in your organisation could potentially benefit from additional investment such as coaching. Work is changing for everyone, regardless of role, and as a result people need to continually develop their skills. But the key to cost-effective use of coaching is to be clear and selective about where in the organisation coaching is going to be offered or an initiative implemented.

In making decisions about how coaching will be introduced into an organisation, there are several factors to think through. One thing that cannot be ignored is cost. HR practitioners must consider how resource constraints will affect the implementation of coaching initiatives or the management of coaching relationships. Without a bottomless pit full of money, it is important to establish parameters about how and where coaching is being implemented. In the absence of such parameters, coaching initiatives can soak up a great deal of resources and time and costs can spiral. An ongoing role for HR is therefore to define the scope of coaching assignments or initiatives and control costs (see the box below).

Making decisions about the parameters for coaching

Some questions for practitioners to consider:

- How far do you want to embed coaching into your organisation?
- Who are you targeting coaching at?
- What are you trying to achieve?
- Will coaching be restricted to individuals of a certain level of seniority?
- Will coaching only be provided in relation to certain development activities?
- Will there be a limit on the number of hours of coaching available to each individual?

The use of internal and external resources

An important decision for HR is whether to use external coaches or to build internal capability within the organisation by training internal coaches and managers. Many organisations, particularly smaller ones, will simply not have the internal capability and it may be more cost-effective to hire an external coach rather than train someone internally. Organisations that are undertaking a lot of coaching, however, may find it more cost-effective to build up their internal capability and only use external coaches in certain specific situations. Apart from the impact of cost and resource issues, there are also some specific situations where either internal or external coaches may be preferable, and these are outlined in Table 7.

Building internal capability

Although line managers are the main deliverers of coaching in organisations, fewer than 20 per cent of respondents to the CIPD 2004 survey have 'all' or 'the majority' of their line managers trained to carry out coaching. The lack of management training in coaching skills forms part of a wider trend. Keep and Westwood (2003) report:

We have more managers than any comparative country – but this does not mean better; in fact for the UK it means more under-qualified, more unprepared managers.

Table 7: | **The use of internal and external coaches**

External coaches are preferable:	Internal coaches are preferable:
• for providing senior business leaders with sensitive feedback; for political reasons this might be difficult for an internal coach	• when knowing the company culture, history and politics is critical
• for bringing specialised expertise from a wide variety of organisational and industry situations	• when easy availability is desired
• when individuals are concerned about 'conflicts of interest' and whether confidentiality will be observed	• for being able to build up a high level of personal trust over a period of time
• for providing a wider range of ideas and experience	• for not being seen to be 'selling' consulting time
• for being less likely to judge and being perceived as being more objective	• for keeping costs under control – and possibly being less expensive

If we do not train our managers in coaching skills, how can we expect them to play an effective role in it? We cannot simply assume they will absorb the skills by osmosis. They must be trained in a variety of coaching skills, models and techniques and have support frameworks within the organisation to go to for advice and help.

If you are training internal coaches to operate within the business, it is probable that they will require more in-depth training since they are likely to work across a broader range of situations and are also likely to be supporting managers coaching their teams. Once training has been delivered, both managers and internal coaches must be given opportunities to reflect on their coaching activities and receive feedback to improve their skills either through supervision or continuing professional development activities.

HR practitioners may need to strengthen their own capabilities because, initially, they are unlikely to be experts in coaching. Being knowledgeable about coaching is crucial to making it work. So if you are given responsibility for managing coaching activities, you should try to build up your knowledge of coaching processes, models, frameworks, and so on. This will enable you to become a more knowledgeable manager of coaching activities and will help you cut through the confusion and jargon that exists in the coaching industry.

The good news is that many of the generic skills held by HR practitioners lend themselves to the effective management of coaching. The skills and experience of selection interviewing, designing efficient measurement systems, supervising projects with multiple stakeholder groups, and many more, are all important parts of managing coaching activities. Training or other development activities to help fill knowledge gaps will ensure that HR's involvement adds value.

Consider the following questions:

- Are you expecting all your managers to coach? If so, have you trained them?
- What level of training have your internal coaches received? Could they benefit from more development?
- How can you sustain the continuous improvement of managers' coaching capability?
- How can you measure progress towards improving coaching skills in the organisation?
- Do your HR practitioners have any skills or knowledge gaps that need addressing? Do they know enough to be knowledgeable managers of coaching activities?

Aligning coaching with other HR activities and business goals

HR holds the responsibility for ensuring that coaching activities are aligned with the strategic goals of the organisation and that they are integrated with other HR/training plans and activities. Coaching must not be a stand-alone initiative. However, recent CIPD research indicates that this is not always happening in practice. Although coaching is linked to 'some' or to a 'great' extent to business goals in around 90 per cent of organisations, it is worrying that only 27 per cent feel that coaching activities are completely integrated into wider HR strategy and processes (CIPD, 2006). Time and time again research has demonstrated that performance improvements can only be delivered via bundles of HR practices that are self-reinforcing, rather than one-off initiatives (eg EEF and CIPD, 2003).

In some organisations, individual managers or executives arrange their own coaching. When this happens and the HR department does not play a co-ordinating and overseeing role, the organisation loses a valuable opportunity to create a coaching strategy aligned with organisational goals and the overall training and development strategy. HR needs to engage with stakeholders in the business and discuss how coaching can help to support business initiatives and goals, and then ensure that coaching activities remain aligned with other HR initiatives.

MANAGING STAKEHOLDERS AND GAINING THEIR BUY-IN

Stakeholder relationship management and dealing with politics

Stakeholder relationships must be carefully managed for maximum benefit to be gained. HR practitioners must ensure that all stakeholders in coaching interventions buy into the process and understand their roles. The multiple stakeholders in coaching relationships create some difficult issues that require consideration. For example, who is the primary client (the client organisation or the individual)? HR must work to ensure that the needs of all stakeholders are met.

Underlying the effective management of stakeholders in coaching are a number of sensitive political issues that require diplomatic and tactful handling. This is particularly the case when HR first introduces or gets involved in managing coaching activities. Some examples of these issues are given below. It is helpful for HR practitioners to consider these points in advance and think through how they should attempt to address them.

Dealing with the political landscape: some sensitive issues

Potential issues that HR practitioners may face when dealing with stakeholder groups:

- *Opening closed doors* – A key problem for HR is when coaching happens behind 'closed doors' because senior-level employees bring in their own coaches and the activities are not co-ordinated by HR. This means that there are no reporting structures or accountability for the coaches being used. Organisations cannot learn from such coaching engagements and HR must find ways to get the senior managers to co-operate and align their coaching arrangements with the wider strategy for coaching in the organisation.
- *Meeting the needs of both the organisation and the individual* – Any HR practitioners who currently have a responsibility for designing or buying coaching initiatives will be aware of the challenge of meeting the requirements of both the organisation and the individual being coached. The onus is on HR to consider the needs of both groups and try to build this into the design and implementation of coaching initiatives.
- *Information flow and confidentiality* – Another issue to think about is how information from coaching conversations is used within an organisation, regardless of whether the coaching is external or internal. From the start, it is essential that HR is clear about what information the organisation wants so that the coaches and clients are clearly working towards specific goals. The clearer the goals, the easier it will be for HR to measure the results.

Building support at senior levels

A strong and active commitment from senior management is universally agreed as essential for the long-term success of all HR initiatives. This is because it is a vital ingredient for securing buy-in further down the organisation – particularly with time-pressed managers. Vocal senior management support and commitment reinforces the message that coaching is important to the business and is something for which employees are expected to make time. Encouraging leaders to champion coaching and act as role models can really help to embed coaching into the organisation so that it becomes part of 'the way things are done here'.

Getting senior-level buy-in and support for coaching (both in terms of their time/energy and committing resources to it) requires HR to make a strong case for investing in coaching and illustrating how coaching will benefit the organisation by supporting the achievement of its strategic goals. This is not an easy task. Recent CIPD research revealed that only 30 per cent of respondents felt that senior managers were 'completely' or to 'a great extent' supportive and committed to coaching (CIPD, 2006).

Consider the following questions:

- Are your senior managers role models for coaching?
- If they are, how can you best use them to help build support for coaching across the organisation?
- If there are no role models, what can you do to change this and gain senior managers' support?
- Are there any situations coming up where you can make the case for coaching by linking it to issues that senior management is concerned about or to support business objectives?

Getting manager buy-in

Line managers are critical to making coaching work. They are the people best placed to identify the development needs of their teams by assessing their capabilities, readiness for new roles and potential for growth. But securing manager buy-in is a significant, and ongoing, challenge. Only 21 per cent of respondents to the 2006 learning and development survey felt that their line managers took their coaching responsibilities seriously to a 'complete' or 'great extent' (CIPD, 2006). Unfortunately, in many instances developing people is not at the top of many managers' priority lists. However supportive they are of coaching in theory, it is always likely to take second place to running their department or delivering their immediate business objectives. Because of this, there is a need for HR to invest time 'selling' coaching to managers and explaining how it can help them achieve their team's objectives. This will encourage and strengthen managers' commitment. HR must convince managers by discussing the business case and involving them in the design and delivery of coaching so that they can see the personal and business benefits that can be achieved (see below).

Convincing managers and gaining their buy-in

Some ideas for obtaining manager support for coaching can be gleaned from previous CIPD research:

- demonstrating the link between training and business performance, value-added results and productivity
- providing support for the line and communicating clear messages about coaching and how it can help
- defining managers' coaching responsibilities in their job descriptions
- rewarding and recognising managers who act as role models and encourage coaching behaviours
- building assessment of managers' skills and results in developing their teams into appraisal systems

Communicating about coaching

When it comes to introducing coaching, there is a major role for HR in communicating and creating understanding. Coaching may be unknown or have little meaning for the average employee, or employees may have negative preconceptions about it – a common one being that it is 'fluffy'! HR must take time to explain what coaching is and be clear in creating understanding about how it links and supports what they are trying to achieve individually and as a business.

HR must communicate why coaching is being introduced and what the benefits are, and open up forums for discussion. Creating dialogue about coaching gives the opportunity for employees to voice concerns and provide input to help shape the design and implementation of coaching programmes.

Results of coaching must also be communicated back to the business to convince sceptics of the benefits and gain their support. Recording and communicating successes is important for sustaining enthusiasm and momentum.

PREPARATION AND SETTING THE SCENE

Setting expectations and preparing the individual

Coaching works best when the individual is both a willing and an informed participant. As Clutterbuck and Megginson (2005) say: 'A good coach will produce great results with a willing coachee.' The more the individual understands about the coaching process and is engaged with it, the easier it will be for him or her to be coached. Before the coaching begins, HR (in conjunction with the line manager) has an important role in providing the individual with information and preparing him or her for a role in coaching (see below).

Key messages to convey to individuals
- The organisation values you and wants to further develop your skills.
- Investing time developing your skills will help you in your future career progression.
- This is an opportunity for you to have some one-to-one personal development time.
- The coaching will be confidential. (Be clear about what information, if any, will be fed back to the organisation.)
- You are not being forced into this – you have to want to participate.
- You will have to do the work – there's no magic button to be pressed here.

In the past, coaching has often had negative connotations, being seen as a remedial activity. It is therefore essential that HR practitioners and managers spend time carefully explaining the purpose of the coaching, and making sure that individuals do not misinterpret why it is being suggested. It is also important to understand that individuals may feel apprehensive. So time should be taken to explain how the process will work in order to allay fears and start everything off on the right foot. It is equally important not to 'over-promise' anything to the individual at this stage – making clear, for example, that by taking part they are not guaranteed a promotion or any other specific career opportunity. These activities are crucial for setting realistic expectations.

Engaging employees in their own personal development is vital. CIPD research has revealed that 41 per cent of respondents reported employee reluctance to learn as a key barrier to organisations when trying to upskill their workforce (CIPD, 2005). If learners are not motivated to improve their skills and performance, it is unlikely that the coaching will achieve anything. HR must work with individuals to help them uncover 'what's in it for me.' The box below provides some examples of information that managers or HR might use when briefing individuals about coaching.

Areas to consider discussing when briefing individuals
- the purpose of the coaching and what it's expected to achieve
- why they have been selected for coaching
- the objectives for the coaching from the organisation's perspective
- what's in it for them
- the length of the coaching arrangement (number of sessions, length of each session)
- who the coach will be
- typical outline of a coaching session
- confidentiality and reporting back of information
- who to go to for advice or to ask questions
- how the coaching will be evaluated.

Being clear and supportive from the outset will help to motivate individuals. As early as possible, they should be encouraged to consider what they would like to achieve from the coaching sessions and identify specific areas they would like to focus on.

Briefing managers and external coaches

Managers must also be confident of their role in coaching, and an important role for HR is building understanding of what this involves. The exact role of managers will depend on whether they are delivering the coaching or whether they are supporting an individual who is receiving external coaching. The box below provides some tips for HR in conveying messages about the role of managers and ensuring that they take it on board.

The role of managers in making coaching work

HR must ensure that managers understand their role in making coaching work by:
- explaining what coaching is, and what it is not – building realistic expectations of outcomes

- explaining how the coaching will benefit the individual, but also how this will translate into improved contribution to the team
- helping the manager understand issues of confidentiality
- managing expectations about how much information they will receive back on the progress of the coaching
- explaining how to look out for signs that the individual is finding the coaching too demanding, which may result in stress.

Specifically, HR must explain that to support external coaching initiatives, the manager:
- must provide the individual with time to undertake the coaching
- must not expect to get information back from the coach on the individual, unless it has been explicitly agreed with the individual and the coach
- should not put pressure on the individual to meet unrealistic goals or to meet goals in unrealistic timeframes
- should discuss progress with the individual and what he or she feels he or she has gained
- should recognise progress and reward the achievement of coaching goals.

External coaches should be briefed by HR so that they have a good understanding of the broader organisational context, as well as to ensure that they are clear about the objectives and desired outcomes. The box below provides a list of areas that you should consider discussing with the coach or giving to him or her in the form of handouts.

Areas to consider covering during external coach briefings
- organisation vision, mission, strategy, values, locations, products, customers, competitors, etc
- organisational objectives for the coaching initiative – what you are trying to achieve
- how it fits into overall HR/training strategy
- the coaching process and model
- the outcomes/benefits you expect to achieve
- the estimated timescales
- clear information about roles and responsibilities (coach/HR)
- evaluation of progress and attainment of goals
- confidentiality arrangements
- administration – time and expense records, notice of cancellation, updates on progress, etc

If you are providing the coach with any sensitive information about the organisation, make sure that he or she has signed a confidentiality agreement. It may also be helpful to have a discussion about how the coach should handle typical coaching dilemmas so that potential problems are considered and thought through.

Choosing partners to work with

The complex coaching marketplace makes decisions about what to look for in a coach (or a partner coaching organisation) unclear and difficult to establish. There is little agreement about the characteristics of a 'good' coach and considerable debate over what kinds of coaching methods and techniques work best.

Because of this, HR practitioners have to be clear about their expectations. They need to build up their own knowledge of coaching so that they can make good decisions during selection and recruitment. Thinking through and setting criteria for selection decisions is well worth the time spent. Apart from the right cultural fit and personal style, try to establish other coaching credentials such as evidence of a positive track record, having a structured approach, relevant qualifications, adherence to professional standards and evidence of supervision.

Providing effective conditions for coaching

An essential role for HR practitioners is creating effective conditions for coaching by ensuring that the culture and climate within the organisation is supportive of learning and development activities. In the 2004 training survey, 80 per cent of respondents agreed that 'coaching will only work well in a culture that supports learning and development.' Much of creating the right conditions for coaching has been covered elsewhere in this chapter, including communicating clear messages, engaging stakeholders, selling the case to senior managers, gaining buy-in from the line and managing the expectations of participants.

But many practitioners and academics go further and suggest that, ideally, a 'coaching climate' should exist within organisations (eg Clutterbuck and Megginson, 2005). This, however, involves implementing a long-term, organisational development programme and is therefore not a light undertaking.

ONGOING MANAGEMENT AND OVERSEEING

Overseeing the matching process

Research has demonstrated that the relationship between coaches and their coachees is the single most important factor for successful outcomes. HR must therefore spend time devising matches between coaches' expertise and individuals' needs. This activity can often help to support a decision as to whether a line manager, internal or external coach will be most appropriate.

When using internal or external coaches rather than managers, HR should ideally offer the individual a choice of coaches who have an appropriate skill set, experience and personality. In this way, HR establishes the coach's track record, but allows the individual an element of choice so that the final selection decision can be based on a degree of 'chemistry' between the individual and the coach. This is essential to ensuring that the coaching relationship works.

Monitoring effectiveness and capturing knowledge

Assessment of the tangible benefits of coaching is critical. This is necessary for accountability on the part of coaches, data to prove the value of the initiative for HR, and closure for individuals. However, formal evaluation of coaching initiatives is often lacking, a large proportion of organisations relying on little more than anecdotal evidence to measure effectiveness. More information about this can be found in Chapter 11.

Reporting progress

Part of the ongoing role for HR is to monitor satisfaction and report progress on coaching via regular discussions and updates with stakeholders. HR should report broad or common issues that surface in coaching (without breaching agreed confidentiality guidelines), progress towards goals, results of evaluation activities and learning points to date. As part of these discussions, HR can also gain input and support for any necessary adjustments to the scope, delivery or management of coaching as a result of feedback and evaluation activities.

TO SUM UP ...

HR's role in coaching can be complex and varied, but without doubt is extremely important to success. Unless HR oversees and manages coaching activities it is difficult to get a clear picture of what coaching is taking place and how effective it is. In such cases, the evaluation of coaching activities is impossible and you lose an opportunity to build up a body of knowledge about lessons learned. An overall perspective allows the HR team to identify pockets of good and poor practice and to plan any necessary remedial action. All in all, HR has a critical role to play in drawing up a framework for coaching activities, gaining stakeholder buy-in, ensuring value for money and making sure that activities are grounded in the organisation's strategic goals. A pretty tough job, whichever way you look at it!

Part 2

Reviewing the evidence

4
Does coaching work? An organisational perspective

This chapter aims to provide some preliminary answers to the question: Does coaching impact on individual and business performance? It is based on an analysis of information provided by about 30 organisations that have introduced coaching and which kindly agreed to share their experiences for this project. Given the relative scarcity of research about the impact of coaching in business settings, this data has proved to be a valuable mine of information about UK organisations' current experiences and use of coaching.

Before taking part in telephone interviews, most of the organisations filled in a questionnaire designed to provide information about their coaching activities and their views on the effective use of coaching. The case study organisations were chosen to represent a wide range of sectors, size and ownership. The organisations that took part in the research are listed below. Some of these organisations have worked with us to produce detailed case studies that can be found in the Appendix.

Organisations involved in the CIPD research project
BBC
Blackrock International
BPB Paperboard
Bovis Lend Lease
Boxwood
Canada Life
Castle Cement
Courtenay HR
Dixons
Everest Limited
Exeter City Council
Glasgow Housing Association
Glenmorangie plc
Greater London Authority
High & Mighty
Kwik-Fit Financial Services
Lloyds TSB

London School of Economics and Political Science
Loughborough University
Midland Area Housing Association
Nationwide
Norfolk, Suffolk and Cambridgeshire Strategic Health Authority
Panasonic Europe
Perkins Shibaura Engines
Pertemps Recruitment Partnership
Regal Fish Supplies
Rugby Cement
Selfridges
Shell
Stephenson Harwood
Surrey and Sussex Strategic Health Authority
Tate
The Children's Society
United Utilities

The core research questions we wanted to address were:

1 Does coaching work?

2 Is there any hard evidence that coaching impacts on individual and organisational performance?

3 How does coaching work?

4 What helps or hinders the success of coaching initiatives?

5 What are the lessons learned so far from those who have been involved in the delivery and management of coaching in organisational settings?

In-depth and high-quality research data were shared with us by the organisations and this has enabled us to provide some initial answers to our core questions, which are reviewed in turn in this chapter.

DOES COACHING WORK?

Our case study organisations were asked to specify the types of coaching used in their organisation and to rate them in terms of effectiveness. The results are shown in Table 8.

All of our case study organisations used a mixture of different coaching practitioners to deliver their coaching activities. Ninety-six per cent used coaching by line managers, and coaching by external coaches was the second most common form (92 per cent). Coaching by

Table 8: | ***Which types of coaching are currently used in your organisation, and how effective have they been?***

	Percentage saying this form of coaching is ...				Percentage using this form of coaching
	Very effective	Effective	Not very effective	Ineffective	
Coaching by line managers	13	54	33	–	96
Coaching by external coaches	39	52	9	–	92
Coaching by internal coaches	16	84	–	–	76
Coaching by members of the HR department	10	74	16	–	76

internal coaches and members of the HR department was less common, but was still used by about three-quarters of our organisations. Coaching therefore tends to involve a variety of internal and external practitioners, with organisations choosing to use a complementary selection to deliver their coaching requirements.

But on to the crucial question – do they think it works? The results of our survey paint a positive picture. The vast majority believe that coaching does work. However, there are some differences in how effective the different types of coaching are thought to be. External coaching receives the highest endorsement (ie 39 per cent rating it as 'very effective'). However, some organisations also reported situations in which external coaching has not delivered the anticipated results (9 per cent of organisations rated it as 'not very effective'). Coaching by internal coaches also received a very positive endorsement, despite barely featuring in the research literature to date. Not a single organisation reported it as 'ineffective' or 'not very effective', but the percentage who rated it as 'very effective' was lower than that for external coaches. Coaching by line managers is generally considered to work, but a significantly higher number of organisations reported problems with this type of intervention (33 per cent). Finally, the vast majority of organisations felt that coaching by members of the HR department (a form of internal coaching) was 'effective', but a small proportion were less impressed – almost one-fifth rated it as 'not very effective'. Looking at these results together, there appears to be a very high level of belief in the effectiveness of coaching from our case study organisations, although there were some indications of teething problems – particularly when using manager-coaches and internal coaches from HR.

We wanted to get beyond generalised beliefs in the overall effectiveness of coaching and find out whether the organisations felt that coaching interventions had specifically resulted in improved organisational and individual performance. The results of the responses to this question are shown in Table 9 on page 56.

Table 9: | ***Overall, have the coaching initiatives you implemented had an impact on the performance of (a) the individual and (b) the organisation?***

	Percentage answering ...		
	Yes, overall, a positive impact on performance	Yes, overall, a negative impact on performance	No, overall, no impact on performance
Individuals receiving coaching	96	4	–
Organisation	87	–	13

Again, the results are very positive. The vast majority of people firmly believe that coaching creates improvements in the performance of individuals, which translate into results for the organisations they work for.

> *Coaching was offered as it is considered to be the best way of allowing employees to grow and develop and thus improve the performance of the business.*
>
> Ola Adams and Pamela Tilt, Nationwide

> *Coaching is a support tool we use to be the best, with great results. Year on year, we see improvement in the attitude of the business shifting towards a more performance-orientated environment.*
>
> Camilla Aitchison, Dixons

However, coaching is not a miracle intervention. Although coaching was almost always considered to deliver improved individual performance, this did not automatically translate into visible benefits for the organisation. For 13 per cent of our case study organisations, coaching had no overall impact on business performance.

The high level of belief in coaching has led to its use to address and support a whole host of different organisational issues, as is outlined in Table 10.

The most common issues coaching is being used to address are those relating to individual performance. Beyond this, coaching is being used for a variety of training and staffing reasons, including skills deficits, supporting organisational change, support for career progression and job changes. Interestingly, a relatively high proportion of organisations said that they were also using coaching to address employees' non-work issues such as work–life balance, which indicates that organisations recognise that issues in employees' personal lives often spill over into their work lives and affect their job performance.

So, does coaching work? Well, according to our case study organisations, the initial answer appears to be 'yes' – not a single organisation described any form of coaching as ineffective (Table 8). And organisations appear to be using coaching successfully in a wide variety of situations and to address a series of different organisational issues. However, there are

Table 10: | ***Issues that organisations are addressing through coaching***

	Percentage of organisations that report using coaching for this purpose
To address individual performance issues	89
To address skills deficits	79
To address transition issues (to a new role or area of work)	79
To enhance career progression	75
To address team issues	71
To address transformation issues (major change initiatives)	71
To address personal non-work issues	57
To address work–life balance issues	50
To address diversity/equality issues	25

clearly some instances when organisations struggle with using the different forms of coaching to their full advantage. Consequently, there appears to be a caveat to the answer 'yes, coaching works': coaching can work, but it seems that we need to understand the limitations and barriers to coaching activities that organisations are currently experiencing.

IS THERE ANY HARD EVIDENCE THAT COACHING IMPACTS ON INDIVIDUAL AND ORGANISATIONAL PERFORMANCE?

Rather than solely relying on participants' perceptions about the impact of coaching, we also asked our organisations about how they were measuring and assessing the impact of coaching. The results show that organisations are making considerable efforts to assess the impact of coaching, understanding that it is vital for the long-term sustainability of their activities. Respondents reported undertaking a wide range of evaluation activities, as shown in Table 11 on page 58.

Unsurprisingly, asking for feedback from participants and their managers is the most common activity. Some may argue that this is simply because it is the easiest option. But given the individual focus on coaching, whether the individual feels that it has helped him or her learn and develop has to be one of the most important indicators of success – as are the views of the manager, colleagues and direct reports about whether the individual's behaviour has changed as a result of coaching. The most disappointing finding is the fact that only just over half of our organisations reported assessing whether the goals set at the beginning of the coaching had been achieved. It is likely that this is because goals were not set at the outset or because time was not set aside for reviewing whether goals had been achieved. Either way, it seems that organisations may be missing important data about whether coaching is actually achieving the goals it was introduced to address.

Table 11: | **The use of different evaluation techniques**

	Percentage of respondents using this technique
Asking for feedback from individuals receiving coaching	*89*
Asking for feedback from participants' line managers	*75*
Assessing changes in individual performance or career progress	*64*
Assessing achievement of goals set at the beginning of the coaching	*57*
Assessing changes in employee attitude survey ratings	*39*
Assessing changes in the culture of the organisation	*36*
Assessing changes in organisational performance	*32*

However, it is pleasing to see that some of our organisations are trying to assess changes in individual and organisational performance, even if it is only a minority. Organisations that are attempting to measure the impact of coaching on performance are trying to adopt meaningful measures that are aligned to the business area or context in which the coaching is taking place. The result is that individuals are being coached in relation to targets that are meaningful for the organisation. This is illustrated by Isobel Aitchinson (Learning and Development Team Leader, Glasgow Housing Association):

> *Measures used are not directly related to coaching as an exercise. Measures relate to the operating key performance indicators for the organisation (and local housing organisations) and the impact on targets – for example, reduction in arrears, void properties, customer complaints, etc.*

This attention to careful measurement was a feature of many of the case study organisations. Overall, the types of measures used can be grouped into three types of data: targets, performance ratings, and success stories.

Targets

Targets are used when the organisations think that coaching will result in clearly identified changes that directly relate to measurable outcomes valued by the business (see the box opposite). Examples include:

- increases – sales, revenue, profitability, productivity

- decreases – cycle times, absence, downtime, quality failures

- instilled practice – employees using a defined procedure or a new skill.

Targets used by our case study organisations
- achievement of business key performance indicators/goals
- measures of increased skills
- quantifiable business improvements
- increased sales per full-time employee
- time taken for new recruits to reach minimum performance levels
- productivity levels
- product quality levels
- reduction in absence through sickness measured through days lost at work
- revenue generated
- market share
- cycle-time improvement
- cost reduction
- profit from sales
- number of team members who set objectives and development targets

Performance ratings and survey results

Performance ratings and survey results are often assessed when coaching aims to achieve changes in behaviour that result in measurable changes in aspects of an individual's job performance. They are also used when coaching is used to collectively change behaviours and attitudes at the department or organisational level. Activities to obtain this kind of information typically include ways to acquire data referring to changes in: customer feedback, 360-degree assessments, ratings of competence/skills, organisational cultural indicators and employee satisfaction scores (see below).

Examples of performance ratings measures used by our case study organisations
- performance rating from coach, coachee, mentor, manager
- 360- or 180-degree feedback
- mystery shopper/customer feedback
- cultural survey scores
- performance ratings
- ratings of competence
- employee satisfaction survey scores
- quality percentage improvement
- achievement of Investors in People (IiP) status
- customer survey results
- skills matrix – percentage of key tasks covered by the teams
- position in surveys such as '100 Best Companies'
- more focused management style leading to greater compliance and better outputs

Success stories of quantitative business improvements

Success stories are commonly used by organisations when they are trying to encourage and build visible evidence of the results achieved via coaching. The stories can help organisations gain support for coaching and illustrate when coaching has helped to support a cultural change or achieve business improvements. They can include:

- stories about changes in customer perceptions

- accounts of individual or departmental successes

- stories of significant improvements in performance or results as a result of coaching

- vision statements and events to publicise achievements.

Success stories based on a quantifiable business improvement
- stories from individuals across the business about how coaching has improved their performance
- stories about how coaching has resulted in significant improvements/changes in business results or other important business performance indicators
- stories generating awareness of customer needs

So organisations are making significant attempts to gain quantitative information about the impact of coaching by using a wide range of measures. Notably, organisations are trying to use measures that specifically relate and are meaningful to the individual and the organisation. Some specific examples of measures organisations are tracking with regard to their coaching activities are described in the case study below.

CASE STUDY

Examples of evaluation activities and measures being tracked by our case study organisations

Glasgow Housing Association
- Coaching activities are reviewed through the use of agreed actions ('next steps') after each coaching session.
- On-the-job coaching for technical-type activities are measured though the use of competency-based checklists.
- The individual's manager and other colleagues are asked to rate progress in specific areas through the use of the personal development plan process.

United Utilities
- Coaches who have completed their training are surveyed to gain information about how it has helped them in their jobs and how it has helped the business. They are also asked to rate their skills/competence.

- Coaching clients are surveyed to assess the impact of coaching on their performance and behaviour.

Canada Life

- When internal coaches coach business performance review teams, the coaches look at a variety of quantitative measures: quality improvement, improvements in customer-response times (cycle-time improvements), improvements in feedback from customer surveys, productivity improvement, higher revenue and/or market share, cost reduction, etc.
- Coaching is also assessed on a qualitative basis, the internal coach looking for evidence of team commitment to tasks, team involvement in and outside of meetings, application/implementation of process steps, grasping the opportunity to make change, etc.
- When coaching is used for leadership development, the internal coaches look for qualitative data to assess the impact of coaching on improved management/leadership skills including: improvements in staff satisfaction via the regular staff survey, the number of staff going through capability procedures, improvement in team members' job performance, etc.

Norfolk, Suffolk and Cambridgeshire Strategic Health Authority

- A Coaching Skills Review Tool provides a culturally sensitive way to collect quantitative measures on coach performance and to review coachee experience through a 360-degree adaptation and a self-review questionnaire.
- Measures that are tracked include promotion of coachee, ratings of effectiveness of coach, 360-degree peer and coachee ratings versus coach self-ratings, etc.
- Evidence/testimonials are sought about how coaching can impact on service delivery and patient care.

Shell

- A variety of qualitative web-based surveys are undertaken to assess attitudes towards and experiences of coaching in terms of staff satisfaction with the quality and quantity of coaching they receive.
- Internal and external coaches are questionned about the benefits they have personally gained from being trained as coaches as well as what positive results they have seen emerge from their coaching relationships.
- A bi-annual organisation-wide employee attitude survey is undertaken containing some questions related to coaching.
- Coaching is correlated with improved competence via a new online competence-based development system.

London School of Economics and Political Science

- A questionnaire is sent to the coachee and coach at the end of the coaching assignment.

Nationwide Building Society

- Measures associated with business initiatives that delegates undertake are tracked.

- A coaching behaviour questionnaire and self-awareness tool are used to measure participants' progress as coaches.
- A validation questionnaire following the coaching programme is used to assess participants' satisfaction.
- An online survey, called Back Web is undertaken three to six months after the coaching programme. The survey randomly surveys a cross-section of delegates, their team members and managers to provide feedback on the coaching skills of the delegates.

Pertemps Recruitment Partnership
- Feedback from line managers is sought to establish how coaching support (by internal coaches) for their new starters affects their ability to manage the rest of their business.

Perkins Shibaura Engines
- The impact of coaching is assessed using a range of business measures including product quality, sickness absence, and the performance management process.
- Employee performance against the company values and behaviours is measured and an assessment made on whether coaching has helped embed those values into the company culture.
- Indirect measures are also monitored, such as the type of issues being raised in the works association, views from 'opinion pulse checks' and 'talkback sessions'.
- An employee opinion survey provides a measure of employee satisfaction.

Everest
- There are regular discussions with sponsors and line managers of the coachees. Triad meetings take place at strategic points in the coaching where relevant. HR overviews how things are going.

Selfridges
- The company's system involves a case study approach, applying interviews and observations with a group of coaches that have recently completed a coaching course and who are coaching the talent/leadership group.

Midland Area Housing Association
- There is peer assessment and review of performance and 360-degree appraisal. Progress against specific personal targets is measured, and short-term action points are checked between coaching sessions.

Alongside these activities, organisations also reported a whole host of informal activities aimed at gaining a feel for how coaching was working in the organisation. This includes talking to managers and senior managers on an informal basis about their views on how coaching is working within the organisation, as well as talking to coaches working with the organisation to gain their feedback. Satisfaction with coaching and the impact of coaching behaviours in the organisation is also assessed during wider business or HR processes such as employee attitude surveys and employee consultation activities.

What results have been achieved?

Organisations are making inroads with the measurement and evaluation of their coaching activities, but what are they actually finding? Overall, they report seeing a wide range of improvements at both individual and organisational levels. Some of the positive results that have been achieved are described below. Readers will find more detail in the full-length case studies in the Appendix on page 245.

Sample comments from our case study organisations about the impact of coaching in their organisations

Performance

'Improved performance by the individual and the team'

'Fewer human errors and thus less time spent correcting work and/or mitigating the effects of incorrect actions'

'Increase in visible performance noted by line manager or coachee'

'A decrease in managerial time required to monitor and check team members' work due to increased confidence in the individuals' performance'

Confidence and motivation

'Individuals have become more proactive as their confidence levels increase'

'Improved confidence and performance at work'

'Early feedback is mainly positive. Those being coached are motivated by the levels of support provided and attitudes towards self-directed progress are enhanced'

Behaviour change

'Re-engagement with role and organisation, greater clarity and perspective, increased proactivity and capacity for addressing issues, increased confidence, greater awareness of management/leadership styles, more effective management of challenging people, greater awareness of career options and choices'

'Change in some managers' work styles – higher commitment, more focused on actions'

'Behavioural changes in targeted individuals; improved performance in specific areas'

'There have been behavioural changes such as leadership development, confidence, resilience and greater coaching skills'

Culture

'Increased two-way communication'

'Improved employee engagement scores'

'Achieving IiP status from zero starting point within 12 months'

'Surveys indicated organisational values are better embedded'

'Results seen so far include benefits for the coachee, such as improved relationships, promotion, greater responsibility and new roles'

Leadership

'More confident and effective leadership is being demonstrated'

'Improved leadership from team-leader level'

'Decision speed has improved at senior levels'

'Management committee and general managers are "singing from the same song sheet"' '

'Improvements in confidence and motivation among the individuals being coached and a general impression from line managers that the individuals are more engaged and enthusiastic in their day-to-day work'

It seems that coaching can result in improved performance, positive behaviour change, more effective leadership, and improved confidence and motivation. These collectively contribute to positive changes to the organisational culture. This is seen in terms of greater employee engagement, better working relationships, a more effective environment and a more positive attitude towards development and change.

HOW DOES COACHING WORK?

Looking broadly at our first two questions, we can conclude that within our case study organisations there is a perception that coaching works and that there are identifiable measures that evidence their successes. However, we were also interested in finding out what our organisations thought was responsible for the improvements that coaching delivered within their organisations. How does coaching work to create improvements in individual and business performance?

There are considerable differences in the types of coaching being used, the level of training considered adequate, the presence or absence of supervision, the breadth and variety of coaching models and techniques, and the behaviours to which they are applied. Coaching therefore can work differently (and successfully) in many different situations. This makes it more awkward to draw straightforward conclusions about the conditions for effective coaching. Nevertheless, a number of common themes emerge about how coaching works to drive performance improvements. The process of coaching appears to have some specific characteristics and attributes which, in combination, help to support learning and change. Our case study organisations identified a range of attributes of the coaching relationship as well as a series of mechanisms that form part of the coaching process by which coaching is said to 'work'. The main themes from the responses are shown below.

Attributes of coaching relationships that help to explain how coaching works

Several characteristics of coaching as a form of development were felt by our case study organisations to help give an indication of how coaching works. These include:

- *a focused form of development* – Respondents provided examples of how coaching enabled individuals to take time out and maintain focus on an issue:

If you want to get the best out of people you have to invest time in their development. Coaching focuses on the individual. It is about taking the time to listen to what individuals want to achieve and what stops them.

Karen Boanas, Canada Life

- *support for change* – Respondents mentioned that the one-to-one coaching relationship enabled individuals to develop a positive perspective that change would occur and was possible. This encouraged individuals to stick with their goals and not give up:

We use coaching to develop personal effectiveness in our managers, encouraging them to move away from reactive management to proactive management and thinking more about high-leverage activity. By stepping back with them and then supporting them as they experiment with their 'ideas' we can give them a pat on the back as they start to see and feel the positive difference they are making.

Karen Boanas, Canada Life

Improving basic skills and knowledge is covered by conventional training interventions and management practices. Coaching is the vehicle used to achieve a behavioural change that can eventually change the culture within the organisation.

Ola Adams and Pamela Tilt, Nationwide

- *support for other learning and development initiatives* – Coaching was considered to be an intervention that could easily align with and support other learning and development initiatives and therefore did not operate as a stand-alone developmental intervention:

As a group we are keen to make coaching a development tool that is available to employees at every level. In a lot of cases coaching is given in conjunction with a specific development course to give the delegate support whilst change takes place.

Camilla Aitchison, Dixons Group Plc

It takes the learning from the broad brush of the Management Development Programme through to the specific aims of the individual in terms of their continuing work with their line manager and team.

Morag Mathieson, Glenmorangie plc

We work with key players addressing change to coach them to lead and manage change effectively considering the business results required as well as the 'human' results. We coach those affected by change to make the transition.

Karen Boanas, Canada Life

- *tailored, flexible support for the learner* – We all have different learning styles and preferences and one of the chief benefits of coaching was considered to be the fact that it can be tailored specifically to align with the learning style of the individual learner and the particular issues or development areas they are seeking to address:

Coaching has impact because it can be delivered flexibly – it is 1:1, tailored to the individual's needs, and confidential.

Jackie Kernaghan, London School of Economics

Coaching is a very flexible breed of training, where the syllabus or agenda is informal and changes with the mood or circumstances of the moment.

David Anderson, BPB Paperboard

- *evidence of an organisation investing in its staff* – Being offered one-to-one attention to their development was interpreted as a commitment to participants' success. This helps to build motivation and commitment to the organisation:

Formal coaching can represent a positive experience for individuals seeking development as they are given 'special attention' to grow through a series of pre-arranged coaching sessions demonstrating a commitment from the business to work with an individual to the required level of competency.

Karen Boanas, Canada Life

- *the ability to address a broad range of interconnected issues* – The fact that coaching can cover multiple areas of development was also felt to be an important part of 'how coaching works' as well as the fact that it is highly flexible. The agenda in a coaching relationship is continually reviewed and sessions can respond to issues that arise over the course of the relationship. Other forms of development were considered unable to achieve this:

Coaching covers a wide area of issues that could not have easily been addressed by a training course.

Gareth Jones, Courtenay HR

Coaching is valuable in addressing specific issues such as dealing with career plateau, career transitions, refocusing, redesigning job role, work–life balance, interpersonal relationships, understanding own management styles and others', managing conflict, dealing with change. However, it is the potential to take a more holistic view of issues and the individual's needs that differentiates it from many traditional training courses.

Jackie Kernaghan, London School of Economics

- *confidentiality and trust* – The confidential environment of a coaching relationship was felt to be a critical part of the success of coaching because it enables the coachee to explore the issues he or she faces over a series of sessions:

During the course of a coaching conversation, many kinds of issues may arise. What is actually dealt with is agreed between the coach and the client.

Roger Williams, United Utilities

It is so valuable to have an impartial, no-strings and confidential sounding-board.

Client of BBC internal coach, Aquilina 2005

The confidentiality, and objectivity to the organisational situation offered by an external coach allows people to be more fully open and honest about their issues in a way that would not be possible within the line management relationship.

Jackie Kernaghan, London School of Economics

- *a deeper form of development* – Coaching is also seen to offer a more personal and deeper form of development for individuals. Because of this, many people felt that coaching had a greater impact:

We just felt that traditional development programmes did not go deep enough. Many development courses or programmes require learning or absorbing stuff. Coaching requires a lot of immersion and experience review. It's deeply personal and, as a result, people tend to take it more seriously and it has a more lasting and profound effect on the individual.

Gareth Jones, Courtenay HR

- *individual ownership of learning* – Because the focus (and often the agenda) is chosen by the individual, a greater sense of ownership is generated, and this often results in a higher level of commitment from participants:

Coaching does not offer me the solution, but facilitates my own thinking so I can make sense of it.

Client of BBC internal coach, Aquilina 2005

Mechanisms that form part of the coaching process and that help us to understand how coaching works

Coaching is believed to embrace a series of activities and techniques that work in combination to result in positive outcomes. These include:

- *goal-setting* – Setting and monitoring targets that hold the coachee to account for his or her behaviour were frequently mentioned as important in ensuring that coaching worked:

It is about establishing goals to work towards and building a sense of achievement. The more people achieve, the more they feel they can achieve.

Karen Boanas, Canada Life

I now have a plan and a goal to address some areas around personal performance that had been frustrating me.

Client of United Utilities internal coach

- *reflection* – Coaching provides 'time out' for people to actually think about what they want from their jobs and how they can improve their performance and relationships at work:

Coaching has provided an opportunity for individuals to reflect on their contribution to and impact on the organisation, along with the support to enhance and improve their position.

Donna Baddeley, Midland Area Housing Association

- *questioning and challenging* – Coaches can challenge and question individuals about their attitudes and experiences so that they reflect and think carefully about their behaviour or what they want to achieve:

Questioning skills are such a key factor in the success or failure of coaching in order for the individual to maximise the time with the coach.

Clare Gardner, Rugby Cement

Coaching skills lie at the foundation of higher-performing leaders and teams. A skilled coach can help managers think differently about what they do and how they do it.

Roger Williams, United Utilities

- *self-awareness* – Coaching combined with a 360-degree feedback process is an effective way of increasing an individual's self-awareness and identifying any development issues or blind spots. Coaching offers a supportive environment for encouraging individuals to act and change their behaviour in the light of the feedback they receive from the 360-degree process:

Coaching helped the senior team to agree a common purpose, develop confidence as a team, identify how to recognise, modify and develop self-awareness and to better understand the team dynamic.

Extract from BPB Paperboard case study, page 249

The questions helped me look beyond my own frame of reference.

Client of a BBC internal coach, Aquilina 2005

- *structured exploration of options and decisions* – Coaching promotes individual ownership for learning but in an environment where they are both challenged and supported. Alternatives and different options can be explored before decisions are made. This combination was felt by many of our case studies to result in a highly effective climate for learning:

Through coaching, other alternatives may appear that have not been considered before. The principle is that if alternatives and action plans can be developed and owned by the individual, then supported through the line manager and coach, they are more likely to be effective.

Name not supplied

When carried out well it can be a very powerful tool. However, all too often, it is just carried out as if it was 1:1 training as opposed to getting the coachee to explore the solutions for himself/herself.

Clare Gardner, Rugby Cement

Coaching helps us to get people to think about solutions, being smarter about work issues. We have seen changes put in place where staff apply the ideas to their normal work tasks and standards.

Ellie Casey, Loughborough University

- *feedback* – Gaining feedback from a variety of different sources helps individuals to develop a realistic view of how others view their performance at work and where they need to focus their efforts. Although some feedback can be hard to take, receiving it in a supportive environment helps individuals to accept it and plan ways of making changes as a result.

- *structured, regular meetings* – Coaching meetings help to pin the learning down for the individual as the coach guides the process and keeps it on track. Triad meetings with the line manager were also felt to help ensure that learning was fully transferred back to the workplace.

Overall, our coaching case study organisations seem to believe that coaching works by providing a process to analyse issues faced, gain feedback, select options, plan approaches to deal with them, enact change and adapt in the light of feedback. All of this is discussed within a confidential and supportive relationship which ensures that the coachee feels fully supported throughout the process.

WHAT HELPS OR HINDERS THE SUCCESS OF COACHING INITIATIVES?

It is still early days for the world of coaching. We are still trying to understand the conditions in which coaching has maximum impact. We are not there yet, but our case study organisations were asked to identify both barriers to effective coaching as well as activities that can help to embed and support coaching. Our analysis of their comments indicates that organisations are currently facing six major barriers to the effective use of coaching (see below).

Barriers to effective coaching (quotes from case study questionnaires)

Lack of understanding of the value of coaching

'Lack of understanding of what coaching can achieve'

'Perception of validity of coaching and cost-effectiveness by senior managers'

'Initially, confusion over what coaching was about – eg the role of the executive coach v the role of the line manager as a coach'

'Lack of listening to individuals who attempt to implement coaching activities and see it as possibly time-wasting'

'The lack of understanding of some – ie that there are no real benefits'

Not seen as a priority for the business

'No idea of coaching as a priority activity to be implemented as part of the overall learning and development strategy'

'Organisational buy-in to coaching. It is not seen as a valuable business process (yet!)'

'Ensuring that it is positioned as part of a wider culture change process rather than an isolated development activity'

'A belief that coaching is a "nice to have"'

The organisational culture

'Lack of integrating coaching as part of the overall culture that tends to be "tell and sign" rather than letting individuals work issues out for themselves'

'Organisational culture which tends to be driven by red tape'

'Existing leadership culture is the single biggest barrier to implementation – ie mainly dictatorial non-supportive leaders who "tell" or manage by threat to improve short-term performance levels, rather than seeing the benefit in using more directive and supportive behaviours that result in longer-term sustainable performance'

'The nature of the remuneration and commission culture which rewards indvidual achievements and does not reward those that might help underperformers or good performers to improve further'

'Ensuring that the business is in the right place to embrace such a change in culture'

Overcoming resistance

'Overcoming initial resistance. Coaching is seen as something only for underperformers'

'The receptivity of coachees; good coaching example should be set from the top down; there should be consistent follow-through of relationship and actions'

'Senior executives were initially reluctant to use internal coaches'

'Coaching by line managers tends to get a lower priority than other tasks and therefore tends to be intermittent and not always effective'

Low levels of skills and experience in the organisation

'The coaching skills of line managers have been shown to vary greatly. An underlying issue is the recognition of coaching as a core leadership skill'

'Educating established managers in using a coaching style. This takes time and education and must be embedded and maintained'

'There needs to be expertise and ownership of the process within the organisation, and it does require ongoing management, promotion, communication, refreshing the pool of coaches, etc, and this has resource implications'

'Accepting the outcomes can be a real challenge for those managing the team. Coaching gives you a healthy dose of reality, which many do not have the strength of character as managers to manage and address'

Time and resources

'Coaching needs to be properly funded. Resource is needed to support the whole process'

'High workloads are the main barrier'

'"I don't have time" is a common comment'

In particular, it seems that the chief barriers concern obtaining buy-in for coaching and building understanding about what it can help the business to achieve. The lack of understanding of the value of coaching seems to translate into other barriers such as a lack of resources and managers failing to make time for coaching. Some organisations felt that elements of their organisational culture also acted as barriers to coaching, while others felt that the lack of skills and experience of managing and delivering coaching within the organisation was a major barrier.

Barriers to coaching are to be expected. It is unlikely that any organisation's implementation of a coaching initiative goes completely smoothly – there will always be sceptics and people who think it is 'just another HR initiative'. When coaching is first introduced, it also often represents a significant change in the organisation in terms of the culture or management/ leadership style. This can invoke feelings of resistance to change, particularly if people lack understanding about how it can help them in their role. As with any other organisational change, it has to be effectively managed and communicated, and barriers must be identified and tackled.

There was similar clarity about the factors that helped to generate success with coaching. And unsurprisingly, many of these reflect the barriers discussed above. The box below lists the main factors believed to support coaching activities.

Factors that help to promote effective coaching (quotes from case study questionnaires)

Providing support for coaches

'Make sure there are support groups of coaches, formed of employees who have been through the training to support each other'

'A buddy system for 'new' coaches with those who attended early on'

'Managers must take responsibility for coaching and development'

'Encourage participants to identify opportunities for coaching from the start and use the support group to discuss their experiences'

'It works best with an effective sponsor for the learner. Individuals who have experienced coaching are keen supporters of it and make excellent sponsors and are keen to do so'

'Opportunities must exist to support experiential learning'

Internal expertise and training

'Qualified personnel undertaking and supervising coaching'

'Learning about coaching ourselves and not contracting out the whole process to another organisation'

'Set up universal framework of coaching/mentoring so that we could clarify what we mean and our approach, explain structures and processes and how strands interrelate'

'Establish local ownership with local co-ordinators, set up tools and resources for support'

'Coaching needs to be designed to address the underlying issues that impact on personal performance A clear training process'

'Coaching/training must be in line with the individual's abilities and expectations'

'Getting a critical mass of people through the coaching programme'

Communication

'Communication of the benefits and allaying the fears of the possible negative aspects of coaching which individuals tend to perceive is a very important start point before coaching or any other soft skills initiative can be implemented'

'Sell it, case studies, stories, results, etc'

'Be prepared for change to take place over time. There are no quick fixes. We would put more effort into communicating about coaching and its benefits if we were starting again'

'It takes time to change from direct management styles to a coaching style, and this time must be allowed for when seeking results'

Evaluation

'There need to be clear business measures, formal accreditation and evaluation of benefits to the organisation'

'Quantifying the benefits'

'Evaluation, as in any other intervention needs to have clear defined outcomes'

Senior management buy-in and support

'Senior executives have to be willing to make the necessary investment without cast-iron guarantees or immediate payback'

'Having a senior management champion was critical to the impetus to introduce coaching in a more structured and systematic way'

'Coaching first needs to be recognised as a key tool to achieve business goals and given the necessary priority when it comes to role descriptions, tasks and targets and therefore performance appraisal and development'

'Always keep department managers and directors involved. This keeps buy-in high on the agenda'

'Needs support from top down – managers must buy into and support'

'Buy-in from the top may appear genuine but if their own leadership style does not model what they want and expect from their subordinate line, then the whole change is in jeopardy or at least may be short-lived'

Forming part of wider change or strategy

'The introduction of coaching is most effective when introduced as a part of a 'bigger picture' of organisational and cultural change'

'Cascading a coaching culture'

Preparation

'Before the coaching intervention starts, think through *all* possible outcomes, not just the positive ones you hope to achieve'

'Sessions need to be properly managed and outcomes agreed at the beginning of each session'

'Clear objectives must be set for the coaching'

'Expectations must be managed'

Rewarding and recognising coaching behaviours.

'Leadership behaviours that support continuing improvements via coaching need to be measured and rewarded or at least recognised as contributing to successful businesses in order that the link between the two is apparent and understood'

Organisations should aim to build these features into the design of their coaching programmes if they want to achieve the best results from their activities.

LESSONS LEARNED FROM THOSE WHO HAVE BEEN INVOLVED IN THE DELIVERY AND MANAGEMENT OF COACHING IN ORGANISATIONAL SETTINGS

Across our case study organisations there is a wealth of experience and understanding about how to manage and deploy coaching. Because of this, we thought it important to ask them what lessons they have learned so far. We hope that tapping into this expertise will prove to be useful for other organisations who are thinking of implementing coaching or looking to refine their current coaching activities. Learning lessons in coaching involves trial and error (seeing what works), evaluating the impact of activities and gaining feedback from coaches, coachees and external providers who have helped to shape the design. All of these sources of information allow our organisations to continually update and improve their activities to ensure that they are as effective as possible. It is without doubt an ongoing process and all our organisations said that they were still in the early stages of the learning curve. However, they were all strongly committed to improving their activities and to learning from the experiences of other organisations. Some examples follow of the issues raised by our case study organisations about the important lessons they have learned to date – broadly these fall into eight main areas.

Build understanding and communicate

- *Define a clear purpose for coaching* – There is a consensus that for coaching to be effective organisations must agree defined objectives for their activities. These should form part of an overall strategy.

- *Create a shared perspective* – Those involved in giving, receiving, supervising or supporting coaching as champions need a shared perspective on what it is for and how it will operate, and a belief that it can deliver value.

- *Select a clear model and definition for coaching* –The model of coaching adopted by an organisation must be appropriate to the issues it is designed to address and the expertise of the coaches who will be using it. Generally, manager-coaches tend to be taught single models of coaching, although in our case study organisations there were exceptions. Internal and external coaches on the other hand tended to use multiple or more complex models based on performance and developmental coaching models.

- *Communicate clear messages* – Communicate clearly that coaching is not aimed at poor performers, but is instead a tool to be used by everyone in the organisation to improve their performance and develop their skills. Another message that has to be made clear is that individuals are responsible for their own development and that being coached is not a passive activity – it requires commitment and hard work for sustainable results to be delivered.

Obtain buy-in

- *Engender belief and positive attitudes towards coaching* – This is without a doubt easier said than done. But a belief within the business in the benefits of coaching and an acceptance that coaching can contribute to business performance were thought to significantly enhance the effectiveness of coaching. This requires HR to persuade others and demonstrate the results that can be achieved.

- *Build managerial support* – Managers were felt to have a crucial role in setting the scene for coaching. If they were unsupportive of coaching, their view was likely to influence people in the team and resulted in the setting up of a number of barriers to effective coaching. Spending time getting managers on board with coaching was therefore felt to be a hugely worthwhile investment.

- *Get the investment, role-modelling and endorsement of senior executives to ensure high visibility* – This point was consistently stressed by our respondents as being vital for effective coaching due to the impact it has on buy-in across the organisation and the availability of resources for coaching.

Plan and prepare

- *Think through implementation and roll-out* – Planning and thinking through the implementation of coaching helps with the roll-out in the organisation and to gain people's buy-in to the process.

- *Prepare and brief all stakeholders in coaching* – This was felt to be important in setting expectations and building support for coaching. Stakeholders include coaches, coachees, managers and senior managers.

- *Understand and assess your organisational culture* – Examining your current culture was thought to be crucial because it allows you to anticipate the questions, issues and pockets of resistance you may face.

Measure and demonstrate results

- *Gain measurable outcomes in terms of quantitative and qualitative data* – Thinking about how you are going to measure the impact of coaching should be considered early on when planning a new coaching initiative. This is necessary for setting expectations about the results you can measure, as well as when making decisions about what evaluation methodology you are going to use. Measuring the results of coaching was felt to be important by our case study organisations because it allowed HR to prove the value of their activities, build their credibility and build the case for ongoing investment in coaching.

Be selective

- *Select who you train to be coaches* – If you are initially only training a small number of people as coaches, choose those who show the most commitment to learning and development. Select managers as coaches who are already effective at enhancing the learning of others. Coach training was felt to work best on managers who already have some basic coaching skills, are experienced at facilitating the learning of others and have a positive attitude towards coaching.

- *Choose development needs best suited to coaching* – Our organisations believed it was important to think about which type of issues/development needs coaching would be used to address (eg work issues, development needs, personal life issues, etc). Coaching is not the only option, and in many cases other forms of development might be more appropriate.

- *Choose participants who will be responsive to coaching* – Our case study organisations rarely applied coaching to everyone and it was recognised that some people were not able to benefit from coaching, or had alternative, preferred ways of learning.

- *Make good decisions about when and how coaching is applied* – HR must be prepared to use professional judgements to decide to what, when, if, and how coaching might be applied. Setting criteria for when coaching would or would not be used was felt to provide a useful framework for understanding how best to use coaching as a resource, alongside other available development options.

Take care over good selection

- *Choose the right coaching providers and build an effective partnership with them* – Making time for selecting the right type of providers was felt to pay significant dividends to our organisations. Efforts should be made to establish exactly what is needed from a provider and these criteria should be used during selection. Once a provider (or providers) has been selected, time should be spent forming an effective working relationship on an ongoing basis.

- *Ensure that coaches have core competencies, skills and knowledge* – At the very minimum, potential coaches must have the ability to listen actively and facilitate the creation of clear action plans.

Link with strategy and culture

- *Use coaching as a tool to support business objectives* – Coaching was felt to be most effective when it was explicitly linked to wider business goals. This helped to build credibility and gain buy-in as people could see that it was designed to support them in achieving their own goals.

- *Coaching should form part of the culture of the organisation* – A culture based on learning and coaching was found to support the introduction of coaching initiatives and increase the likelihood of effectiveness.

- *Align with HR processes and business strategy* – If a coaching initiative is positioned as part of a wider culture change process, ensure that it is closely aligned with other HR development initiatives so that it is not seen as a stand-alone intervention.

Provide training and support

- *Provide a range of learning opportunities to support and develop newly-trained coaches* – Newly-trained coaches are most often still fairly inexperienced in their role as coaches. Organisations therefore felt it was important to offer them ongoing support, professional development and supervision so that they could continue to build their skills and expertise.

- *Understand professional boundaries* – Respondents felt it was important that coaches should make good professional judgements and place boundaries around the coaching they provide. Because many manager-coaches had very limited training, such boundaries created important safety-nets. Some organisations took greater steps than others to make these boundaries clear during coach training or when assessing external coaches.

SUMMARY CONCLUSIONS

Our case study organisations firmly believe that coaching works. There are measurable impacts at the individual and organisational levels and the factors that help and hinder effective coaching are identifiable and consistent across a wide range of different organisations. However, although measuring the impact is achievable at the individual level, many organisations are still struggling to gain meaningful data at the organisational level, particularly in determining return on investment. But it is early days and organisations are still learning how best to demonstrate the impact of coaching, by experimenting with a range of different measures. Respondents have already learned a great deal and are increasingly understanding the factors that help and hinder coaching activities. We can conclude that the results from our case study research indicate that coaching is a valuable intervention as long as it is well targeted, appropriate to the issues faced and properly supported, and that those undertaking it have the skills to be successful as coaches.

Before turning to whether the research literature supports this view and our examination of the specific issues facing external coaches, manager-coaches and internal coaches, we end this chapter with the words of some of our respondents:

I have personally found coaching of value to me in my professional development. I have also had very positive experience in coaching others. I think it is something we will see more of in our sector and organisation over the coming years.

Sharon Green, Stephenson Harwood

The introduction of a coaching programme and the extension of coaching skills across the management group is part of a wider programme of cultural and organisational change. It forms a key part of our thinking about leadership and the development of high-performing teams and individuals. It is still early days and we haven't got our heads around specific 'quantifiable' measures for the impact of coaching and recognise that we have to improve in this area. We are seeing plenty of subjective evidence to say it works and have already found spin-off benefits that we had not anticipated. However, the thing that still gives me the biggest buzz is seeing the obvious and sustained enthusiasm of our coaches and continued support from the business almost two years on since we began the programme. This, coupled with the stories from managers and individuals who have benefitted from coaching, reinforces the belief that organisational and personal performance will increase over time, and it will be a sustainable increase.

Roger Williams, United Utilities

I believe that coaching has been shown to have a range of benefits in the organisation. This view is also supported by our senior management so we are introducing more ways to encourage coaching and development of staff.

Lester Desmond, Shell

Coaching is seen as a key tool in helping our people deliver the business plan, through recognising that all employees posess the skills and talents required to reach their goals, but with the added confidence of knowing that support from peers and management in delivering the goals is there when you need it.

Nigel Briers, Perkins Shibaura Engines Limited

Coaching is very close to our hearts here at KFFS. We believe it has helped changed our culture.

Tracey Smith, Kwik-fit Financial Services

5
Executive or external coaching

External or 'executive' coaches are a growing resource for UK businesses. It is estimated that the global demand is doubling every year and it is currently a $500 million industry in the USA (Shearman and Freas, 2004). But the UK is not far behind – the *Financial Times* recently reported there were some 4,000 professional coaches operating in the UK (Sanghera, 2004). The origins of executive coaching are relatively hard to establish; however, these days few industries or sectors exist where executive coaching is not being used. This high level of investment and usage means there is an increasing demand for evidence to verify its value and impact.

Although it is clear that external or executive coaching is widely used, it is less clear why companies use coaches, the exact role they play, the profile of skills and attributes they hold, and in which areas they specifically add value. It is these questions that we will try to answer in this chapter. We will also discuss a key difference emerging in the literature and noticeable in our case study organisations: external coaching with an open agenda (where the individual solely determines the content) and external coaching to a specific organisational agenda. We follow this with a consideration of the research on the effectiveness of these approaches and review what impact they are having in organisational settings. Finally, we outline key issues in the use of executive or external coaches.

WHAT IS EXECUTIVE OR EXTERNAL COACHING?

The terms 'external coaching' and 'executive coaching' are often used interchangeably to refer to the same type of coaching. For the remainder of this chapter, we will use the term 'executive coaching' to avoid repeating both terms throughout.

As with many other forms of coaching, a number of definitions exist. One useful example is offered by Hall *et al* (1999) who define it as

> *a practical, goal-focused form of personal, one-on-one learning for busy executives that may be used to improve performance or executive behaviour, enhance a career or prevent derailment, and work through organisational issues or change initiatives. Essentially, coaches provide executives with feedback they would normally never get about personal, performance, career and organisational issues.*

Several commentators have argued that executive coaching is really a case of 'the emperor's new clothes' (eg Tobias, 1996) because they feel it is simply a repackaging of activities and techniques borrowed from other disciplines such as counselling, psychology, learning, consultation, and so on. However, many others would argue that executive coaching is something specific and unique in its own right. In several ways, executive coaching is defined as much by what it is not as by what it is, and this has contributed to the vociferousness of the debate in this area.

Although a large number of definitions of executive coaching exist, they commonly highlight a number of specific characteristics:

- It is delivered by coaches operating from outside the organisation.
- It is generally provided for senior-level employees or executives.
- It consists of one-to-one developmental discussions.
- It provides people with feedback and aims to build self-awareness.
- It is used to address a wide range of issues, but often focuses on improving behaviour or performance or developing/enhancing skills.
- It works on the premise that clients are self-aware and do not require a clinical intervention.

There are two main types of executive coaching assignments: those which focus on the individual's agenda for change (sometimes called 'free agenda' coaching) and those which stem from a specific organisational agenda. The main difference between these two roles is the freedom of the individual to choose the coaching agenda, although the time-span of the intervention may also differ significantly. In free agenda coaching, the agenda is driven by the individual with little or no direct input from the sponsoring organisation. It has a broad scope addressing a number of personal, developmental and organisational issues. The second type of executive coaching is introduced to specifically address defined organisational aims. It often forms part of, or follows, a development event and seeks to develop the executive's skills and performance in alignment with organisational goals. Within both these types of coaching, a wide variety of issues can be discussed and dealt with, including interpersonal, communication or leadership skills, performance issues, personal impact and style, transitions to new roles, self-awareness, and so on. Organisations do sponsor both types of executive coaching, but many feel more comfortable investing in executive development into which they have some input.

Organisational agendas for executive coaching can stem from a variety of different activities, but are frequently a consequence of strategic initiatives and wider leadership development activities. At the heart of the rationale for offering executives this form of development is the assumption that by developing greater self-awareness, working through issues/problems and developing new skills or styles, their contribution and effectiveness will improve. And by enhancing the performance of the most influential people within the organisation, it is believed that the performance and results of the organisation as a whole will improve.

WHO ARE EXECUTIVE COACHES?

One of the remarkable features of the burgeoning executive coaching industry is how little is known about the coaches themselves, their areas of competence and the selection processes used to appoint them. Given the cost of employing them and the influential position they often hold with very senior-level business leaders, the absence of this basic information is worrying.

The lack of regulation and accreditation in the coaching industry means that executive coaching services are currently being delivered by a diverse group of individuals and organisations. Executive coaches come from a variety of different professional backgrounds. Examples include human resources, occupational psychology, training and development, sports psychology, counselling and management development. Many coaches are self-employed or operate within small firms. However, there are also coaching consulting firms for whom executive coaching is the major part of their practice, and many large HR/management/ outplacement consultancies have added executive coaching services to their portfolios, aiming to secure large multinational contracts. Naturally, all these different 'types' of executive coaches bring with them very different skills and experience. And this is where opinion begins to diverge on which skills, qualities and experience executive coaches should have.

But what can the research tell us about who executive coaches are? A few of the professional bodies have published details of their membership, but probably the most extensive information is provided by the International Coach Federation (ICF) (Grant and Zackon, 2004). This surveyed 2,529 of its member coaches and found that most (57.3 per cent) held some specific credentials, although the level was not defined. The majority were female (73 per cent) with an average age of 45–54 years. Member coaches came from a broad range of prior professions ranging from teachers through to executives. Thus even within one of the professional bodies there is a wide variety of experience, practice and credentials.

The education level of coaches appears to vary internationally as was indicated in a three-country survey by i-Coach Academy (information from i-Coach Academy, personal communication, May 2004). In the UK, some executive coaches are operating at the highest level with no coach-specific training, while others hold doctorate-level awards (see Figure 11).

Information about the profiles of executive coaches is not, however, helped by the fragmentation and the differences of opinion within the coaching industry itself. Membership of professional bodies can be obtained on the basis of as little as five days' training or as many as 2,000 hours' plus. And significant differences also exist in respect of the criteria (experience, skill and knowledge-base) required for membership of the different coaching professional bodies. For example, one group (the Association of Professional Executive Coaches and Supervisors) requires a combination of business and psychological experience for membership as an accredited coach. Coaches who are members of the Association of Business Psychology will also combine these areas in their experience base, whereas the Worldwide Association of Business Coaches places a strong emphasis on senior business experience to gain membership. Membership of the Special Group in Coaching Psychology inevitably requires a core education in psychology for practitioner status.

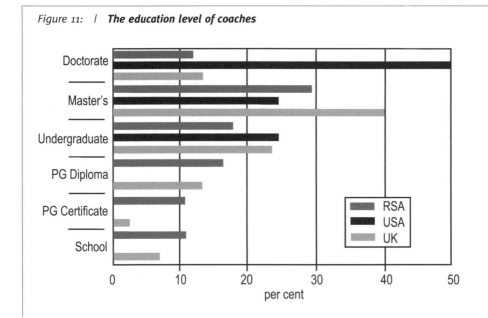

Figure 11: / *The education level of coaches*

We can obtain more understanding about the profile of executive coaches by reviewing studies that investigated what requirements organisations requested when recruiting executive coaches. Organisations employing external coaches differ in the preferred experience and qualifications that they require. In particular, there is a debate within the literature and for organisations about whether coaches should hold psychological qualifications or at least develop psychology alongside business or human resourcing competencies. A recent study by consultants Beam Pines (Ventrone, 2005) noted that organisations using executive coaches looked for business experience (85 per cent), psychology qualifications (50 per cent) and organisational development knowledge (45 per cent) as the preferred credentials when selecting coaches.

The information we have reviewed here demonstrates that there is no typical profile for an executive coach – this may change in the future as the industry becomes more professionalised and issues such as regulation and accreditation are formalised. It may be that executive coaching does enable people from differing backgrounds and experience to bring to the table their own unique contribution. However, the caveat to this is that these coaches clearly understand and articulate where the boundaries to their coaching abilities lie. Because this may not be the case at present, it is clear that organisations must exert considerable care when assessing the competence of the coaches they employ.

THE HISTORY AND DEVELOPMENT OF EXECUTIVE COACHING

Exactly when the practice of executive coaching first came into use is fairly hard to establish in the literature, but there is a general agreement that the term 'executive coaching' came into usage in the early 1980s (Tobias, 1996; West and Milan, 2001), and had become widespread by around 1990. Views on its exact determinants are more contentious, many commentators pointing to origins in sports coaching and the performing arts (West and Milan, 2001) which they believe is evidenced by the number of sports professionals and actors transferring their skills into the business arena. However, others feel that the origins of executive coaching stem from other 'helping' disciplines such as counselling and consulting, whose professionals moved their practice into the business world.

In the past, there was a tendency for executive coaching to be used as a remedial activity. An external coach was brought in by a company as part of a 'rescue fantasy' (Wasylyshyn, 2003) – the last chance for an underperforming executive. For organisations, executive coaching provided an opportunity to undertake pre-emptive and proactive interventions to improve their performance (Greco, 2001; Kilburg, 1996). However, the tide has turned and executive coaching is now increasingly offered to the most highly valued staff in the organisation as a means of maximising their contribution. As pointed out by Pirie (2004), the perception of coaching has undergone 'a transition from stigma to status symbol'.

As with many bespoke services, engagement of an external coach has taken on aspirational qualities. There is a growing trend for senior executives to equate the offer of an executive coach as an indication of their worth and status. Palmer (2003) claims that 'the executive coach has become the new must-have corporate accessory'. Indeed, it was noted by researchers at the Institute for Employment Studies that the phenomenon of 'coaching envy' is a reality for the members of its research forum (Carter, 2001). As Hall *et al* (1999) observe:

> *Executives like the confidentiality and personal attention: they also like what coaching does for their careers.*

Media hype and the increasing popularity of coaching more generally has led to a huge growth in the use of executive coaches. Ninety-two per cent of our case study organisations employed external coaches, and 64 per cent of respondents to the CIPD's 2005 training and development survey reported using coaching by external practitioners. Moreover, 36 per cent of respondents to the survey said they expected their use of external coaches would increase in the next few years. Despite this, some signs of the executive coaching market maturing are starting to appear – the majority (51 per cent) of respondents felt that they would keep their use of executive coaches at the same level in the next few years, while 13 per cent said they might decrease their use.

WHAT HAS CONTRIBUTED TO THE GROWING POPULARITY OF EXECUTIVE COACHING?

The popularity of executive coaching seems to result from a series of characteristics that make it highly suitable for the development of time-pressurised business leaders. Executive coaching can be undertaken in short sessions delivered at times that fit in with their other work commitments (eg while travelling, early/late in the day, and so on). And it can also be a huge support for executives trying to deal with rapid change and pressure. Executive coaching can be a flexible, responsive resource for business leaders that can be delivered 'just-in-time' when they need support or guidance.

The fact that the coach is external to the organisation is also viewed as being highly beneficial – particularly by the executives themselves. Coaching by executive coaches is often perceived as being more independent and confidential. This is illustrated by a quote provided by one of our case study respondents in the questionnaire they completed.

The confidentiality, and objectivity to the organisational situation offered by an external coach allows people to be more fully open and honest about their issues in a way that would not be possible within the line management relationship. One coachee said that if their manager had given them the same feedback that the coach had, they would have felt criticised and defensive.

For senior-level managers/executives it can be 'lonely at the top' because they have few people they can confide in, and develop ideas and discuss decisions and concerns with. An external coach can be used as a 'safe and objective haven' for executives to discuss issues and provide support (Masciarelli, 1999). An opposing view identified executives' lack of access to people who ask questions, provide advice and give counsel as the greatest difficulty facing senior executives. He observed how people who work closely with executives are often afraid of, or do not know how to confront them regarding their behaviour or decision-making. Executive coaches can fill this gap by providing the executive with feedback about his or her behaviour and its impact upon others. Kampa and White (2002) state,

We view a major purpose of the executive coach's role as being to provide feedback for the executive about the executive's behaviour and its impact on others, both those within and outside the organisation.

The growing acceptance of the costs associated with the poor decisions or leadership style of senior managers/executives has resulted in executive coaching's providing HR with an opportunity to undertake pre-emptive and proactive interventions to support them (Greco, 2001; Kilburg, 1996).

External coaches are also felt to be more appropriate than other coaching practitioners (eg internal coaches) in particular situations. For example, internal coaches can be less suitable when highly sensitive or confidential issues have to be addressed or when a coach with extensive and diverse experience is required. This is illustrated by the following quotes from our case study respondents.

Independent coaches, rather than internal coaches, are thought to be the best solution for coaching at a senior level in Panasonic due to trust and confidence issues.

Extract from Panasonic Europe case study, p. 278

Executives often welcome the added value of an external perspective that an external coach brings and the coaching may also be seen to be more confidential.

Extract from Shell case study, p.286

The CIPD's guide to coaching (Jarvis, 2004) offers the following advice:

External coaches are preferable:

- *for providing sensitive feedback to senior business leaders. For political reasons, this can be difficult for an internal coach*

- *for bringing specialised expertise from a wide variety of organisational and industry situations*
- *when individuals are concerned about 'conflict of interests' and whether confidentiality will be observed*
- *for providing a wider range of ideas and experience*
- *for being less likely to judge and being perceived as more objective.*

Executive coaching is also considered one of the best forms of development for senior managers and leaders. The CIPD's 2005 training and development survey interestingly found that although external, executive coaching was not among the most frequently reported activities for leadership development (31 per cent reported using it), it was rated as one of the most effective (84 per cent rated it as effective). And this is supported by a recent study by Cranfield that investigated innovative approaches to developing future-oriented strategic thinking in senior leaders (Clarke, Bailey and Bristow, 2003). They surveyed a range of private sector organisations across Europe and the USA, as well as senior managers and clinicians across the NHS. The respondents in the NHS survey were participating in an internal leadership development programme and were asked what they considered the most effective development process for preparing future senior-level leaders. The top three most effective processes were considered to be:

- on-the-job training with support and a good mentor – 46 per cent
- off-the-job personal development – eg MBA programme – 27 per cent
- coaching/mentoring – 15 per cent.

It therefore appears that executive coaching is seen as a part of a coherent approach to successful executive development.

All of these characteristics of executive coaching have fuelled the growth of executive coaching in recent years. However, there is also little doubt that its increased popularity has also been partly stimulated by the hype of the popular press.

WHAT ARE ORGANISATIONS USING EXECUTIVE COACHES FOR?

Several research studies have attempted to investigate the reasons organisations provide for hiring executive coaches. For example, research by the Institute of Employment Studies identified six main business reasons for engagement of an executive coach (Carter, 2001):

- supporting the induction of a senior manager
- supporting individuals identified as high-potential or as targets for extra support to increase the proportion of those from minority groups likely to reach senior management positions as part of an affirmative action plan
- supporting individuals or teams through the introduction or implementation of major structural or cultural change
- as a critical friend or sounding-board for a senior manager where mentors are not appropriate or practical

- supporting the personal effectiveness of individuals by underpinning wider development programmes or processes such as 360-degree feedback programmes or development centres.
- the reward or retention of senior managers.

Similarly, a survey of 1,153 UK organisations by Origin and the University of Central England found that organisations used executive coaching for three main reasons (Sparrow and Arnott, 2004):

- to support a strategic initiative
- to support leadership development
- to respond directly to individual request

The explanations our case study organisations gave for using executive coaches also reflect these same reasons, as is illustrated by the quotes below:

The organisation undertook a major restructuring and culture change programme to meet the changing demands of the external business environment. The managing director specifically requested personal support via external coaching for the entire senior team throughout the change process and encouraged the development of coaching skills internally.

Extract from BPB Paperboard case study, p. 249

Use of external coaches is largely linked to the executive coaching programme. Shell has arrangements with a selection of external providers. When people in leadership positions are looking for a coach, individual needs are assessed and then individuals are put in touch with a suitable coach following a discussion with their manager.

Extract from Shell case study, p. 286

The goal and vision was clear – to develop a client-centred organisation where people naturally focus on and think about their clients.

Extract from Bovis Lend Lease case study, p. 245

Taken together these studies indicate that executive coaching can be offered in support of either an organisational or individual need. A company might thus offer coaching to help a senior manager assist his or her team to undergo a major change process but might also offer coaching in response to an individual request where no organisational imperative is identified.

WHAT TYPE OF WORK DO EXECUTIVE COACHES DO?

Cavanagh and Grant (2005) categorise three different types of coaching in their work with executives:

- *skills coaching* – This can be of short duration and requires the coach to focus on specific behaviours. The coach may model behaviours and encompass a rehearsal and feedback process.

- *performance coaching* – This focuses on the process by which the coachee can set goals, overcome barriers, and evaluate and monitor their performance.

- *developmental coaching* – This takes a broader, more holistic view, often dealing with intimate personal and professional questions and involving the creation of a personal reflective space. This is a core area in which external coaches rather than internal coaches are usually but not always preferred as a resource.

Reviewing the experiences of case study organisations, it seems that executive coaches are indeed used for all three of these reasons. However, although executive coaches were occasionally involved in skills coaching, more often our case study organisations preferred to train internal coaches to fulfil this role.

The technical skills coaching is undertaken by technical experts throughout the business – these people have undertaken training to develop their coaching expertise so that they can act as effective technical experts.

Lester Desmond, Shell

The size of the organisation and regularity of need for skills coaching may influence the extent to which executive coaches are used for this purpose.

Performance coaching and developmental coaching were the main types of coaching that our case study organisations hired executive coaches to deliver, although it seems that executive coaches play a particularly strong role in developmental coaching. It is likely that this is because of the complexity of this type of coaching (ie supporting changes in individual behaviour) and the in-depth skills and experience needed to deliver it effectively. This is illustrated by comments provided in the initial questionnaire we gave to our case study organisations:

Where a shift in behaviour is required to assist the person in a new role. For a senior person where a development course cannot meet the specific need and we have the ability to source a coach to address the specific need.

Behavioural change; opening minds; expanding horizons; organisation change.

Looking more closely at the specific remit executive coaches tend to address, we find that helping senior managers and executives develop their interpersonal skills and deal with change are the most common reasons for hiring executive coaches. A study by Horner (2002) confirmed that impact, influence, transitions, culture change and self-awareness are the areas executive coaching is most commonly used to address (see Figure 12 on page 88).

This is supported by research by Hay (2002), who also pointed to developing interpersonal skills, change management style and building team effectiveness as the main reasons for using executive coaching.

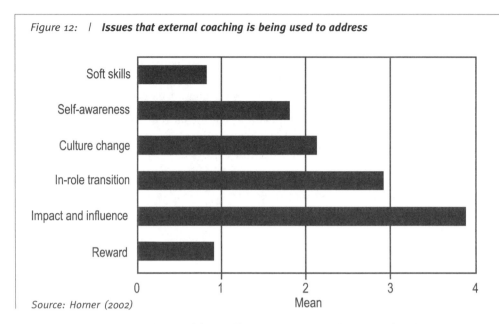

Figure 12: | *Issues that external coaching is being used to address*

Source: Horner (2002)

Our case study organisations additionally reported a similar focus for their executive coaching activities:

Panasonic is also encouraging its senior leaders to consider executive coaching as an effective tool in their own personal development. Aimed at harnessing personal leadership development, executive coaching – provided through an external supplier – can focus on some key areas:

- *enhancing personal presence and influence*
- *improving risk-taking and decision-making*
- *boosting creativity and collaboration during times of change.*

Extract from Panasonic Europe case study, p. 278

Ross Gorbert concludes: 'We didn't set out to embed coaching in our culture, but as we created development programmes, including a coaching element has proved to be the most beneficial and most sustainable way of achieving behaviour change.'

Extract from Bovis Lend Lease case study, p. 245

Two further rapidly developing roles for the external coach, which were often reported by our case study organisations, are to consolidate learning from training or development events (eg 360-degree assessment) through follow-up coaching, and to support the development of internal coaching capability within the organisation. This latter role involved either providing coaching or supervision for manager or internal coaches to support their training, or providing advice about the design of internal coach-training programmes.

Managers were initially trained by a coaching skills programme delivered by an external provider, but now that has been incorporated into general leadership modules that are run within the company.

Extract from Perkins Shibaura Engines Ltd case study, p. 281

The two-day programme is followed by a confidential one-to-one session with the external coach. This allows participants to discuss issues that arise during the programme, as well as giving them an opportunity to receive coaching themselves (and it allows them to see the coaching approach in action again).

Extract from Tate Museums case study, p. 292

To prepare the coaches for their role, an external coaching consultancy was commissioned to run a series of performance workshops to develop the skills of the coaches. ... Following on from the workshop, coaches take part in two action learning set events over the next six months. These are again facilitated by the external coaching company and provide an opportunity for the coaches to talk about their experiences and any issues that have arisen and to explore how they should be tackled. The coaches can also contact the external coaching company for ongoing support during the lifespan of the projects.

Extract from Surrey and Sussex Strategic Health Authority case study, p. 289

After the programme, the external coaching company runs external supervision days for the internal coaches so that they can share learning and receive independent advice and coaching on difficult situations they experience. It is a minimum requirement to attend two supervision days every six months.

Extract from United Utilities case study, p. 296

In several of our case study organisations, these activities were connected to aspirations to develop a coaching culture within their organisations and often resulted from the initial engagement of an external coach for a senior executive. Once the benefits of coaching became clear to the executive, he or she recruited the coach to assist with the roll-out of coaching to other parts of the organisation. It is not always clear whether the external coach is acting as a trainer, management consultant or coach in this role.

Following the MD's own positive experience, coaching was offered to a senior search consultant who was feeling demotivated and at a crossroads in her professional and personal life. This was resulting in a number of things including tensions within the team. She, too, found the coaching hugely beneficial ... Although Courtenay HR is a small business, a coaching programme was introduced for all client-facing staff (12 people). The coaching programme comprises 6–8 sessions, generally over 12–15 months.

Extract from Courtenay HR case study, p. 255

The evidence suggests that high on the list of priorities for organisations using executive coaches are areas such as interpersonal, leadership and change skills which require a developmental style of coaching due to the need to change behaviours. However, support and consultancy for wider coaching initiatives also came through strongly as a theme.

HOW DO EXECUTIVE COACHES DIFFER FROM OTHER COACHING PRACTITIONERS?

It is fairly obvious how executive coaches differ from manager-coaches. It is a full-time job, they are more experienced and knowledgeable, and they operate outside the managerial relationship (and the organisation more generally). However, more confusion exists about how executive and internal coaches differ in terms of their remit and skill base.

Research by the School of Coaching that compared external and internal coaching found that their activities were provided in response to the same mix of organisational and individual objectives: to improve individual performance (81 per cent), to support personal development (79 per cent) and to improve company performance (78 per cent) (Kubicek, 2002).

So do internal and executive coaches do the same thing? Apparently not. The research indicates that although there are some similarities, external coaches do generally have a different remit for their coaching activities compared to those of internal coaches. Interestingly, the most common use for both internal and external coaching was 'enhancing overall leadership skills' (Ventrone, 2005). However, apart from this, the data revealed little overlap in the uses of the two types of coaches. More specifically, enhancing job performance and developing communication skills ranked among the top uses for external coaching. However, these items were much less common uses for internal coaching. In contrast, developing technical skills ranked as one of the preferred uses for internal coaching but was the single most low-rated item for external coaching. In addition, respondents indicated that they are more likely to use internal rather than external coaches to prevent derailment.

Broadly speaking, the other main differences between internal and external coaches are that executive coaches tend to have a broader base of experience and expertise, gleaned from their work across organisations in different sectors and of different sizes. Differences between internal and executive coaches is covered more extensively in Chapter 6, which focuses on research looking at the internal coach. However, it is important to note here that the more complex and varied coaching that executive coaches often deliver does raise issues about their training and skill base. The range of competencies and skills required of the external coach tends to be broader and more in-depth, going beyond the more restricted range of coaching skills required for a manager or internal coach. This is a topic that is discussed at length in Chapter 8. However, organisations must still be careful to consider the type of work (eg performance, skills, development coaching) that they are hiring executive coaches to undertake, and must exert considerable care to explore the competence of the coaches they employ.

Two particularly controversial issues surround beliefs about the required skill bases of executive coaches. The first centres on the argument that because in-depth coaching often involves addressing psychological processes a psychology background may be required. An article by Berglas in the *Harvard Business Review* makes much of the need for coaches to be aware of potential psychological problems with clients. Berglas (2002) wrote:

> *I believe that in an alarming number of situations, executive coaches who lack rigorous psychological training do more harm than good. By dint of their backgrounds and biases, they downplay or simply ignore deep-seated psychological problems they don't understand.*

However, this much-cited article takes a very limited view of the evidence base, promoting what would be a minority position even within the psychological community. Other parties argue that although coaches need a good understanding of relevant psychological principles and theories, it is unnecessary for them to be formally qualified as a chartered psychologist. This is because several other types of qualifications (eg coaching specific courses) cover relevant psychological theories in enough depth to provide individuals with a necessary grounding for them to operate as a coach. Worries emerge when executive coaches are operating without any relevant training that covers psychological theory and principles at all, whether specific coaching or psychology qualifications.

The second contentious issue is whether executive coaches must have similar experience and background to the senior-level employees that they coach (eg relevant industry experience). This is an area that has not been subject to detailed study, and assumptions are often made in coach selection about the relevance of past roles or experience which in fact may have little to do with the task facing the coach and their client. Most people would agree that executive coaches do need a strong understanding of organisational dynamics and the business world to be effective. However, direct experience of a particular industry or role is unlikely to be necessary for a person to be an effective coach – their real contribution is their ability to help individuals learn and develop. But opinions do differ. In some cases, industry experience is viewed as highly desirable often because it helps to establish the 'face validity' of the coach (ie for coaches to have credibility with the executives being coached). The competence and credibility of the executive coach is a major part in the process of winning over the individual and creating a good working relationship. Other commentators point out, however, that hiring a coach on the basis of specific experience can be counterproductive in a coaching relationship. One of the main benefits of using executive coaches is their neutrality and objectivity. This can uncover limiting beliefs, values and assumptions that may be obstructing the strategic objectives of the individual and the organisation. It makes sense to assume that executive coaches should be hired for their ability and skills to help people make changes in behaviour and performance rather than anything else.

So it does appear that there is a different emphasis in the focus and breadth of the work of internal and executive coaches, and in the skills and experience they should hold. This is likely to have implications for their required training, experience and knowledge base. More information on these issues appears in Chapters 6 and 8.

DOES EXECUTIVE COACHING WORK?

So does executive coaching actually work? Is it worth the expense, and does it deliver greater results than other types of coaching such as internal coaching or manager coaching? The bulk of the research that exists investigating the impact of coaching in business settings has focused on organisations' use of executive coaches. This is partly because it has a longer history of use, but also because it is a more obvious (and often higher) cost to organisations than using internal resources. Furthermore, coaches and coaching organisations themselves have been investing in research to prove the value of their activities, and this has additionally fuelled the research programme in this area. This factor has to be kept in mind when reviewing the research in this area – as David Clutterbuck warns: 'Senior HR professionals are rightly highly suspicious of 'research' by coaching companies' (personal communication, June 2005).

Of our case study organisations 92 per cent employed external coaches and 91 per cent considered them either a 'very effective' or 'effective' developmental resource. This almost exactly mirrors findings from other CIPD research which found that 92 per cent of survey respondents believed that coaching by external practitioners was effective (CIPD, 2005). A number of studies are emerging which attempt to go beyond measuring perceptions of whether executive coaching is effective. In particular, there have been increasing attempts to measure the changes that occur as a result of executive coaching – both for individuals and the organisations in which they work.

One investigation explored the development of 24 executives from a variety of different organisations (Feldman, 2005). They were coached for 40 hours over 13 months, and also attended three peer round-table events to share experience and gain support. The executives were given a choice of coach from a pool of 12 coaches recruited for their diversity of background and interest. The coachees all had less than four years' experience at the executive level but no prior experience of coaching. A learning contract was drawn up for all coachees and the research design included a survey before, in the middle, and at the end of the study, semi-structured interviews (over the phone for 20 participants) and detailed case studies of five participants. The impact of coaching was assessed around six themes:

- leadership, management and technical skills
- organisational structure and capacity
- attitudes and beliefs
- personal life
- job satisfaction
- tenure.

At the end of the study coachees' overall satisfaction level with the coaching experience was measured as 4.6 on a scale of 5 (positive). One notable point was that significant improvements in leadership and management skills were achieved. There was also an increase in the coachees' effectiveness at balancing the demands of their personal and professional lives. Although no significant change over time was noted in the level of job stress and burnout, several coachees felt the coaching had encouraged them to take vacations and personal time. One notable point was that these changes became apparent within six months of starting the study.

Another interesting study looked at the perceived effectiveness of executive coaching across various measures and also considered the perceived effectiveness of different coaching methods (Dawdy, 2004). Sixty-two participants took part in the study, all from a large engineering firm. They had participated for at least six months in a coaching programme, which was provided by a single firm using an in-house framework. A survey of the participants was conducted at the end of the programme to gain their views on its effectiveness. Of the respondents, 90 per cent considered coaching to be effective. Additionally, 91 per cent thought it was valuable to their relationships outside work, while

75 per cent thought it was valuable to their relationships within work. On the question of whether it had facilitated behaviour change on a scale from 1 (not met) to 7 (met far beyond expectations), the mean score was 4.34.

Interestingly, there was no significant difference in the perceived success of various coaching techniques used by the coach (eg interviews, feedback, listening). Eighty-eight per cent of those who had experienced 360-degree feedback rated it as positive or neutral, and a similar result was found for communication with the coach (82 per cent), acquiring new skills (74 per cent) and the coach's encouragement (87 per cent).

A rapidly developing area of research explores the executive coaching process itself. One example is a study by Dingman (2004) who investigated whether there was a significant relationship between the quality of the coaching process and coachees' job-related attitudes (eg job satisfaction, organisational commitment and work–life conflict) and self-efficacy. The researchers looked at the evidence for executive coaching efficacy using the Kirkpatrick (1967) training evaluation criteria and then attempted to establish whether these factors related to the success of executive coaching, in this case measured by changes in the self-efficacy and job-related attitudes of the coachee. The assumption implicit in the work is that positive job-related attitudes correlate with high job performance. Executives were asked to rate their coach in terms of three specific behaviours: interpersonal skills, communication style and instrumental support.

The quality of the coaching relationship was found to have a positive effect on self-efficacy but there was a negative effect on job satisfaction. This may have been influenced by the fact that some of the executives were being coached out of their jobs. There was no support for a relationship between coaching and coachees' levels of life–work conflict and organisational commitment.

When reviewing the existing research, it is useful to separate the studies which looked at executive coaching where the individual has set the agenda himself or herself (free agenda coaching) versus instances when the individuals were working to a set agenda identified by the organisation (coaching to a specific agenda).

Executive coaching to a specific organisational agenda

This type of coaching often follows on from other developmental activities such as leadership development programmes and 360-degree feedback activities where the individual has undertaken some self-assessment or diagnostic work resulting in feedback. As such, the organisation is prompting the type of issues the executives will address during the coaching by making them more aware of their personal style and areas they need to develop in. Many commentators believe that follow-on activity such as coaching is critical to making the investment in development programmes such as 360-degree feedback actually pay off. Where these diagnostic interventions often fall down is in providing the means for participants to actually make lasting changes to their behaviour. It seems that 'knowing what you need to change' is only one piece of the jigsaw – it is not enough to bring about actual changes in a person's style or work habits. This is where executive coaching is felt to fit in, because of its change orientation and support for ongoing development. It is a viewpoint supported by

Locke and Latham (1990), who demonstrated that it is the goals that people set in response to feedback which promote change. So that is the theory – but does the research evidence support it?

A recent student asked the question, 'Did coaching following participation in a leadership programme make a difference in individual leadership development, and if it did, in what ways?' (Hernez-Broome, 2004). The research involved 43 graduates from the Centre for Creative Leadership's 'leadership development programme' (a five-day intensive programme including a $3\frac{1}{2}$-hour coaching session near the end to determine the objectives to work on in the coming months). Twenty-two participants were offered follow-on executive coaching using the same coach they had worked with in the programme. At the end of the coaching intervention structured interviews were carried out with the coached individual and a paired non-coached subject to determine whether behaviour had changed. The overall results were:

- The coached subjects were more specific about where they had sought and achieved behaviour change, whereas the non-coached subject tended to report broad areas of change.

- The behaviour changes identified were focused on leadership behaviour with the coached group, whereas the non-coached group identified work–life balance as the dominant theme.

- The coached group also developed a focus on their own coaching behaviours, whereas only 10 per cent of the non-coached group mentioned this.

- The coached group reported greater success in achieving their objectives (as indicated from a 7-point scale – however, no statistics or primary data are given in the paper).

This research indicates that coaching conferred a number of benefits in terms of providing individuals with more focus and support in achieving both their own and the organisation's goals to change and develop their leadership behaviours

Coaching following development programmes is often considered helpful, because of the overwhelming amount of information that participants receive as well as the emotional response that unexpected feedback can trigger. Discussing the results with a coach and setting goals can help people to make sense of the issues raised and ensure that positive steps are taken to begin addressing them. An early CIPD study (Lane, 1994), focusing on small to medium-sized businesses, reported that coaching can aid 360-degree feedback in the following ways:

- focusing on behaviours seen by staff and the individual as priority areas, rather than trying to deal with every area

- reconciling differences between self and others perceptions by considering both performance and the importance attached to certain behaviours by staff in facilitated sessions

- providing guidance and help to the individual to identify the areas of concern and agree actions on how they could be improved.

One of the most frequently-cited studies to date in this area looks at the effectiveness of coaching after a development event by comparing the performance of coached and non-coached individuals (Smither *et al*, 2003). The aim of the research was to find out whether coaching could enhance the impact of feedback from multiple sources in promoting improvement in performance. The participants in the study were 1,361 senior managers in a global corporation who received multisource feedback in autumn 1999. After feedback, 404 of the managers received coaching and then responded to a brief online questionnaire. In the autumn of 2000 another multisource feedback programme was carried out in which 88.3 per cent of managers from the initial survey received feedback. In July 2002 a further brief survey was carried out in which raters evaluated the progress of the manager towards goals set by the manager himself and based on the initial feedback.

The research found that managers who worked with a coach were more likely to set specific (rather than vague) goals and to seek ideas for improvement from their supervisors. They also had a higher performance improvement in the 360-degree feedback from their direct reports and supervisor – however, the effect observed was small. When considering these results, some issues must be considered. The multisource feedback was being used within an appraisal system in a high accountability culture (ie salary and resources were all linked to the results). In these circumstances the effect of the coaching might be masked by this driver for change. Also, this was a very short intervention, 55 per cent of the managers having three or more conversations, 29.4 per cent having two, and 15.6 per cent having just one. Nevertheless, this limited coaching intervention did produce identifiable and beneficial impacts.

In a similar vein, Thach (2002) investigated the quantitative impact of coaching and 360-degree feedback on the leadership effectiveness of 281 executives within a single company. The programme was split into three phases: phase 1 involved 57 executives, phase 2 involved 168 executives, and phase 3 involved 113 executives. The coaching concentrated on one to three development actions identified from their 360-degree feedback and participants received four coaching sessions before a further 360-degree and participant survey was undertaken. There was no choice of coach and the duration of coaching was short, although many participants paid for further sessions from their own funds. Unfortunately, unlike the Smither study discussed above, no comparison was made with non-coached executives.

The overall percentage increase in leadership effectiveness was 55 per cent in phase 2 and 60 per cent in phase 3. The coaching impact was also analysed by the average number of meetings with the coach (3.6), but it was noted that the higher the number of sessions the higher the scores obtained. The qualitative feedback gained from the participants revealed that the factor of greatest impact was felt to be the relationship with the coach, while the information gained from the 360-degree feedback was seen as the second most important factor.

On a smaller scale but with a similar remit Luthans and Peterson (2003) again investigated the impact of multisource assessment in conjunction with executive coaching. They noted that there is usually a discrepancy between the higher ratings of self and the lower rating given by others, and this often results from a lack of self-awareness. They proposed that 360-degree programmes should attempt to raise performance to match the higher self-rating score rather than lowering the self-rating to match the views of others. To determine how effective coaching was at making this performance improvement happen, they conducted a study involving all 20 managers in a small firm. At the start of the study, and again three months later, 360-degree ratings were collected. After the initial assessment the managers met for a coaching session to analyse the results. All managers met the same coach and followed the same process. The feedback was confidential to the client and the coaching was developmental, not assessment-oriented. The process was structured around the following themes: what discrepancies exist, why are they present, and what needs to be done to reduce the discrepancies? The final part of the session concentrated on ensuring that the individual took responsibility for making the changes. Follow-up checks were carried out randomly and participants were asked whether they had made the changes discussed.

Given the short time-scale of the study and duration of the coaching it is perhaps surprising that the initial discrepancy between self and others' ratings were eliminated in all three factors tested (ie behavioural competency, interpersonal competency and personal responsibility). As hoped, the reduction in discrepancy was brought about through the elevation of the others' rating, not the reduction in the coachee's ratings. There was an improvement in both the managers' and their employees' work attitudes, involving a significant increase in job satisfaction with the work itself, supervision and co-workers. Organisational commitment also increased.

The research discovered that executive coaching can help individuals and organisations to maximise the results from 360-degree feedback programmes, and can produce a wide array of benefits for both parties such as increases in satisfaction, attitude and reduced turnover. The authors also found evidence of an improvement in organisational performance – eg in sales figures (seasonally adjusted) – following coaching and feedback. However, because these are systems-level indicators they were not deemed sufficiently controlled to link directly with the individual coaching intervention.

Clarke (2000) reports on a ten-year programme in a health authority. As part of a management development programme candidates undertook a 360-degree competence assessment. Following this, a development plan was drawn up which put forward a project that would make a difference to their organisation but which also enabled them to develop their skills in line with their personal development plan. Thus organisational benefits were defined as well as objectives to meet personal needs. Achievement of the development plan was supported by mentor-coaches. Over the period during which the programme ran, a number of benefits were identified, including staff development, workplace changes, subsequent promotions, effective introduction of quality systems, and achievement of individuals' and the organisation's development objectives. A similar programme is reported by Kidd (2000) in relation to a scheme in a scientific institute where more effective linking between individual and organisational development was enabled.

So looking at all these studies together we are able to see that executive coaching has beneficial effects when delivered in conjunction with other developmental activities for senior managers and leaders. While some shortcomings exist in some of the published studies, research is increasing in sophistication and is beginning to produce credible results which demonstrate the value of this type of executive coaching.

Free agenda executive coaching

A few studies exist in the literature that investigate the effectiveness of free agenda executive coaching. Because of the lack of set organisational goals for this type of coaching, it is necessary to focus on changes in the individual's patterns of behaviour and performance. While this may translate into benefits for the organisation, the immediate concern is achieving the individual's goals for coaching. This can create issues for HR in terms of evaluating the success because of the confidentiality that exists within the coaching relationship.

One such study looked at a group of 16 managers within a large bank coached for a year while the organisation was undergoing major change (Wales, 2003). A self-report question-naire was used that looked at six levels of learning and change which impacted on an individual or the organisation.The main benefits seen in terms of the individual's internal development were improved self-awareness and confidence. Self-awareness consisted of four elements:

- the ability to understand one's past and learn from it
- openness to one's own and other's feelings
- the ability to reflect on situations before moving into action
- the ability to make appropriate choices.

However, alongside this the managers also showed marked improvements in several external behaviours, including leadership and management skills, assertiveness, stress management, work–life balance and understanding difference. The improvements in these external behaviours was felt to arise via improved communication skills. The authors concluded that free agenda executive coaching did bring about individual change in self-awareness and confidence (a developmental issue), which through enhanced communication skills (skills issue) led to changes in their external behaviour (performance issue).

A further study investigated the mental/emotional growth of six executives coached to a free agenda over 14 months (Laske, 2004). They found significant improvement in nearly all participants (as assessed by a novel psychometric assessment questionnaire that determines the level of attainment in adult development levels). They were also assessed as to their performance capability and given an efficiency index as to how much of their capability was currently being used. This marker was also found to improve over the course of the study. It is unclear how widespread the use of this assessment tool is, and the generality of the findings are thus quite restricted.

MEASURING THE RETURN ON INVESTMENT (ROI) OF EXECUTIVE COACHING

Measuring the ROI of executive coaching seems to be the current 'holy grail' for everyone in the industry. However, unfortunately few successful attempts have been made – mostly because it is an extremely complicated calculation to undertake. Yet it is a central question – are the benefits from executive coaching worth what organisations are spending on it?

One of the rare (and much-touted) studies that attempted to measure a return on investment for executive coaching was conducted by Right Management Consultants and published in the *Manchester Review* (McGovern *et al*, 2001). The quoted figure for ROI of 5.7 was achieved through coachee's own estimates of their increased productivity. No details are available as yet on the specific elements of the ROI calculation.

An interesting approach to executive coaching that combined individual and organisational needs was reported by Philips (2005), who worked with a global hotel chain in a highly competitive and market-sensitive sector. Executive coaching was introduced in the organisation to achieve bottom-line improvements that resulted from addressing individual development needs. For example, staff turnover rates might be directly linked to the need for an executive to develop his interpersonal skills. The progress of 25 executives randomly selected from a bespoke Coaching for Business Impact programme was examined. The engagement lasted six months (weekly sessions were encouraged but monthly sessions were required as a minimum). The study focused on tangible benefits but also attempted to measure intangible benefits such as improved communication, job satisfaction, etc. The researchers reported that the hotel received a return on investment of 221 per cent.

Attempts to measure ROI-style calculations for executive coaching is being promoted in a number of joint initiatives in the field. For example, the Worldwide Association of Business Coaches has teamed up with the Return on Investment Institute to encourage such initiatives and provide training for organisations and coaches to undertake such studies. Hopefully this will result in the publication of some interesting findings in the next few years.

However, in the meantime a few unpublished studies are emerging from organisations that have attempted to identify the ROI as part of internally-run evaluation activities. We have easily identified a score or more well-conducted studies that have identified specific impacts from coaching – however, unfortunately most of these remain confidential to the organisation. One good example nonetheless is a study by Colone in a major international bank (Colone, 2005).

During this study, changes to areas such as turnover, achievement of targets, time taken for new recruits to reach competence and comparisons between coached and non-coached individuals were carefully monitored over a number of years. This data was used to assess the return on investment for the company. As part of these calculations, it was worked out that the company had spent approximately $900,000 on executive coaching for 101 managers in one department over a period of three years. This equated to an investment of approximately $3,000 per person per year. From a purely financial perspective, this was a large investment, and was unprecedented in the company as an investment in the development of their managers. When evaluating the return on investment, they considered:

- the executive competencies the coaching focused on, as recorded in their development plans
- the employee climate survey results for the three-year period along with previous

results as a baseline for comparison (measuring employees' responses to questions about values, partnership/teamwork, results, attitude and communication)

- 360-degree feedback results received by the managers over the three-year period, which provided scores on overall leadership effectiveness, values, partnership (teamwork), results, attitude and communication

- the impact executive coaching had on the performance of the management team gathered from interviews with the managers themselves.

They found significant results in a number of areas, including:

- staff retention v turnover rates – Turnover rates decreased from 20 per cent in 2000 to 8 per cent in 2003, but in addition virtually all of the group's 101 highest-performing employees stayed with the organisation. From the company's perspective, this high retention rate translates to higher productivity as a result of having extremely experienced and knowledgeable staff.

- decrease in recruitment costs – The savings on executive recruiting fees as a result of the high retention rates was substantial during 2000 to 2003. Conservative estimates by the organisation claim an expense saving of $540,000 per year in executive recruiting fees for the three years, 2001, 2002 and 2003 for a total saving of approximately $1,620,000. A comparison of the company's turnover rates to peer companies in the industry shows a markedly lower turnover rate than peers in each year except for 2001.

- decrease in executive development costs – Another area in which savings were realised during this time period was executive, leadership and management development. They compared the cost of 360-degree feedback combined with executive coaching (averaging $3,000 per client) and the resulting impact on each individual manager's growth and development, to the cost of executive, leadership or management development training (averaging between $4,000 and $20,000) and the return from this, both from the individuals' and their senior managers' perspectives. The results of this comparison indicated that executive coaching as a development strategy was more cost-effective than training and had more impact on the executive's leadership behaviour and in influencing organisational change.

- productivity gains – Productivity was measured in terms of the number of projects completed annually versus available resources (number of staff available) to complete those projects. Results indicated that while the number of projects either increased or remained stable in the period 2001 to 2003, the number of resources used to get the work done decreased, translating into higher productivity overall.

This data provided hard evidence of the impact that executive coaching had on the performance of the senior management team of this organisation during the period 2001 to

2003. They concluded that the 'return on investment' in executive coaching is measurable as long as the organisation maintains management information that can be compared over time. What is required of the researcher who is documenting this return is an understanding of the business and thoughtful reflection on how executive coaching has affected the work and performance of the participants alongside how measurement can be used to demonstrate the return on the investment in executive coaching. This study also proves the value of organisations undertaking internal studies themselves, particularly because of the internal researcher's close understanding of the people and the meaning of the data. At present, few of these studies find their way into the literature due to issues of commercial confidentiality, but hopefully in the future these research studies can reach a wider audience because they are of great interest to the profession.

Results from our case study organisations

The experiences of our case study organisations provide us with further insights into the results seen from executive coaching. Here are just a few examples of some of the benefits and results they have achieved:

> *Coaching has enabled us to move from justifying our existence to becoming creators of value to our parent group, and in two year-long phases deliver significant shareholder value and both strategic and competitive advantage. Our restructuring and the exploitation of unique market circumstances would not have happened without the coaching initiative. We are in the process of evaluating this, so my assessment thus far is based purely on my observations. But it is based on the fact that we have created tens of millions of pounds in shareholder value and improvements in safety and other key performance indicators measures on management performance.*

Extract from BPB Paperboard case study, p. 249

> *One of the spin-offs has been that managers receiving coaching are beginning to use a coaching style of management themselves with administrative staff. While they aren't formally receiving training in coaching skills, they are receiving tips from the coach on managing issues and communication in their teams. This is resulting in managers adopting some coaching skills in their day-to-day management style, which, again, is having positive effects.*

Extract from Courtenay HR case study, p. 255

> *Too often in the past, the concept of executive coaching has been undermined by its 'touchy-feely' associations – it hasn't been considered a substitute for practical training courses, and has often been seen as a remedy to be applied to those who are poor performers. Bovis Lend Lease's experience has been quite the opposite – coaching has been a highly tangible, results-driven part of their organisation's development. Outstanding results have been achieved as a result of coaching the talent within the organisation.*

Extract from Bovis Lend Lease case study, p. 245

> *The most significant change for the organisation is a raised awareness of people's different interpersonal styles and shortcomings when dealing with other people. People now give each other more time and try to understand the other person's perspective. There is a lot less conflict and fewer misunderstandings which has created a healthier, more positive working climate.*

Extract from Courtenay HR case study, p. 255

As you can see from these quotes, our case study respondents felt that executive coaching delivered good results for both individuals and organisations as a whole.

ISSUES FACING ORGANISATIONS WHEN USING EXECUTIVE COACHES

Although both the literature and our case studies report positive outcomes from executive coaching, some specific challenges for organisations related to this type of coaching have also emerged. They include:

- navigating the unregulated coaching industry and recruiting high-quality executive coaches

- evaluating executive coaching, particularly free agenda executive coaching

- balancing individual and organisational agendas for coaching

- costs and lack of scalability.

Navigating the unregulated coaching industry and recruiting high-quality executive coaches

For some time now, concerns have been raised about the lack or regulation of the coaching industry and the resulting number of 'coaching professionals' operating in the market who are inexperienced, have little relevant training and lack the appropriate knowledge and skills. Part of the problem lies in the fact that the coaching industry is highly fragmented, with no single professional body or set of standards and qualifications to guide buyers of coaching services. This has left many HR practitioners wary and uncertain about how to approach the selection of executive coaches. The CIPD 2004 training and development survey provided insights into the concerns of the HR community. The results indicated that HR feel that the lack of accreditation and regulation is 'worrying', that finding high-quality coaches is 'a difficult task' and that the terminology can be confusing and off-putting (CIPD, 2004). A significant proportion of our case study respondents indicated that in the absence of external standards they still relied on word of mouth to identify good executive coaches.

We hope that the current initiatives between professional bodies focusing on standards, supervision and kite-marking will help to address these concerns. In the interim the hugely variable quality of executive coaches has resulted in practitioners realising that they need to adopt a more discriminating approach in order to identify high-calibre coaches and secure a top-quality service.

> *We would like to have external coaches we can trust. However, we are often subjected to the hard sell and there is no current way to verify their qualifications or their competency ... There is a need for transparent ethics and process and a need for standards which identify the level of ability.*

Sharon Green, Stephenson Harwood

But what criteria are organisations considering when recruiting external coaches? According to a study by the University of Central England and Origin Consulting (Sparrow and Arnott, 2004) organisations are now regularly applying the following criteria during selection:

- a cultural fit and personal style that works for the organisation

- evidence of a positive track record

- a structured approach to coaching (for example, a model they can describe)

- qualifications relevant to the type of coaching they offer

- adherence to professional standards

- evidence that they are being supervised as coaches.

The CIPD guide *Coaching and Buying Coaching Services* (Jarvis, 2004) advised that organisations should consider whether executive coaches have:

- an appropriate level of experience

- relevant business/industry experience (if deemed important)

- references

- an appropriate background

- relevant qualifications and training

- knowledge of a variety of tools, techniques, models and assessment instruments

- membership of professional bodies

- professional indemnity insurance

- an understanding of ethical boundaries and the need for referral

- specific personal attributes and qualities

- involvement in supervision.

A more detailed discussion about each of these areas can be found in the CIPD guide (Jarvis, 2004).

Difficulties in evaluating executive coaching, particularly free agenda executive coaching

A paradox exists at the heart of the evaluation of executive coaching, particularly when it has a free agenda but is sponsored by an organisation. In this situation, issues around confidentiality affect the ability of organisations to assess the full impact of the coaching because they are unlikely to have full information about the objectives that the individual and coach are working to address. Any organisational benefits achieved will be the indirect consequence of changes in individual attitudes and behaviours, and hence organisational measures will only ever tell part of the story. It is the recognition of this difficulty that leads many of our case study organisations to rely heavily on feedback from the individual himself or herself. However, researchers are often critical of self-report measures, arguing that this type of 'happy sheet' feedback does not provide *evidence* that executive coaching has had a real impact. This gives HR practitioners and researchers some challenges in painting the full picture of the results that executive coaching is delivering.

Balancing individual and organisational agendas for coaching

A related issue that HR practitioners often face with executive coaching is balancing individual and organisational agendas for coaching. Again, this is particularly problematic with regard to free agenda coaching. Allowing an individual to dictate the agenda for coaching can mean that the individual's objectives for coaching fail to align with those of the organisation. A recent evaluation study carried out by 13 organisations confirmed this, reporting that the coaching agenda is often the individual's, and thus did not wholly reflect that of the organisation (Pirie, 2004). In some situations this can have very negative results for the organisation – which was something that some of our case study respondents also commented on.

> *There is the question of who is the client? An external coach will sometimes unlock things we wouldn't. There have been some instances of coaching 'out of a job'. This is an issue, and time needs to be spent so that the coach's perception of what is needed agrees with the organisation's view of need.*

Nicky Hillier, High & Mighty

> *Some people have left Tate following coaching. Sometimes during coaching, employees realise that they aren't happy in their jobs.*

Extract from Tate Museums case study, p. 292

There was evidence within our case study research that this has become a serious consideration for companies when considering the deployment of executive coaches in their organisation. The perceived risk in terms of recruitment and induction costs to replace a cherished performer can weigh heavily on the minds of HR professionals. This risk is not to be easily discounted because coaching has come to be seen as a reward for the higher achievers in the company – precisely those employees the organisation will not wish to lose.

To minimise these risks, executive coaching where the objectives are fully defined by the sponsoring organisation is becoming more popular. This has benefits to the organisation in providing predetermined criteria for success and hence a more direct route to effective evaluation. This move is generally welcomed by executive coaches:

> *Organisations embarking on coaching programmes should not be afraid to ask 'What's in it for us?' Where accountabilities are clear and the individual can link improvements in their own performance to business improvements, these can be discussed and agreed as goals to achieve ... Often it's just a question of raising the point, 'What changes can the business expect to see as a result of the individual demonstrating new behaviours?*

Alison Williamson

Costs and lack of scalability

A factor that cannot be ignored when discussing the use of executive coaches is cost. Few organisations can afford the high costs of executive coaching for large numbers of employees, and several of our case study organisations reported that this resulted in problems with scalability. Unless the organisation has a bottomless pit full of money, parameters in respect of the use of executive coaching must be set (who is eligible, how many sessions they receive, etc). Without these, confusion and resentment can arise because of a lack of understanding about why certain individuals are receiving this form of development. Research has illustrated that 'coaching envy' is a reality within many organisations (Carter, 2001) and HR must be careful to try to avoid this because of the bad feelings it can engender.

CONCLUSIONS

Nearly all the studies we reviewed in the literature have shown executive coaching to be effective either as an intervention with a free agenda or when it has a specific organisational agenda. Unfortunately, the robustness of the research designs varies significantly, so caution should still be preserved when interpreting these results. Several studies lack detail that allow for full comparisons to be made, while others are clearly seeking to prove the value of a particular framework. However, even with these caveats a body of academic work is now accruing which gives us a degree of confidence in the effectiveness of executive coaching.

The academic literature is further supported by CIPD survey data and the findings from our case study organisations. Whether you look at performance of individuals or organisations there is generally widespread agreement that executive coaching works. However, organisations have also reported facing a number of difficulties in achieving full value from their executive coaching activities. Recruiting high-quality coaches remains a challenge because of the lack of regulation, standards of practice and accredited qualifications and training programmes. Yet a number of professional bodies are making serious inroads into this area through a variety of initiatives aimed at improving standards of professional practice throughout the coaching industry. Organisations are also experiencing problems with the evaluation and alignment of free agenda coaching interventions. With pressure to prove the value of these activities growing, organisations are increasingly demanding that organisational objectives for executive coaching are borne in mind.

Executive coaches offer organisations a number of features that differ from internal coaching practitioners: they tend to have greater experience, to have more in-depth skills and to be perceived as more objective and confidential. However, they are very expensive and costs can quickly mount if organisations want to offer coaching to large numbers of senior managers/executives. Organisations therefore have to make good decisions about when it is best to use executive coaches by considering where they add the most value.

6

The manager as coach

Much of the coaching literature focuses on the use of external coaches, but organisations are increasingly looking to develop their internal coaching capability by training staff in coaching skills. The two main options are to train internal coaches (most commonly senior managers or HR professionals) or to encourage and facilitate coaching by managers. This chapter is concerned with manager-coaching.

Despite the scarcity of research investigating organisations' use of manager-coaching, we fortunately have a rich source of information on current organisational practice from our case study organisations, who are actively encouraging their managers to coach. In this chapter, we start by looking at how and why manager-coaching has become established in UK organisations. We then discuss the remit for manager-coaching, the issues manager-coaches commonly address and the skills that are needed in order to be effective manager-coaches. Issues with the effective implementation of manager-coach programmes are unfortunately relatively common, and we will discuss the most frequently-cited ones that organisations report experiencing. Finally, we examine what results have been seen from these initiatives and review what has been learned so far about gaining maximum value from manager-coaching activities.

HOW IT ALL BEGAN

There has been an explosive growth in organisations training their managers in coaching skills in recent years. However, it is a mistake to assume that manager-coaching is a new phenomenon. The role has been around since the first description of coaching. Indeed, the earliest reference we found in our literature review was published in the 1930s and looked at the role of sales managers as coaches (eg Bigelow, 1938).

The sales sector has a long tradition of coaching by managers. It became a prominent activity because sales jobs require a high level of 'soft skills' to develop trust/rapport with the customer and to close sales, alongside having the ability to deal with hard numbers and targets. One-to-one personalised learning (coaching) developed as an effective mode of transferring these skills from managers to team members. By observing staff selling, managers could see where problems lay and coach them to develop new or more effective sales behaviours. These early forms of sales coaching aimed to pass the wisdom of sales managers ('experts') on to the next generation because it was believed that set techniques would remain relevant over time. This approach worked within a clear command-and-control management structure and at a time when the business climate was more predictable. However, contemporary organisational life has changed. The working environment now moves at a much faster pace and this means that organisations and the people working in them must learn and adapt quickly. Alongside this, as management theories moved away from command and control, the model of the manager-coach has also evolved.

The soaring popularity of manager-coaching

All of a sudden, organisations are expecting their managers to act as coaches. The CIPD's training and development survey 2005 found that 88 per cent of respondents are now using coaching by managers within their organisations, and 74 per cent of respondents indicated that they intend to increase their use of them in the next few years. Furthermore, the previous year's survey confirmed the belief that coaching is now an essential part of managers' jobs. Ninety-seven per cent of the HR practitioners surveyed believed that coaching was a necessary part of any manager's skill set (CIPD, 2004).

The CIPD survey data is supported by other research data that also reports a widespread prevalence of manager-coaching. A slightly earlier survey of 179 senior HR managers in the UK found that four-fifths of organisations (79 per cent) were providing coaching by line managers (Kubicek, 2002). Interestingly, this research found that despite the prevalence of manager-coaching, most organisations did not have a stated vision or policy to develop a coaching style of management (67 per cent), although 30 per cent had one or were working to develop one.

WHAT IS DRIVING THE INVESTMENT IN MANAGER-COACHING?

But why has it become so popular? At first glance, the cynics among us may argue that the current popularity of coaching by managers may simply be part of an exercise in cost savings. Are organisations simply trying to reduce costs spent on external coaches by training their managers to coach instead? Organisations that invest in initiatives to develop manager-coaches are likely to have specific reasons for doing it – and for some of our case study organisations reducing their reliance on external coaches was one of the drivers. However, reducing costs was rarely the primary reason. For the most part, the desire to reduce reliance on external coaches arose because organisations realised that coaching could benefit a much wider audience in the organisation. To deliver large-scale coaching, organisations realised that alternative ways such as developing internal capability within the organisation were required. A further reason provided for reducing the reliance on external coaches was that organisations felt they were losing an opportunity to build up a body of knowledge and expertise about how coaching works in their organisation. Many argue that if coaching is to become a core part of their organisation's learning and development strategy, it makes sense for them to begin investing in developing coaching skills internally. And for many organisations, training their managers in coaching skills was the primary method for doing this.

However, what quickly became clear from our case study organisations is that training managers as coaches should not be viewed as a cheap or easy option. Gaining results from manager-coach programmes is not guaranteed, and requires considerable effort and investment. Managers require training and ongoing support/supervision to become effective coaches, as well as monitoring to make sure that they are actually making time to deliver coaching alongside their numerous other managerial activities. Just getting the programme off the ground and finding managers who believe that it is not a waste of their time can be a challenge in itself.

Our research suggests that a number of other drivers apart from cost may be playing a role in the growth of manager coaching. One reason is that coaching by managers is perceived as both a timely and tailored response for meeting employees' development needs in an increasingly uncertain business environment. This rationale was reported by our case study organisation Perkins Shibaura Engines:

> *Coaching is felt to be a critical mechanism for keeping employees' skills updated in line with the fast pace of the business environment. As Change Manager Nigel Briers explains: 'The rate of change in the industry means that employees can't be continually retrained, so they are coached to understand the elements of change and move with them.'*
>
> Extract from Perkins Shibaura Engines case study, p. 281

It seems from our case study organisations that manager-coaching is also frequently being encouraged as part of a drive to make changes to the organisation's culture, often to move from a directive form of management/leadership to one that is more facilitative and collaborative. This is illustrated in several of our case studies:

> *Camilla Aitchison, Dixons Group's director of management development says: 'You're not going to get high-quality customer service by applying the dictator model of leadership.' One of Dixons' main business objectives is to change the culture in the business from a directive culture to one in which leaders/managers act as coaches. By building coaching skills, they intend to motivate employees to achieve high performance and encourage them to work out solutions for themselves, resulting in improved service for the customer.*
>
> Extract from Dixons case study, p. 258

> *Ross Gorbert, Head of Learning and Development at Lend Lease Europe, explains: 'The construction industry has traditionally been known for having a command-and-control management culture. What we've started through coaching is a more empowering and creative culture where people don't need to wait to tell someone what to do or wait to be told themselves.'*
>
> Extract from Bovis Lend Lease case study, p. 245

As discussed in Chapter 2, a wealth of research has predicted and identified discernible shifts towards managers taking a greater role in supporting the learning and development of their teams. Many of our organisations accepted that managers could better support their staff if they had strong coaching skills. This is illustrated by our case studies from Tate Museums and Perkins Shibaura Engines:

> *As part of his new role, the L&D manager produced a learning and development strategy for Tate. The cornerstone of this strategy focused on creating a shift towards managers taking responsibility for facilitating the learning and development of their team members. Employees would also be encouraged to play a more active role in identifying their own development needs*

linked to their jobs and career aims. The L&D manager had experienced coaching in previous jobs and firmly believed that it would help to make this shift happen.

Extract from Tate Museums case study, p. 292

This move to 'just in time' learning is part of the organisation's interest in encouraging lifelong learning and continual support for employee development from managers and peers.

Extract from Perkins Shibaura Engines case study, p. 281

Manager-coaching is also frequently introduced to support wider change programmes in the organisation or in response to demanding business goals. Changing the leadership style or improving the skills of business managers often formed part of these change initiatives:

As global competition has grown there has been more and more pressure on management to achieve their targets and grow sales year on year. To achieve these targets it was felt important that managers not only focus on the targets themselves but also on how to achieve them by getting the best from their people. Panasonic want to increase the focus on leadership and people development within the business and believe that a stronger coaching culture is vital to achieving this. As a result they have been working to develop a coaching style of management, believing that it helps people to take more ownership for their work, supports personal development and encourages people to come up with solutions to issues they face. In this way, coaching is believed to be able to greatly impact on bottom-line success as well as supporting the personal development of their staff.

Extract from Panasonic Europe case study, p. 278

Two years ago, David Anderson, Managing Director for BPB Paperboard, introduced coaching as a means of encouraging his senior managers to think more laterally, develop a more open perspective and examine their interactions to see how working relationships could be improved. ... At the time, the company was experiencing a period of change ... The organisation undertook a major restructuring and culture change programme to meet the changing demands of the external business environment. The managing director specifically requested personal support via external coaching for the entire senior team throughout the change process and encouraged the development of coaching skills internally.

Extract from BPB Paperboard case study, p. 249

Another common reason for the introduction of manager-coaching programmes was that organisations had received feedback that managers lacked sufficient managerial skills to effectively support their teams. An illustration of this was provided by Glenmorangie plc:

Coaching had been carried out in Glenmorangie on an informal basis for a number of years, but two years ago the company ran an employee satisfaction survey which kick-started them into taking coaching more seriously. Training and Development Manager Morag Mathieson explains: 'The survey identified that the employees did not feel that our managers had good interpersonal skills. We therefore formally instigated a new management development programme.' As a result, the company embarked on designing a coaching programme to quickly and efficiently upskill the 60 management staff employed at the plant.

Extract from Glenmorangie case study, p. 262

WHAT IS THE REMIT OF MANAGER-COACHING, AND HOW IS IT DIFFERENT FROM OTHER FORMS OF COACHING?

Manager-coaching is generally viewed as a fairly narrow form of coaching – primarily because of the influence of the managerial relationship. It has a number of positive characteristics that differentiate it from external or internal coaching:

- The coaching is solely focused on the fulfilment of business objectives.
- The coach-manager will be aware of the performance and perception of the coachees within the organisation.
- The relationship is ongoing, allowing timely intervention (just in time ...).
- The coaching is available to all staff.

However, it is generally felt that manager-coaching is a very different style of coaching relationship. Primarily this is because the managerial relationship is not one of equals – after all, managers hold more senior positions with more power and responsibility than their direct reports – but the relationship is a mutually beneficial one. The manager depends on the employee to accomplish tasks and work towards team goals, and the employee relies on the manager for recognition and to set the conditions for success. During coaching, the manager and coachee set goals that help each other to achieve their own objectives at work. Manager-coaching therefore tends to have a very different dynamic from other coaching relationships.

As a result of the existing managerial relationship, the coaching agenda for managers tends to be more restricted and rarely has an open agenda (ie one solely determined by the individual and covering both personal and work-based goals). Manager-coaches are usually solely concerned with improving and developing employee performance in line with organisational requirements. Managers with strong coaching skills are able to help individuals improve their performance by building understanding about:

- what effective performance looks like
- how to achieve it
- what skills are required to perform under different circumstances
- what models of problem-solving help and hinder performance
- how to build competence for the future.

What kind of issues do manager-coaches most commonly work on with their teams? Each organisation will have different expectations about the level and type of coaching managers are expected to deliver. Some organisations expect their managers to act as technical coaches, helping to drive up skill levels in the team. Others see the role as being focused on performance improvements to support the delivery of key targets and goals. Another more complex role is development coaching, where managers coach staff to develop new skills and behaviours. A survey of 221 personnel and HR specialists investigated the use of internal and manager-coaches and found the principal purpose was to improve job-specific/technical skills

(64 per cent) although management development, leadership skills and supervisory development were also common reasons at 50 per cent, 47 per cent and 42 per cent respectively (The Work Foundation, 2003).

In some organisations, manager-coaches are seen as the 'first port of call' or the 'gateway' to wider coaching services. In these organisations, staff are expected to have an initial discussion with their manager about their development needs before they make a joint decision on how those needs can best be met – whether by the manager or more experienced internal or external development coaches. Shell is a good example of this approach:

> *The default coach for an individual is the line manager as all managers have a coaching element inherent in their roles and responsibilities. Coaching by managers generally takes place as part of ongoing discussions about development and performance. But Shell also recognises that managers aren't always best equipped to coach (eg if technical skills coaching is required or if an individual needs a greater level of coaching expertise). Within the technical areas of the company the vast majority of formal coaching isn't delivered by the manager but by other coaches in the organisation who act as technical coaches or internal development coaches. If someone requires coaching to improve their technical skills, they agree with their manager to approach a local expert in that subject to receive some coaching.*
>
> Extract from Shell case study, p. 286

In this situation, the key to successful coexistence of a variety of coaching practitioners is a clear identification of the needs of the coachee by the manager-coach (with the help of HR), allowing each type of coach to be used to their best advantage. For manager-coaches it is critical that they understand the boundaries of their expertise and know when to refer people on to alternative sources of support. All of the different types of manager-coaching require different skills of the manager-coach, and this has significant implications for their training.

THE LIMITATIONS OF MANAGER-COACHES AND THE ISSUES THEY CAN ADDRESS

As we have previously discussed, for the majority of manager coaches, improving the performance of their team members is the main focus of their role. But to do this, manager-coaches must have a good understanding of the factors that impact on performance as well as the ability to analyse issues and devise solutions. This is not a simple job. Manager-coaches must be able to understand a whole host of factors that can influence job performance and determine whether they are playing a role in the work of a particular individual. There are a huge number of factors that can impinge on someone's performance at work, including: targets, resources, recognition/reward, support, feedback, satisfaction, work–life balance and working relationships (eg Purcell, Kinnie and Hutchinson, 2003; Lane *et al*, 2000).

Helping the individual to analyse the factors hindering his or her performance is part of the role of the manager as coach. However, the coaching techniques taught in many of the training programmes (eg simple problem-solving models) often treat as simple a situation that may be more complex. Manager-coaches using such techniques are unlikely to be able to identify or address the multifaceted issues that can arise during coaching, including limitations in the way the coachee approaches problem-solving, misperceptions of feedback and issues that arise when dealing with ambiguous data. Inexperience and low levels of training also create a tendency to stop looking once a single causative link has been found (Sterman, 2000; Lane and Corrie, 2006).

So even within the reduced coaching agenda of the manager-coach, challenges can arise that may be beyond their expertise. As a result of this, it is essential that manager-training programmes build understanding about boundaries of expertise and help managers recognise when they need to refer individuals on for more specialist support. The limited knowledge and experience of many manager-coaches also presents a powerful case for them to be involved in supervision and for organisations to develop clear, ethical frameworks of practice to identify these boundaries and explain how managers should work within them.

WHAT KIND OF SKILLS DO EFFECTIVE MANAGER-COACHES NEED?

Before we look at research that has attempted to identify the skills and attributes of effective manager-coaches it is important to understand that they do not just need good coaching skills – to start with, they must be good people managers. Our case study organisation Midland Area Housing illustrates this point:

> *To effectively coach staff, managers had to hold staff to account, make changes, and focus their energy and resources to meet the targets.*

But what does the research literature say about the required skills of manager-coaches? Some early CIPD research looked at the roles of the manager as coach, mentor and guru and identified some characteristics of managers who were working as effective people developers (CIPD, 2000). Effective manager-coaches in the study were found to:

- devote time to selecting and developing team members
- be able to use different management styles
- adopt learning behaviours – eg asking questions, experimenting, reviewing success and mistakes
- be good facilitators
- delegate appropriately
- communicate and share learning from different experiences.

The research clearly indicated that managers who were getting it right were doing a number of related people management activities well. It is not a simple question of teaching managers a few coaching techniques. The complexity of the skills that effective manager-coaches need to demonstrate means a quick course to learn a selection of managerial/coaching skills is unlikely to work. Effective manager-coaches must have a base of strong people management and development skills, and then be supported in developing some specific coaching skills.

A number of research studies have explored which particular coaching skills managers need to develop. A recent review identified the three major constructs of sales coaching by managers: supervisory feedback, role modelling and trust (Rich, 1998). On a more general note, Kenton and Moody (2001) state that a coach requires various core skills to ensure an effective coaching relationship: being able to create rapport, paying attention to content and process, keeping an open mind, paraphrasing and reflecting, asking probing questions, identifying limiting assumptions and beliefs, and giving and receiving feedback. These are the skills that managers should be looking to develop if they want to become effective coaches. However, overall, it was the commitment to their own personal development and self-awareness of the coach that was essential to their competence.

A study by Ellinger and Bostrom (1998) tried to define the way effective manager-coaches behave by collecting detailed descriptions of 12 managers from four companies. The managers were considered to be excellent at assisting the learning and development of others. From their analysis, 13 behaviour sets demonstrated by effective manager-coaches were identified. These were grouped under two headings – empowerment and facilitation:

Empowering behaviours

1   Question-framing to encourage employees to think through issues

2   Being a resource – removing obstacles

3   Transferring ownership to employees

4   Holding back – not providing the answers

Facilitating behaviours

1   Providing employees with feedback

2   Soliciting feedback from employees

3   Working it out together – talking it through

4   Creating and promoting a learning organisation

5   Setting and communicating expectations – fitting into the big picture

6   Stepping into the other person's shoes to experience his or her perspective

7   Broadening employee perspectives – getting them to see things differently

8   Using analogies, scenarios and examples

9   Encouraging others to facilitate learning.

These research studies show that effective manager-coaches need to learn a whole host of coaching skills and behaviours in order to operate as good coaches. Organisations should consider these when designing their manager-coach training programmes.

DOES MANAGER-COACHING WORK?

Finally, what do we know about whether manager-coaching actually works? We asked organisations to make a judgement on the effectiveness of coaching in the CIPD training and development survey 2005. Overall, the response was positive – a fifth felt coaching by line managers was 'very effective' and a further two-thirds felt it was 'effective'. The majority of companies do believe that coaching by managers is an effective development tool (see Table 12).

Table 12: | ***Coaching by line managers – is it effective?***

| Percentage of respondents saying ... | | |
Very effective	Effective	Not very effective
19	65	16

Source: CIPD (2005)

Similar views were seen in our own smaller selection of case study organisations – 64 per cent identified coaching as 'effective' or 'very effective', although 32 per cent rated the activities as 'not very effective'. So the vast majority of HR people involved in the management and overseeing of manager-coaching do believe that it is broadly effective, but clearly there are some issues or barriers in making it work in all situations.

Research indicates that developing the coaching skills of managers can result in more positive employee attitudes towards the employment relationship generally (Lane *et al*, 2000). Staff who felt that their managers were acting as effective coaches (ie who really encouraged them to learn) also believed:

- 'I have plenty of opportunities for training in my current workplace.'
- 'My ideas are valued by my employer.'
- 'It is important to me that I do a good job.'
- 'I work in an environment that encourages me to learn.'
- 'I feel that I am consulted about workplace changes.'
- 'I am encouraged to share useful ideas with others.'
- 'The opinion of my employer towards my learning matters to me.'

However, despite this initially positive feedback, the impact of manager-coaching on business performance is much less well understood. There has been a distinct lack of research in this area which is likely to stem from the complexity of evaluating these kinds of programme. As noted earlier, programmes to encourage and implement manager-coaching often accompany or support other organisational changes (eg culture change programmes) and, as a result, it is difficult to separate the impact of coaching explicitly from the other changes taking place in the organisation. This has reduced the type of research that has been undertaken so far, but there is a wealth of individual case studies reported in the professional journals (eg Landale, 2004; Eaton and Brown, 2002).

One example is a case study illustrating how a manager-coaching programme helped to turn around the culture at Vodafone from a command-and-control culture to one characterised by respect and empowerment (Eaton and Brown, 2002). Staff development was highlighted as a central role for the manager and the coaching programme itself involved 85 managers at three levels of seniority. The move from a 'heads down' command-and-control culture to one based on coaching was identified as a significant contributor to Vodafone's turnaround from slipping behind BT Cellnet and Orange to regaining the top market position.

Although there are many books and articles on the subject of manager-coaching (we reviewed 203), few address the subject of outcome research in any detail and even fewer attempt to calculate a return on investment. A rare study was conducted by Wageman (2001). It investigated the effectiveness of managers as coaches and their ability to improve the performance of their teams by encouraging them to be self-managing. The findings suggested that the principal reason for failure is a lack of motivation by the coachees and the inability of managers to create the right conditions for teams to thrive. In this field study at Xerox, two factors were investigated: the design of the team and the quality of coaching by the manager. Thirty-four teams were assessed and labelled as either consistently high-performing or consistently poorly-performing teams. Quantitative measures of performance were measured which related to bottom-line indicators such as response rate, parts expenses, machine reliability, etc. The data analysis was rigorous and large effects were seen.

Unsurprisingly, well-designed teams were found to exhibit more self-management and were more effective than teams with design flaws. However, well-coached teams exhibited more self-management but did not come up with better task performance. Manager-coaching alone did not influence bottom-line results. Instead, it was found that coaching and team design interacted positively. Use of 'positive' coaching techniques (eg providing cues, informal rewards, problem-solving consultancy, etc) produced improved results in well-designed teams, while the use of 'negative' coaching techniques (eg identifying team problems and task intervention) had a greater impact on poorly-designed teams. It therefore seems that for manager-coaches to achieve improved business results, they must be able to flex their coaching style to meet the specific needs and structure of their team.

There have been attempts to measure return on investment for executive coaching (discussed in the previous chapter) but the research on manager-coaches flounders on the pragmatic approach taken by companies. The majority of organisations are not taking steps to evaluate their manager-coach programmes or to evaluate the results that manager-coaching is delivering to the business. For example, research by the School of Coaching found that only 27 per cent of companies formally evaluated their coaching skills initiatives. And where evaluation did take place, very few organisations were doing so at the level of business performance (Kubicek, 2002). As a result of this and the relatively recent emergence of manager-coaching, there is unfortunately very little hard research evidence available investigating the impact of manager-coaching.

Results achieved by our case study organisations

Our case study organisations reported a wide array of different results from their manager-coach programmes. Clearly, there will be a range of outcomes, depending on the issues manager-coaching is intended to address and the model of coaching an organisation adopts. But our case study organisations give us some ideas about the range of results organisations are seeing from the programmes they have implemented. Our analysis revealed that the type of results achieved broadly fall into ten main areas:

1   making changes to the organisation's culture or helping to embed a coaching culture

2   improved management skills and capability

3   behaviour change in the coaches

4   benefits for the coachees as a result of receiving coaching

5   greater employee engagement and commitment

6   improvements to business indicators or results

7   savings in HR time/costs

8   achievement of external awards and recognition

9   unexpected spin-offs

10 accelerated talent development.

1 Making changes to the organisation's culture or helping to embed a coaching culture

Many organisations reported that one of the most significant results they have seen from the introduction of their manager-coach programme were positive changes in their organisational culture:

Ross Gorbert explains: 'The construction industry has traditionally been known for having a 'command-and-control' management culture. What we've started through coaching is a more empowering and creative culture where people don't need to wait to tell someone what to do or wait to be told themselves.'

Extract from Bovis Lend Lease case study, p. 245

KwikFit Financial Services firmly believes that coaching has helped to change their culture.

Extract from KwikFit Financial Services case study, p. 268

Coaching is now accepted as 'the way we do things around here'.

Extract from High & Mighty case study, p. 267

They also measure employee performance against the company values and behaviours and have found that coaching has helped to embed the values into their culture.

Extract from Perkins Shibaura Engines case study, p. 281

In many cases, organisations felt that the manager-coach programmes were resulting in coaching cultures beginning to emerge:

The culture of learning and coaching is continuing to evolve and managers are now coaching outside their core remit and direct reports.

Extract from Glenmorangie case study, p. 262

The propagation of a coaching culture is gathering pace. Having provided managers with the skills and the mindset to 'coach' their own managers and staff, the result has been a proactive learning environment where people think more for themselves and where the customer remains at the forefront of the business.

Extract from Bovis Lend Lease case study, p. 245

2 Improved management skills and capability

The training programmes organisations had delivered were believed to have increased the range and depth of managers' skills and their ability to manage their teams. These changes were noticed by their direct reports, managers and HR staff alike:

The L&D manager firmly believes that coaching has had an impact. Several managers have reported noticing improvements in the management style of their direct reports – eg celebrating successes with their teams as a way of improving motivation. And team members are also noticing differences in their managers, saying 'I've noticed the change in "A" – he used to tell me what to do and now he asks me what we should do.'

Extract from Tate Museums case study, p. 292

Feedback from sponsors and line managers has been positive, and this has resulted in requests for more coaching for other people in the business.

Extract from Everest case study, p. 261

Coaching managers to coach and giving them the necessary tools to develop, empower and coach their own teams brought tangible results within Bovis Lend Lease.

Extract from Bovis Lend Lease case study, p. 245

3 Behaviour change in the coaches

Taking part in the coaching skills training programmes was felt to have resulted in managers learning new and more effective coaching behaviours:

The managers who took part in the coaching programme gave very positive feedback, believing it helped them develop their coaching and management skills. Behavioural change was observed in the coaches by their managers and peers in terms of their confidence, resilience and leadership skills, as well as their improved coaching skills.

Extract from Selfridges case study, p. 283

Feedback from participants' managers was positive – they noticed improvements in their performance and ability to manage their teams. And comparison of the initial and final 360-degree feedback results demonstrated real improvement in leadership and management competencies.

Extract from Glenmorangie case study, p. 262

Interviews with senior leaders indicate a positive behavioural impact and improved ease of dealing with change.

Extract from Shell case study, p. 286

4 Benefits for the coachees as a result of receiving coaching

The improvements in managers' coaching skills also resulted in improved performance and behaviour in their team members – ie the people on the receiving end of their new skills. Coachees were also considered to be more satisfied and engaged with their jobs and to have higher levels of motivation and confidence:

> *Benefits have been reported by the coachees as a result of receiving the coaching. These include: improved relationships, promotion, greater responsibility and new roles.*
>
> Extract from Selfridges case study, p. 283

> *The Back Web survey results have shown that coachees saw an improvement in the way they were coached. Feedback from the coachees is that managers have created better working relationships and were more effective in communicating with their teams – resulting in improved team results.*
>
> Extract from Nationwide case study, p. 269

> *The organisation has identified clear performance differences between those who are coached and those who are not in terms of meeting targets and quickly addressing issues that arise.*
>
> Extract from KwikFit Financial Services case study, p. 268

> *It indicates that staff are generally satisfied with the coaching they receive. … The most common benefits reported from those who have received coaching are that they are able to do their jobs better and have greater confidence in their abilities.*
>
> Extract from Shell case study, p. 286

Coaching by managers was also felt to offer non-threatening development opportunities to people who didn't feel comfortable in traditional training/education settings:

> *As Nicky Hillier, H&M's Personnel Manager, points out: 'Coaching can have a very positive impact on individuals for whom traditional learning modes such as classroom teaching have very negative associations. It is possible to spot and develop the potential of employees and hence their contribution to the organisation through coaching.' Coaching is considered to have worked well for the company in this situation and Nicky illustrates her view by describing the development of a return-to-work employee whose personal development plan a few years ago included 'learn to send an email' and who is now responsible for the payroll of the company.*
>
> Extract from High & Mighty case study, p. 267

5 Greater employee engagement and commitment

The changes to the management style and culture filtered down and encouraged changes in the way employees felt about their jobs. As a result, many organisations reported improvements to employee engagement, job satisfaction and commitment:

> *The feedback is that the employees enjoy the coaching culture, they feel their ideas are valued and their efforts are appreciated. As one employee noted: 'In my previous jobs, the only time I had been in an office was when they was going to let me go. Here I was in the office and someone was trying to help me – I kept waiting for the punch line but it didn't come.'*
>
> Extract from Perkins Shibaura Engines case study, p. 281

Shell also carries out a biannual organisation-wide employee attitude survey that contains some questions related to coaching. The latest results demonstrate that a majority of employees think they receive effective coaching, with a slight increase on the results two years before.

Extract from Shell case study, p. 286

Business results were growing steadily and the staff survey results were improving so the programme must have been doing something right.

Extract from Glenmorangie case study, p. 262

6 Improvements to business indicators or results

Some of our case study organisations had tracked improvements to business performance indicators as a result of their coaching initiatives:

The company has made attempts to measure the impact of coaching using a range of business measures. Examples include product quality measured in parts per million (ppm), sickness absence measured by number of days lost from work, and the performance management process measured by percentage ratings. Through these efforts, the organisation has seen evidence of performance improvements. For example, product quality was improved by 19 per cent last year and sickness/absence was down from 7 per cent to an average 2.4 per cent.

Extract from Perkins Shibaura Engines case study, p. 281

Even though Regal Fish Supplies is a small business, the company has assessed the impact of a coaching style of management/leadership using both qualitative and quantitative measures. They look for changes in key performance indicators such as sales and profits, while also looking for changes in the company's culture and quality of management/leadership. ... Within just five months, the sales team had met their targets for the first time and within a year were continually surpassing them.

Extract from Regal Fish Supplies case study

When measuring the impact of coaching, KwikFit generally looks at the managers' performance and focuses on issues such as attendance and quality. For example, when sales productivity had noticeably declined in a given area, individuals being coached were set achievement targets. Individuals were coached to help them achieve these targets and productivity increased as a result.

Extract from KwikFit Financial Services case study, p. 268

Other organisations reported that the manager-coaching programmes had helped to support wider business initiatives or change management programmes in the organisation:

Change is quicker as well as more focused as a result of the coaching interventions.

Extract from Midland Area Housing case study

7 Savings in HR time/costs

The improvements to managers' skills in managing their teams often led to fewer disciplinaries, reduced staff sickness, and lower staff turnover. All of this was felt to contribute to reduced costs in terms of HR time usually spent dealing with these issues:

With this new approach to people management and development, Regal Fish Supplies achieved an Investors in People award within 12 months and turned around their reputation from being a 'hire and fire' company to a company people actively seek to join. This represents a significant improvement in HR time and costs, as the HR manager explains: 'We used to be hiring every week – and I haven't had to recruit for the last four months.' Furthermore, as a result of this style of management, disciplinary events are much less common and the disciplinary procedures are now designed to 'get them back on track', rather than to take the perceived 'easier' route to dismissal.

Extract from Regal Fish Supplies case study

Sickness/absence was down from 7 per cent to an average 2.4 per cent.

Extract from Perkins Shibaura Engines case study, p. 281

8 Achievement of external awards and recognition

The investment in training managers as coaches also helped organisations to gain a series of external awards such as Investors in People. Others companies reported they achieved improved results or recognition in surveys, such as 100 Best Companies To Work For, or were achieving good results when they benchmarked their activities against other organisations:

The company has gained Investors in People status but is also the only retail company to have been awarded the Matrix standard.

Extract from High & Mighty case study, p. 267

In the Sunday Times poll of 100 Best Companies To Work For we went from 78th to 42nd to 30th and we were voted Scotland's Learning Employer of the Year 2004 by Learndirect Scotland.

Extract from Glenmorangie case study, p. 262

With this new approach to people management and development, Regal Fish Supplies achieved an Investors in People award within 12 months.

Extract from Regal Fish Supplies case study

Results from a 180-degree feedback exercise (provided as part of the CIPD coaching qualifications) has allowed them to benchmark their activities against other organisations. This has demonstrated that their 180-degree coaching results are just above the national average.

Extract from Everest case study, p. 261

9 Unexpected spin-offs

Many organisations mentioned that as a result of training managers to coach, they had noticed some unexpected positive spin-offs within the business. These tended to result from changes to the culture, from now having a greater bank of coaching skills, or as a result of staff and managers feeling more empowered and motivated:

At the end of last year, the L&D manager suggested coaching techniques to get people talking and discussing issues and ideas throughout a strategy/planning day for the directors and department heads at Tate. As a result, the Head of Policy and Planning said that the quality of submissions was markedly improved. He feels this is a tangible piece of evidence demonstrating how coaching techniques can be used to improve the productivity of day-to-day activities.

Extract from Tate Museums case study, p. 292

As a result of the programme, managers are now more confident and willing to contribute to the provision of training themselves – for example, helping to deliver training courses in their area of specialism for employees. ... The culture of learning and coaching is continuing to evolve and managers are now coaching outside their core remit and direct reports. 'Obviously, there must be a bit of give and take as managers have a full workload, but it is a developing area. In the future, we are keen to use the expertise the managers have developed and identify them as champions of an area where they can act as internal coaches.'

Extract from Glenmorangie case study, p. 262

As people have developed, their confidence has improved and they have started to push their ideas forward. An example of this is given by the HR manager: 'A recent internal promotee at his induction interview was able to list 14 separate improvements to his department which he had voiced at the company Works Council.'

Extract from Regal Fish Supplies case study

Coaching is certainly becoming more common in the organisation and one director commented recently that it had provided members of her team with a common language. More and more people understand the benefits coaching can bring and managers who haven't attended the programme realise that there is a tranche of skills that they are lacking and need to develop.

Extract from Tate Museums case study, p. 292

10 Accelerated talent development

Finally, the improved coaching skills of managers were believed to be helping to develop talent within the organisation. Managers were developing their team members' skills and abilities, and this resulted in promotions and other career steps:

Jackie Hoare concludes: 'More and more companies are realising that benefits from coaching can be substantial. When coaching is at the centre of an organisational culture, it can help improve morale and accelerate talent development. It can help Boxwood continue on its dramatic growth path.'

Extract from Boxwood Group case study, p. 247

Promotion of the talent programme coachees is the hardest demonstration of the impact of coaching, but it is difficult to attribute this solely to the coaching. Of the nine coachees who received coaching for the duration of the pilot programme, three have been promoted and another has made a sideways move that's likely to lead to a promotion in the next few months.

Extract from Selfridges case study, p. 283

As you can see, the majority of our case studies were able to identify extremely positive results from their investment in training managers as coaches. However, this was often based on low-level evaluation activities rather than measurement of the impact on business performance indicators. Some of our case study companies justified a lack of any measurement by virtue of the fact that they could see improvements in the performance of managers and the staff and therefore had no need to waste resources measuring it. Although this is a symptom that manager-coaching initiatives were being seen to have positive results, in the long run it leaves organisations open to challenges about the value it delivers because they will lack information to support their position:

> *Many people in the business didn't see the need for formal evaluation because of the high visibility of the results of the programme.*
>
> Extract from Glenmorangie case study, p. 262

Nonetheless, the results discussed above are impressive, even if, for the most part, they are anecdotal. Organisations are achieving significant benefits from their manager-coaching activities.

ISSUES AND BARRIERS TO MANAGER-COACHING

As may be expected with a fairly new area of activity, manager coaching brings with it a host of new challenges for organisations to grapple with. All the organisations we interviewed were well aware that they were just starting out on a journey and realised that they had much to learn. Progress can be slow and organisations must be fully committed to keeping momentum for manager-coaching initiatives high. Just 14 per cent of respondents to the latest CIPD learning and development survey felt that coaching was the predominant management style in their organisations (CIPD, 2006), illustrating the long road ahead for many.

A common issue is the struggle to gain the attention of managers due to their other work commitments and pressures. Coaching is just one of a number of responsibilities managers hold and a common complaint is that managers find it difficult to make the time for this activity. Gaining full senior management support and commitment is also problematic because it links to how seriously line managers take their coaching responsibilities. Only 12 per cent of respondents felt that line managers took their coaching responsibilities seriously to a complete or great extent (CIPD, 2006).

> *Senior managers at Panasonic have been relatively supportive of the initiative. Managing directors across the business are nominating people to attend the programme, but the training team would like more vocal support going forward in order to build momentum for the coaching programme.*
>
> Excerpt from Panasonic Europe case study, p. 278

Many organisations were also experiencing other barriers to their operations. It is felt to be extremely important that manager coaching activities are not seen as stand-alone initiatives – they need to be fully aligned with other HR and business strategies.

> *The Tate view is that it's essential to join up initiatives in the organisation so that people can see how they all fit together. In the future, links between coaching and the managers' objectives (via the performance management system) will be made more explicit, as well as ensuring coaching activities are fully aligned with Tate's strategic goals.*
>
> Extract from Tate Museums case study, p. 292

This is unfortunately not always that easy to pin down. Although coaching is considered to be linked to 'some' or a 'great' extent to business goals in around 90 per cent of organisations, it is worrying that only 27 per cent feel that coaching activities are completely integrated into wider HR strategy and processes (CIPD, 2006).

A related issue is ensuring that managers see the value of undertaking coaching activities. Forty-one per cent of respondents to the latest CIPD survey admit that coaching does not form part of their managers' job descriptions. Furthermore, 54 per cent report that those who are involved in coaching activities are not rewarded and recognised for their efforts (CIPD, 2006). If organisations are serious about encouraging managers to make time for coaching, surely a good place to start would be to make it a clear part of their job descriptions and reward those who demonstrate commitment and skills in this area?

Almost all the organisations were struggling with finding tangible and measurable results, even if the anecdotal feedback was very positive:

> *In Retail, they have attempted to assess changes in member satisfaction questionnaires and sales results as a response to the coaching. But the exercise was found to be inconclusive. It was difficult to relate results specifically to the coaching intervention because it was part of other major changes to the business. It is still early days in the roll-out of the coaching programme, but by the end of the calendar year Nationwide hopes to have some hard data on the success of coaching in supporting these initiatives.*
>
> Extract from Nationwide case study, p. 269

> *High-level evaluation of coaching is felt to be difficult because of all the other factors that are likely to affect business results. So Shell has focused on identifying changes in competence, behaviour and culture as well as gaining feedback from people about the benefits they have seen from coaching.*
>
> Extract from Shell case study, p. 286

Almost all the organisations we spoke to had plans to improve the measurement of results over time:

> *Evaluation is seen to be absolutely crucial as, without it, coaching will be seen as 'just another woolly initiative' from Personnel and Development. The business needs to be convinced that coaching will improve performance and business results or they won't take it seriously.*
>
> Extract from Nationwide case study, p. 269

> *Another area Selfridges would like to improve is assessing and measuring the development of participants' coaching skills. At the start of the future programmes, they will assess participants' starting level of coaching skills and repeat the assessment half-way through the programme (at the four-month stage) and then on a regular basis as a continuous measure of skill development. They will also collect stories of the benefits of coaching to gain information more formally about what has happened as a result of the coaching in terms of the performance and development of the individual coachees. These stories will be used with senior managers to persuade them of the impact of coaching and to convince them that it is a worthwhile investment.*
>
> Extract from Selfridges case study, p. 283

Shell has recently begun to attempt to correlate coaching with improved competence via a new online competence-based development system. ... In the future, the data this tool can provide should identify improvements in competence for coaches before and after coach-training programmes, as well as improvements in those receiving coaching for development. This will help to demonstrate the impact of coach training in developing people's competence as coaches, as well as demonstrating how coaching can support the improvement of other competencies and skills.

Extract from Shell case study, p. 286

Hopefully, in a few years' time some harder business information about the impact of manager-coach programmes in organisational settings will begin to filter through to accompany the positive qualitative feedback that exists at the moment.

Problems with the implementation of manager coaching programmes are to be expected – after all, this is a very new area of activity and barriers and obstacles affect almost all types of HR and business activity. Having mechanisms in place to gain feedback and evaluate current activities is essential for organisations to understand the issues and barriers to manager coaching that they face. A second benefit of this activity is that HR can also gain useful data to illustrate the results they are seeing from their activities. Keeping a mind open to lessons that can be learned is essential for all who are involved.

CONCLUSIONS

There has been a dramatic growth in the number of organisations investing in initiatives to train their managers as coaches. Training managers in coaching skills helps to embed coaching in an organisation's culture as well as moving the organisation away from traditional management/leadership styles and towards approaches based on facilitation, learning and motivation.

Manager-coaches tend to work to a reduced coaching agenda, the main focus of their activities being to improve individual performance. There are therefore limits to the depth and scope of the results that can be expected. However, our case study organisations clearly illustrate that manager-coaching can deliver a wide array of benefits for the coachee, the manager and the organisation. CIPD survey evidence supports this, revealing a strong belief in the HR community that coaching by managers works.

The literature review found that there is currently a lack of research in this area, making it difficult to draw firm conclusions about the impact of coaching by managers in organisational settings. The few detailed studies that are available indicate that manager-coaching works, but the evidence is less clear-cut in relation to bottom-line business indicators. Detailed controlled studies (of which there are few) show that the impacts are usually dependent on other factors being in place. Hopefully, in the future, as more research emerges, we will be able to confirm some of the findings shown by our case study organisations here.

Manager-coaching works best when it is introduced for specific reasons and is supported by senior management. It is more likely to fail where it does not form part of a coherent process, with minimal or no training and little focus on behaviours amenable to change. The key lessons learned by our case study organisations are to introduce manager-coaching carefully, over time, with proper training and support. A commitment to measuring impacts and learning lessons to improve the programme is essential, because it builds the credibility of the initiative and helps to demonstrate that manager-coaching is delivering benefits to the business.

7
The internal coach

In the last few years, a new type of coach has emerged on the scene: the internal coach. Internal coaches are increasingly becoming a feature of coaching strategies in UK organisations, particularly being used by organisations who are serious about embedding coaching skills and developing a coaching culture.

Because this form of coaching is relatively new, there is a real sense from our case study organisations that internal coaches are still at the point of defining themselves and their work. In the coming years, their role will become further established as they carve out their particular roles and the benefits they can deliver in contrast with other coaching practitioners such as external coaches and manager-coaches. In this chapter we describe the current snapshot and discuss the way internal coaches are being used by organisations in the UK at the moment. Of our case study organisations, 76 per cent reported using internal coaches and 80 per cent reported that HR practitioners were also delivering coaching (a form of internal coaching). We draw on their experiences to illustrate current approaches in this relatively new area of practice. Later in this chapter we review the literature to determine what benefits organisations are seeing from investing in developing internal coaches – but before that we discuss the profile of internal coaches, why they are becoming popular, their remit as coaches, and what their training needs are.

WHAT IS AN INTERNAL COACH?

So, what do we mean by 'internal coach', and how does the role differ from those of manager-coaches and external coaches? One definition has been provided by Frisch (2001):

A one-to-one developmental intervention supported by the organisation and provided by a colleague of those coached who is trusted to shape and deliver a programme yielding individual professional growth.

This definition illustrates several distinct features of the role of internal coach:

- An internal coach is outside the coachee's line management relationship, and so is distinct from the manager-coach.

- Internal coaches do not always use formal assessment techniques commonly used by external coaches because they already have significant background information on the coachee and have access to the results of organisational assessments and other relevant data.

- Multiple interventions are assumed in internal coaching. It is an ongoing relationship or programme, not a one-off conversation.

- An internal coach has a wider remit than a manager-coach, focusing holistically on 'individual professional growth' rather than solely focusing on performance improvement.

At the moment there is some confusion about the role of internal coaches. There is a tendency for them to be confused with mentors – they are both developmental relationships within the organisation but they operate outside the line management relationship. The focus of mentoring relationships is, however, very different from that of the internal coach. Mentors focus on careers advice and advancement and specific development issues. But it is less common for them to address issues connected with performance or behaviour change. Several of our case study organisations also reported receiving questions about how and when internal coaching should be used, as opposed to external or manager-coaching. The confusion is not helped by articles that refer to internal coaches when they actual mean manager-coaches. So it is important for organisations to communicate clearly about the roles of different coaching practitioners in order to build understanding.

So who are internal coaches?

To help dispel the confusion, we thought it would be useful to start by looking at the types of people currently working as internal coaches before moving on to discuss their typical roles. A large proportion of internal coaches come from the HR department itself, and some of our case studies clearly illustrate this:

The HR department is the main source of internal coaches.

Sharon Green, Stephenson Harwood

Coaching is delivered by two internal coaches from the HR department who have the job title 'business consultant'.

Extract from Canada Life case study, p. 251

Internal coaches come from the Staff Development Unit, Human Resources and Development and the Academic Teaching and Learning Centre.

Extract from London School of Economics case study

As part of our leadership development programme run by external consultants, three people were trained as 'super coaches'. These were members of the Resourcing and Development team who were already experienced in coaching.'

Extract from Selfridges case study, p. 283

You could say that HR professionals have always undertaken some coaching activities because it is often inherent in their role, but it is usually fairly informal. These days, internal coaches from HR departments undertake coaching either as a full-time job role or as a significant part of their duties. In many cases it is these people who act as advocates or champions for coaching in the early days when it is introduced, because they understand and have seen the results that coaching can achieve. Their enthusiasm for coaching often helps to drive the initiative and gain buy-in and support within the organisation:

The L&D manager had experienced coaching in previous jobs and firmly believed that it would help to make this shift happen.

Extract from Tate Museums case study, p. 292

The Group HR Director, Linda Booth, and United Utilities Change Manager, Fiona Cameron, were driving the initiative and were very committed and enthusiastic about coaching and had established a track record of success in the business. Having two people like this to drive the initiative helped to get it off the ground as they were very credible in the business.

Roger Williams, United Utilities, p. 296

Alongside members of HR, some large organisations have also trained a network of managers to work as internal coaches. In all but the smallest firms the success of coaching can mean that demand can rapidly outstrip supply and the average HR department can find itself overstretched:

The L&D manager regularly undertakes 'corridor coaching' with people who approach him for advice on problems they face, but because he has limited time, if the person requires regular or in-depth coaching because the issues are more deep-seated or long-term, he talks to them about seeing an external coach for a few sessions.

Extract from Tate Museums case study, p. 292

The result of this is either hiring external coaches or providing specific, in-depth coach training for others in the organisation to build up a network of internal coaches. In this situation, many organisations feel it makes sense to utilise the skills of manager-coaches who already have strong coaching skills and who are keen to further develop their expertise in this area. These managers are trained to coach other managers in their coaching skills or provide non-line-manager coaching in particular situations:

Dixons Group has implemented a coach-training programme in the business to build up a network of internal coaches. Coaching at Dixons began as a pilot in-house programme in summer 2004. Coach training was initially pitched at senior managers/junior directors who run large teams and have an influence across the business.

Extract from Dixons case study, p. 258

Others have trained a mix of HR practitioners and managers as internal coaches, preferring to select a cross-section of people who show the right attitude and approach:

To date, 63 people are active as executive coaches – these have included managers, directors and HR professionals. Selection of coaches for the programme was done by publicising plans to train a body of internal executive coaches and asking for volunteers to apply. The volunteers attended a one-day development centre where their coaching skills and potential, as well as their commitment and interest in coaching, were assessed. Those with the greatest levels of skill and commitment were chosen to go forward for the coaching programme.

Extract from United Utilities case study, p. 296

It therefore seems that internal coaches are a mixture of HR professionals and managers who have received additional coach training so that they can provide broader coaching in the organisation. Organisations seem to be selecting for the role of internal coach people who have demonstrated prior coaching skills as well as a commitment and interest in the area.

WHY ARE INTERNAL COACHES BECOMING MORE POPULAR?

Internal coaches are steadily increasing in number and the distinct role they can play is now acknowledged by many organisations, and in the coaching industry more generally, where they are included for membership and accreditation in many of the coaching professional bodies. Ventrone (2005) investigated the prevalence of internal coaches in the USA and found that companies are also increasingly turning to internal coaching. Seventy-five per cent of respondents reported that they either have (50 per cent) or are considering developing (25 per cent) internal coaching. It is likely that a similar situation will be seen in the UK in the next few years as organisations continue to aspire to developing internal coaching capability and coaching cultures. Initial signs that this trend may be occurring were found in the CIPD's 2006 learning and development survey. When asked what activities were being implemented to support the development of a coaching culture, 18 per cent said that activities involved developing a network of internal and external coaches, while a further 35 per cent reported taking a dual approach and implementing both coach-training for managers and coaching via internal and external coaches.

But why are organisations investing in developing internal coaches? There are a number of reasons why internal coaching is becoming more prevalent. Many of these echo the reasons given in Chapter 6 that lie behind the rapid growth of organisations' use of manager-coaches. The growth of both of these forms of coaching stem from organisations seeking to develop coaching skills and capacity within themselves. As Frisch (2001) argues:

> *Coaching is now seen as an investment in the organisation's future. Perhaps concurrent with this has been the emergence of the internal coach ... which is predictable, but not entirely obvious.*

As organisations have looked to develop coaching skills within the organisation, or to make efforts to build a coaching culture, they have realised that having an internal resource to champion coaching within the business and to provide timely and ongoing coaching services can be both cost-effective and valuable:

> *Coaching at United Utilities developed as a direct result of the U Can programme. Coaching skills were identified as being critical to sustaining the culture change and to improving people development skills in the business. ... They decided to train internal executive coaches to deliver the coaching services within UU.*

> Extract from United Utilities case study, p. 296

Ventrone (2005) reports that large US companies are increasingly turning to internal coaching to cost-consciously meet their employees' development needs. Despite a clear increase in the demand for coaching, the amount being spent on these services has decreased, so that reported spending in the USA is down approximately 3 per cent compared to the previous year. Corporate pressure to reduce spending/costs, coupled with an ever-increasing number of coaches flooding the market, has contributed to the commoditisation of coaching. Internal coaching has become a popular response for organisations looking to deliver more coaching while spending less money.

Research has suggested that companies are using internal coaching, in part to avoid some of the perceived downsides of external coaching (Ventrone, 2005). This was also discussed by some of our case study organisations:

The company had used external coaches in the past but had concerns that externally-provided coaching failed to focus sufficiently on the needs of the business. As Nicky Hillier has noted: 'There can be an issue about who is the client.'

Extract from High & Mighty case study, p. 267

Perhaps not surprisingly, Ventrone's research indicated that 'cost' represented the single most pressing concern, the related items 'measures of success' and 'ROI' following closely behind (Ventrone, 2005). However, the data also indicated that internal coaches seem to present a viable solution to providing coaching for larger numbers of individuals, 50 per cent endorsing 'number to be coached' as a main driver for internal coaching. This rationale is illustrated by the United Utilities case study:

Traditionally, UU used external executive coaches to deliver coaching in the organisation, but given the size of the coaching population (the company wants to make coaching available to all managers), this was going to be an approach that would be expensive and difficult to manage. So instead, they decided to train internal executive coaches to deliver the coaching services within UU.

Extract from United Utilities case study, p. 296

The cost implications of offering external executive coaches to the next management layer were far too high. ... Consequently, the BBC decided to draw on existing internal coaching activity and create a pool of accredited internal coaches. The pool is now over 80 strong.

Quote from BBC case study, Aquilina, (2005)

Another reason for the growth in the use of internal coaches stems from a change in how coaching is viewed. Previously, coaching was seen as a remedial activity – something that was only offered to poor performers. In contrast, these days coaching has a stronger developmental focus and is offered to many employees throughout the organisation – very often the highest performers. With this change in attitude, the need for the coach to be external to or separate from the organisation (eg to prevent defensiveness on the coachee's part) is reduced. In this scenario, the potential benefits of using an internal coach have become clearly apparent. They are readily available to offer ongoing support and have a great deal of knowledge about the organisation and the context within which the coaching is taking place. As Alexander (2001) argues, 'An internal coach can bring an understanding of the organisational environment, the nuances of context and the culture.' An internal coach is also likely to know the coachee and have an understanding of his or her role and responsibilities:

Internal coaches have a good insight into what the organisation expects of its managers and are easily accessible for formal coaching and quick catch-ups.

Karen Boanas, Canada Life case study, p. 281

In this internal model of coaching, the coach is also valued for being able to bring an appreciation of BBC culture and business to the coaching relationship.

Quote from BBC case study, Aquilina, (2005)

Frisch (2001) identified four factors that he believes are fuelling the growth of internal coaching:

- *cost savings* – in comparison with the fees for external coaching programmes which are more expensive … and internal coaching resources can be applied more widely.

- *existing knowledge of the organisation* – internal coaches can use their knowledge of the organisation to make faster initial progress.

- *more effective feedback channels* – an internal coach is more likely to be able to observe or hear about how those being coached are performing: this can then be used in further coaching sessions.

- *a wider organisational commitment to learning* – internal coaching is seen as a sign of a learning organisation.

It is likely that a combination of factors has contributed to the rise of internal coaching, but the growth in the use of internal coaches certainly seems to indicate that organisations see a clear business case for using this form of coaching. This is likely to be a trend that will continue developing in the next few years.

WHAT IS THE REMIT OF THE INTERNAL COACH?

In previous chapters we discussed external coaches and manager-coaches, but how do internal coaches compare? Are they highly trained coaches capable of coaching to an open agenda and of supervising manager-coaches? Or are they simply akin to manager-coaches with a small degree of further training?

Internal coaching differs from manager-coaching because it tends to address a broader range of issues and has a more individual focus. Manager-coaches primarily work to a fairly fixed and reduced agenda because of the direct nature of the managerial relationship. Their training is relatively limited and will often be constrained within a particular model of practice. In contrast, the executive coach often works with a free agenda, the coaching addressing a wide range of deeper issues to unlock changes desired by the individual. Executive coaches require a flexible model of practice with knowledge of more tools and methodologies. The internal coach seems to sit somewhere between these two forms of coaching – focusing on the individual's agenda but with the organisation's goals firmly in view. This has significant implications for internal coaches' training, supervision and ongoing professional development.

Ventrone's study (2005) of 20 organisations identified differences between internal and external coaches in terms of the levels they operated at. Unsurprisingly, external coaches worked at higher management levels within the organisation, some 45 per cent working with chief executive officers, chief finance officers and others with similar levels of responsibility. When asked, 'If you have or are contemplating an internal coaching programme, how will it differ from your external programme?', these differences emerged:

- Internal coaches work at lower levels in the organisation.
- The coaching process is different.
- Different skills are developed.

- More group coaching is delivered.

None of the respondents in the research said that the two roles would not differ.

Analysis of our case studies shows that there are considerable differences in organisations' expectations of the role their internal coaches will play. For the most part, respondents who used internal coaches identified three specific coaching roles for internal coaches:

- the specialist development coach working with a reduced but similar remit to the external coach

- the technical coach or champion

- the business change coach.

Internal coaches who act as skill champions or technical coaches tend to be employees skilled in particular aspects of the business who coach others to develop these skills. The origins of this type of 'coaching' lie within conventional training or mentoring programmes:

Within the technical areas of the company the vast majority of formal coaching isn't delivered by the manager but by other coaches in the organisation who act as technical coaches or internal development coaches. Technical coaches are technical experts trained to develop their coaching expertise so that they can act as effective technical coaches. Within such a large company, the solutions to technical coaching vary. In some parts of the organisation people are picked out to act as full-time technical coaches (eg in business areas where there are lots of graduates who need coaching), while in other parts technical coaching forms a part of people's general job roles.

Extract from Shell case study, p. 286

Some organisations that offer development or executive coaching outside the line management relationship train internal coaches to provide this service (alongside or instead of external coaches):

Traditionally, UU used external executive coaches to deliver coaching in the organisation, but given the size of the coaching population (the company wants to make coaching available to all managers), this was going to be an approach that would be expensive and difficult to manage. So instead, they decided to train internal executive coaches to deliver the coaching services within UU.

Extract from United Utilities case study, p. 296

Dixons Group has implemented a coach-training programme in the business to build up a network of internal coaches. ... Once trained, coaches are expected to act as internal coaches within the business. The coaching is completed on top of their day jobs but is limited to each coach having no more than two or three coachees at any one time. Receiving coaching is open to anyone in the company, but at the moment it tends to be head office staff at management levels.

Extract from Dixons case study, p. 258

This form of coaching was most commonly offered to senior managers or leaders and often concentrates on developing their leadership and change management skills. In many ways, this service is designed to be comparable to that offered by external coaches:

Alongside coaching as part of the business process review initiatives, the internal coaches also coach individuals as part of leadership development activities. They coach leaders on general effectiveness and how best to deal with the challenges they face in their roles, as well as encouraging them to use coaching skills with their own teams. They also coach those leading transformation initiatives in the organisation to help them to lead and manage change effectively, considering the business goals as well as what's required from their staff in order for the goals to be delivered.

Extract from Canada Life case study, p. 251

Many of the internal coaches at Shell are HR professionals who are trained to deliver leadership coaching in the organisation.

Extract from Shell case study, p. 286

Business change coaches are internal coaches who concentrate their activities on helping individuals or teams to improve business processes or undertake change initiatives in line with the organisation's business goals. Their focus is firmly on delivering value to the business, but this is achieved by working with individuals to help them identify ways to make effective and sustainable changes or improvements happen:

Coaching is an integral part of the business process reviews. Each process review team has a clear mandate and an assigned internal coach who meets with them on a regular basis to coach them through a systematic process of continuous improvement which includes speaking to customers, gathering and analysing data, identifying root causes and implementing process improvements. Throughout the review the coach will support the team as they enter new territory, challenging corporate culture and cutting across divisional hierarchies to deliver processes that focus on customer and quality.

Extract from Canada Life case study, p. 251

NSC SHA run a five-day co-coaching programme – aimed at Modernisation Associates – whose remit is to support radical reform and leadership development in health and social care. By the end of the programme participants should be able to support leaders in implementing radical change using a coaching approach and have acquired mentoring skills.

Extract from Norfolk, Suffolk and Cambridgeshire Strategic Health Authority, p. 277

They have realised they can use this internal resource for wider initiatives and have used the internal coaches to help with the ongoing implementation of the change programmes.

Extract from United Utilities case study, p. 296

Throughout our case studies, an emerging role for internal coaches is the support and development of a coaching culture. The way internal coaches are seen to support this evolves as the culture develops. During the initial stages of introducing coaching to an organisation, where buy-in for coaching is being negotiated, the coaching provided by internal coaches (often HR) can provide illustrative examples of the benefits and can familiarise the main stakeholders with what coaching involves:

An evaluation of how this softly, softly approach has worked is by how many people are now asking for coaching and want to improve their own development. The perception has changed from it being 'woolly' to coaching being effective in solving individual issues. One previously anti-training section is setting up its own mentoring programme, for example. Now everyone wants it. It seems like I have gone from zero to hero.

Stephen Williamson, Pertemps case study

The L&D Manager feels that senior team buy-in is ultimately essential to the successful embedding of coaching within an organisation, and he has been working hard with directors to help them understand the link between coaching and performance and hence the value to the organisation longer-term. At first, a gradual approach to the introduction of coaching seemed appropriate, focusing on regularly reporting results and progress with coaching to the senior team.

Extract from Tate Museums case study, p. 292

It seems that a key part of the role of internal coaches is supporting other coaching interventions that are being implemented in the organisation – both supporting the development of manager-coaches and managing and gaining best value from external coaches:

No formal training is given to the managers to develop their coaching skills, although the HR department regularly coaches managers on an individual basis to help them improve the coaching skills they use with their teams.

Extract from High & Mighty case study, p. 267

Managers who are coaching are supported by a coaching champion. She has regular meetings with the coaches, observes them coaching their consultants, and gives feedback on their performance.

Extract from KwikFit Financial Services case study, p. 268

All our new entrants are automatically paired with a coach (a senior manager who is not their line manager) and a buddy. The role here is to develop the soft skills such as negotiation and presentational skills. For a senior manager the coach can be a colleague with particular expertise in a new area.

Extract from Blackrock International case study

Internal coaches are also used to support manager-coach programmes. Several organisations reported using internal coaches to design and deliver the training programme (often in conjunction with an external provider):

To support the coaching initiative, three members of the R&D team were trained as 'super coaches' so that they could help to run the coaching workshops and support the participants throughout the coaching programme.

Extract from Selfridges case study, p. 283

The external coach works with two master coaching practitioners from training and development (T&D) to deliver a five-day in-house coaching programme.

Extract from Dixons case study, p. 258

Once a manager-coaching programme has been initiated, organisations need to offer ongoing support to consolidate learning, embed behaviour change and maintain focus. Many of our case study organisations also felt that supervision of newly-trained coaches was useful and could help to improve their skills. Internal coaches are a useful resource for this purpose because their insider knowledge and ready availability can be of benefit in maintaining the momentum of the change. In this phase, the internal coach may supervise the manager-coaches and/or provide more specialised coaching support:

> *If the issue is unusual, then HR will take the manager through the process and suggest a coaching tool – ie will coach the manager on how to coach their reportee.*
>
> Nicky Hillier, High & Mighty

> *The master practitioners act as an internal resource, helping managers who are training as coaches and also advising and guiding trained coaches in the business as issues arise. The Dixons' T&D team has also designed and produced a booklet incorporating information, tools and techniques for coaches to use after they have completed the coach training. This type of support provides coaches with some guidance materials to use when they are back at work.*
>
> Extract from Dixons case study, p. 258

> *NSC supervisors have two days of training to equip them to take on this role, and can only do this training if they have already completed the other five-day programme and have a significant level of mentoring and coaching experience.*
>
> Extract from Norfolk, Suffolk and Cambridgeshire Strategic Health Authority case study, p. 273

While external coaches can also be used to support internal coaching programmes, many organisations have reported that using purely external resources on an ongoing basis can result in costs spiralling. However, being part of the organisation does mean that internal coaches can rarely offer the same degree of confidentiality and the valuable external perspective that is delivered by external coaches. Because internal coaches operate outside of the line management relationship, there can be confidentiality within the interaction, but this is dependent on the particular definition of the coaching contract adopted by the organisation. Whether the coachee is fully confident of the confidentiality in an internal coaching relationship is a question frequently raised by coachees.

> *Because internal coaches may have multiple roles in the organisation, they may find themselves interacting in different situations with their clients; this raises issues of trust and confidentiality. Therefore there is a need for a clear strategy for ongoing supervision and development.*
>
> Quote from BBC case study, Aquilina, (2005)

As a result of these differences, many organisations feel that using a combination of internal and external coaches offers the most effective solution:

> *External executive coaches are still used across UU for senior executives and in other instances when it is deemed appropriate. It is not seen as an either/or decision. Internal coaches are still relatively inexperienced compared to many external coaches. And the business is also conscious that internal coaches are taking on the coaching part of their role on top of their day jobs, so external coaches can help to relieve the demands on their time.*
>
> Extract from United Utilities case study, p. 296

> *Some people at Tate have said that it works well to have someone within the organisation co-delivering the coaching programme, because they can assimilate themes and ensure that links are made with other initiatives. But an external coach can bring in different skills and challenge participants to think differently. In my view, the two together work very well.*
>
> Colin Coombs, Tate Museums case study, p. 292

Executives often welcome the added value of an external perspective that an external coach brings and the coaching may also be seen to be more confidential. Overall, although a combination of practitioners are involved in delivering coaching within Shell, the vast majority of coaching is undertaken internally.

Extract from Shell case study, p. 286

The NSC believes that a mixed economy of internal and external coaching providers ensures choice and value for money.

Extract from Norfolk, Suffolk and Cambridgeshire Strategic Health Authority case study, p. 273

Using internal coaches to fulfil these functions is not a cheap option for organisations. Just like manager-coaches, they require training, ongoing support and supervision – and at a higher level because of the wider expertise they need to develop. Just how organisations are developing their internal coaches is a topic covered in detail in Chapter 8.

DOES INTERNAL COACHING WORK?

The response from our case study organisations appears to be a unanimous 'yes'. All of the organisations using internal coaches reported that they were either 'effective' or 'very effective'. However, the effectiveness of coaching delivered by HR practitioners (a form of internal coaching) received a slightly lower rating. Twelve per cent reported that they felt this type of coaching was 'not very effective'. The most commonly-cited reasons were the perceived lower level of confidentiality (and therefore trust) or a lack of specific coaching training.

But what does the research say? Unfortunately, because this is a newly emerging area there is only a small amount of research we can draw on to answer this question. A rare study looking at the effectiveness of internal coaching in a public sector municipal agency was undertaken by Olivero *et al* (1997). Although they describe the mode of coaching used as 'executive coaching', within our definition their study investigated the effectiveness of internal coaching. Thirty-one managers underwent a conventional managerial training programme. Then eight of the managers underwent a coach-training programme and then coached their peers every week for two months as they undertook a real-life project. The productivity of the managers was measured after training and after coaching. The measures chosen were appropriate to the specific work of each manager, and were quantifiably of benefit to the organisation. The result was a 22.4 per cent increase in productivity after the management training but an 88 per cent increase after coaching.

Although these figures seem clear-cut, a number of issues should be borne in mind. In particular, we should remember that the projects undertaken by the managers while they were being coached would also have contributed to enhanced productivity. Nevertheless, the research provides scarce information about the positive impact internal coaching can deliver to organisations.

A recent study by the NHS Leadership Centre (Woolnough *et al*, 2004) looked at coaching effectiveness for one specific group of employees – female mental health nurses. This was, in part, a pilot programme with the overall objective to provide leadership and career development for nurses to help them compete for leadership positions and redress the gender balance at senior grades in the NHS. Six NHS mental health Trusts participated in the programme, which compared mentored (but, using our definition, coached by internal coaches) nurses with a control group. They collected data (using questionnaires, repertory grids and telephone interviews) at three time-points from 60 participants who were divided equally between the coached and non-coached groups. The programme ran for 12 months.

During the programme, 41 per cent of the coachees were promoted compared to 15 per cent of the non-coached group. Given the short time-scale of the interaction, this is a significant result. Most of the promotions came towards the end of the programme and 90 per cent of the promoted nurses said their elevation was directly related to their participation in the programme. Those in the coached group who had not been promoted had engaged in some activity to strengthen their roles through professional development. Overall, the level of satisfaction with their careers increased. This was not shown in the non-coached group, where a small decrease in satisfaction was reported, although this was not statistically significant. The coached group scored higher in leadership ability and felt they had more access to those with power in their Trust. Generally, they scored consistently higher than their non-coached colleagues in a range of abilities and attitudes that would equip them to undertake leadership roles. The coached group was also less likely to consider the employing Trust to be favouring males for leadership positions.

Ventrone's study (2005) of 20 organisations examined the perceived effectiveness of both internal and external coaches. Internal coaches were rated as extremely effective in the areas where they commonly practised, with ratings of above 80 per cent for both 'developing technical skills' and 'preventing derailment'. In contrast, external coaches were more effective in 'enhancing overall leadership skills', 'enhancing job performance' and 'developing communication skills'. The implications of this research are that there may be some trade-offs for the lower cost and broader reach offered by the services of the internal coach. Although organisations are increasingly turning to internal coaches to address coaching needs in the organisation, their ability to coach may not be as effective in all situations as that offered by external coaches. This is likely to stem from a lack of training and experience. Organisations therefore need to think carefully about their expectations of the results that internal coaches can feasibly deliver, and complement their use with external coaches in more complex cases or with regard to specific issues as they arise.

The benefits of internal coaching – evidence from the case studies

Despite the relatively recent emergence of internal coaching, our case study organisations have reported a wide array of results from their use of internal coaches. However, it is important to note that it was particularly difficult to establish causal links between the work of internal coaches and improvements in individual and business performance, because internal coaching is frequently used to complement or support other coaching initiatives (eg manager-coach programmes). For this reason, the organisations reported finding it difficult to identify and measure the specific impact of internal coaching as opposed to that being delivered by the other coaching initiatives they were helping to manage and support. Yet organisations were still able to give us a flavour of some of the results they felt had been achieved.

Internal coaching was certainly felt to deliver value to the individuals who were on the receiving end of the coaching. All our case study organisations reported that individuals enjoyed being coached and felt that it had resulted in a variety of positive benefits for them:

Feedback from individuals is that they have never received anything like this before and are grateful for the support. Being picked out for 'special attention' when the intention is clearly positive can be a driver for positive changes in behaviour and a desire to deliver.

Karen Boanas, Canada Life

The net result of the coaching programme to date is that more people at Boxwood feel they have a more structured career path and a clearer understanding of what they need to do to be successful.

Extract from Boxwood Group case study, p. 247

Changes that have been reported include:

- *Managers are better at selecting new team members.*
- *Managers are better at having conversations about issues, and problems are resolved more quickly.*
- *People are going home and having better relationships with their families.*

Extract from Dixons case study, p. 258

The internal coaches have noticed that coaching can inspire people and make them enthusiastic and more engaged in their work. Some individuals have blossomed as a result of coaching, having gained a greater appreciation of the influence and impact of their role. Managers have taken more ownership of their work and the customer processes they manage, moving away from always checking with their boss to actually presenting ideas and solutions instead.

Extract from Canada Life case study, p. 251

The London School of Economics and Political Science uses internal coaching in conjunction with external coaching but reported a series of benefits they are seeing as a result of their activities. In particular, internal coaching was felt to have improved individuals' management skills, commitment and confidence:

We are seeing a number of results:

- *re-engagement with role and organisation*
- *greater clarity and perspective*
- *increased proactivity and capacity for addressing issues*
- *increased confidence*
- *greater awareness of management/leadership styles*
- *more effective management of challenging people*
- *greater awareness of career options and choices.*

Extract from London School of Economics case study

The range of benefits that individuals had received often resulted in HR being drowned in requests for coaching. The positive results seen had also stimulated interest and support for coaching within the business:

> *Demand for the coaching programme is growing as a result of the positive feedback from previous participants, and there is now a waiting list of senior people booked to attend the course, including one managing director ... To build on the success of the internal coach programme, a two-day coaching module for middle managers is currently being developed that will form part of the management development programme.*
>
> Extract from Dixons case study, p. 258

Many organisations reported that their internal coaching programme also resulted in benefits for the coaches delivering the service.

> *BBC internal coaches report the following benefits of being a coach:*
>
> - *'It allows me to develop my own skills as well as those of my client.'*
> - *'As a coach I feel I give value back to the BBC.'*
> - *'Being a coach helps me to improve my own performance in my day job.'*
> - *'It increases my own awareness of how to manage and deal with continuous change.'*
>
> Quote from BBC case study, Aquilina, (2005)

But results were not solely seen at the individual level of analysis. Some organisations were able to provide examples of how internal coaching had delivered clear benefits to the business:

> *Coaching in conjunction with the process review teams has had a positive impact on the business in terms of cost reduction and business growth. It has also made staff more aware of and responsible for delivering the customer proposition.*
>
> Extract from Canada Life case study, p. 251

Several examples were provided in the range of initiatives discussed by Norfolk, Suffolk and Cambridgeshire Strategic Health Authority:

> *In terms of results from the different programmes, evaluation is still ongoing but some of the findings to date are as follows. Three of the original cohort of 12 on the BME coach/mentoring programme were promoted within nine months, and five more have stated that they are now working in broader work streams, with two other individuals stating that 'they are personally developing in unexpected ways'.*
>
> Extract from Norfolk, Suffolk and Cambridgeshire Strategic Health Authority case study, p. 273

> *Addenbrooke's Hospital in NSC has addressed the issue of linking mentoring and coaching to improving the patient experience. They report as follows: 'Coaching has particularly been embraced by the Service Improvement and Human Resources Directorates at Addenbrooke's. The benefits have been at two levels: at the individual level, coaching has helped reduce self-limiting beliefs; and at the team level, coaching has helped teams to work through issues affecting patient care.'*
>
> Extract from Norfolk, Suffolk and Cambridgeshire Strategic Health Authority case study, p. 273

Coaching is having a positive impact on patient care. It has proved particularly valuable when challenging established practice and when problem-solving around service development. One example where coaching has helped is in identifying and escalating issues preventing provision of a streamlined service to patients.

Extract from Norfolk, Suffolk and Cambridgeshire Strategic Health Authority case study, p. 273

Many organisations felt that developing internal coaches had helped to support wider cultural change initiatives, improve working relationships across the business or fast-track their organisation's move towards a coaching culture:

The concept of developing internal coaches within Boxwood was central to the programme. ... As Jackie Hoare explains, the introduction of career coaches outside of reporting lines has also resulted in greater cohesiveness within the company: 'Through regular coaching sessions, many employees are communicating with people they previously had little contact with. It has really added to the sense of collaboration and behavioural change within the company. Rather than people working in isolation in their assigned service unit, today there is a greater awareness of what other people are doing and the challenges they face.'

Extract from Boxwood Group case study, p. 247

Coaching is shifting from being 'the in thing to do', to becoming a way of behaving and managing people at Dixons. This positive shift in the culture and management style is something they have seen develop over the last 18 months.

Extract from Dixons case study, p. 258

As discussed earlier, internal coaches can provide organisations with a rich resource of coaching skills that they can draw on for many other purposes. Many of our case study organisations reported that they had experienced a multitude of positive spin-offs from their investment in internal coaches that directly benefited the business:

Trained internal coaches acquire skills which are transferable to other development programmes providing an internal resource to support other initiatives. This has been a big and unexpected bonus for our organisation.

Roger Williams, United Utilities case study, p. 296

At the end of last year, the L&D manager suggested using coaching techniques to get people talking and discussing issues and ideas throughout a strategy/planning day for the directors and department heads at Tate. As a result, the Head of Policy and Planning said that the quality of submissions was markedly improved. He feels this is a tangible piece of evidence demonstrating how coaching techniques can be used to improve the productivity of day-to-day activities.

Extract from Tate Museums case study, p. 292

UU has noticed some successful spin-offs from the coaching programme and having the internal coaching resource within the business. They have realised they can use this internal resource for wider initiatives and have used the internal coaches to help with the ongoing implementation of the change programmes. ... UU has also provided further training for some of the internal executive coaches to give them more in-depth group facilitation skills – these individuals are now used as team coaches. These coaches also support the senior management team by facilitating meetings. The flexibility and transferability of coaching skills for use in other initiatives in the organisation is considered to be an extremely helpful and unexpected outcome of the coaching programme.

Extract from United Utilities case study, p. 296

However, some organisations reported that coaching can also have some unexpected results:

But there have also been instances where coaching has resulted in people leaving the business as they have realised that they want a change. In these instances, coaching is still considered to have had a positive impact. If people are not engaged in their work, they're unlikely to be performing effectively for the business.

Extract from Canada Life case study, p. 251

Many organisations did, however, report frustrations about not being able to gain quantitative data to prove the value of internal coaching for the business. Often they felt that the anecdotal feedback was extremely good, but that the business would need to see hard evidence before it was truly convinced about the value coaching was delivering:

But despite all the positive feedback, UU want to be able to measure the business benefit of coaching. As Roger Williams states: 'While we have had a lot of good feedback, how do you turn that into cash?'

Extract from United Utilities case study, p. 296

At the moment, Dixons are undertaking some evaluation of their coaching activities, but are finding it difficult to establish quantifiable results. They have received some fantastic anecdotal stories by asking people about their experiences and what they have seen as a result of the coaching programme.

Extract from Dixons case study, p. 258

Our case studies therefore demonstrate that despite the relatively recent emergence of internal coaches on the coaching landscape, benefits to individuals and organisation are already being experienced. The very nature of internal coaching – with its particular emphasis on supporting other coaching initiatives or business change programmes – will mean that it will be harder for organisations to understand and identify the specific ways that internal coaching is delivering value to organisations. HR practitioners will need to think of innovative ways to demonstrate the impact of internal coaching so that an evidence base can begin to be established.

Risks and issues with adopting an internal coaching model

As organisations have introduced internal coaches to their organisations, a number of issues have arisen that organisations must be aware of and try to counter in the design of their programmes.

Frisch (2001) argues that a significant issue is the credibility of internal coaches. Because of this he makes the case for standards to be set for the internal coach comprising an explicit set of guidelines which clearly lay out how a coaching programme works and who internal coaches work with (eg only clients outside of their departments), and which emphasise the purpose. This is something that is backed up by Kilburg (2001), who calls for the 'development and implementation of an adherence protocol by both parties'. Aquilina (2005) also supports this:

> *With greater potential for collusion and coercion, an internal model needs to develop a framework, a set of rules, a protocol which ensures that internal coaches remain detached and do not become part of the problem.*

Many issues relate to trust and confidentiality. As part of her research Aquilina (2005) interviewed a number of different participants involved or with an interest in internal coaching at the BBC: 15 clients, 15 nominators, five key stakeholders, as well as some coaches. Some quotes from her research about these issues are shown below:

> *'There will be a need to work more closely with the internal coaches to get them to understand the inherent dangers of being in this role.' (Stakeholder)*

> *'I can imagine that some people might feel uncomfortable because that coach has relations in the organisation.' (Stakeholder)*

A major issue can be conflicts of interest. A study by Wasylyshyn (2003) found that 79 per cent of respondents felt concerned about an internal coach's potential for experiencing conflicts of interest. This was also raised by the participants in Aquilina's research, as you can see from the following quotes:

> *'An internal coach needs to think very carefully about where they coach – if they are matched with someone who could potentially raise conflict of interest issues, this must be raised and managed.' (Stakeholder)*

> *'People need to observe strict demarcation between their relationship with someone as a coach and then later as a colleague, line manager or member of staff.' (Nominator)*

> *'As the organisation becomes more dynamic and sees a movement of people, there is a risk that today's coach may be tomorrow's line manager or member of staff.' (Stakeholder)*

Another risk that has emerged is that internal coaches end up being used for other development activities, rather than being reserved for the activity they have been trained for – coaching. Frisch (2001) comments on the danger of setting up an internal coaching model as 'an internal advisory role' or 'team-building or training' or 'mentoring'. Furthermore, because the boundaries between clients and internal coaches can feel more 'fuzzy' – they are also colleagues of their clients – a danger also exists that coaching relationships turn into informal relationships in which the coaching process is not fully broached (de Haan and Burger, 2005). Organisations must ensure that they carefully reserve the use of their internal coaches for coaching activities rather than just using them as a general development advisory service.

Although one of the powerful benefits of internal coaches is their understanding of the organisation's culture and context, it has also been found to be a potential risk. De Haan and Burger (2005) argue that the internal coach's knowledge of an organisation can result in a 'corporate blind spot' which prevents him or her from seeing certain patterns or from raising them for discussion. This is echoed by one of the participants in Aquilina's (2005) research at the BBC, who comments:

> *The risk of working with internal coaches is that they become part of the problem ... so that they don't bring in another perspective, but share the same seated view of the world as their clients.*

Several organisations reported that because of these issues, regular supervision for internal coaches was needed.

> *The internal service's philosophy for supervision is to ensure the integrity of the service, but in addition it provides 'a learning vehicle for coaches'. The supervision document goes on to say:*

> *Supervision is:*

> *formative: learning which comes from a reviewing of the journey of client and coaching relationship*
> *normative: best practice/model development*
> *restorative: personal development, self-awareness and self-care.*

Aquilina, (2005)

And careful recruitment and selection of internal coaches was again raised as being critical. One of the participants in Aquilina's (2005) research at the BBC stated, 'You need to have very good training and brutality in selection to ensure that the right people are working as internal coaches.' This view is reinforced by Frisch (2001) who talks about the importance of rigorous recruitment and selection, training for internal coaches and ongoing supervision and development of the internal coach.

A final issue that was raised was that many organisations experience being 'victims of their own success'. In these situations there can be a rapid rise in demand, and internal coaches may be swamped with requests for coaching. This situation has to be carefully managed, particularly if internal coaches are coaching on top of their day jobs.

Although organisations can therefore achieve a number of wide-ranging benefits from internal coaching, a number of problems can also emerge associated with maintaining trust, confidentiality and conflicts of interest. Organisations should be aware of these issues and build regular review and monitoring into their internal coaching activities.

CONCLUSIONS

The internal coach is an emerging role within organisations but one that is finding considerable favour with organisations that are initiating and developing coaching cultures. The use of the term 'coaching infrastructure' in the Norfolk, Suffolk and Cambridgeshire Strategic Health Authority case study is significant because it highlights the real underpinning role the internal coach can play.

Internal coaches are playing a broad variety of different roles, often operating as a supervisor and trainer of manager-coaches as well as coaching in their own right. In some organisations they are offering specialist coaching services to leaders or senior managers, while in others they are acting as technical coaches helping to build up skill levels in the organisation. However, a critical role for internal coaches is supporting other coaching interventions in the organisation and the development of a coaching culture. Within large organisations, their supervision and support role for manager-coaches means that the 'critical mass' of a coaching infrastructure can be achieved quickly and cost-effectively.

The training provided for internal coaches, as exemplified by the best practice organisations within our case studies, gives them a developed skill base which, taken with their insider knowledge of the organisation, confers on them a high degree of credibility with their clients. This, in turn, facilitates the buy-in and take-up of employees and therefore the sustainability of coaching in the organisation more generally. However, their level of competency is not generally equivalent to that of a professional external coach, particularly as it is still relatively early days for many internal coaches operating in their roles. In particular, the research indicates that although internal coaches are effective in developing technical skills and preventing derailment, external coaches are more effective in developing leadership skills. Thus, organisations must think carefully about the training needs of their internal coaches if they are expecting them to support the development of leaders and senior managers.

The studies looking at the impact of internal coaching are still too few to give a fully conclusive answer about whether it is effective or not, but the early signs are positive, as are the results reported by our case study organisations. Together, these results indicate that internal coaching is delivering value at the level of the individual coachee. We will have to wait and see whether the research in the next few years confirms the benefits from our case studies that internal coaching is also delivering value to the organisation's bottom line.

8

Learning lessons about organisations' coach-training programmes

A major area of current activity for UK organisations is designing and implementing coach-training programmes for either manager- or internal coaches. The CIPD's 2006 learning and development survey revealed that 47 per cent of respondents who use coaching are training line managers to act as coaches, while another 35 per cent report that they are taking a dual approach and implementing both coach-training for managers and coaching via internal and external coaches. This large-scale investment by UK organisations appears to be driven by a desire to create a coaching culture, build up internal coaching capability, or reduce reliance on external providers – or perhaps a combination of all of these.

From our review of the literature and the experiences of our case study organisations, some clear themes have surfaced about the effective training of manager- and internal coaches. The training that organisations provide for managers and internal coaches appears not to differ hugely. Often, internal coach-training programmes involve similar types of activities but tend to be more in-depth and take place over a longer time period than that offered to managers. Internal coaches are also much more likely to be offered the opportunity to attend external coaching courses to gain qualifications or accreditation, as well as receive on-going support services such as supervision. In this chapter we firstly consider how easy it is for people to learn coaching skills, before moving on to how organisations are training their manager-coaches. Because the components of training programmes for both manager- and internal coaches are fairly similar, we analyse both types of coach-training programmes together to identify common features, but we then provide comments on how internal coach training is different. Throughout this chapter we draw heavily on the experiences of our case study organisations who have been implementing these programmes over the last few years. It is hoped that by reviewing the lessons they learned, other HR practitioners can pick up ideas and advice for when they design their own programmes.

CAN ANYONE BE TRAINED TO BE AN EFFECTIVE COACH?

Developing and learning new coaching behaviours and skills is not a simple process. An important initial question is that of nature versus nurture – is it possible to *teach* managers key coaching skills? There are a few studies in the literature that have looked at this question, and the good news is that the answer seems to be 'yes'. Graham *et al* (1993), for example, studied 87 account representatives who worked for 13 sales managers and found that as a result of training, managers could develop coaching skills. Seventy per cent of the account representatives indicated that they had observed a positive change in their managers.

However, it appears not to be just a question of sending managers on a short course. CIPD research (Lane, 2000) found that effective manager-coaches were actually doing a number of related people management activities well. The research suggested that if organisations want effective manager-coaches, they must ensure that they have a base of strong people management and development skills, as well as learning some specific coaching skills and techniques.

For the trainee coach seeking to improve or develop his or her coaching skills, there are a number of practitioner books and articles available providing good-practice guides and a range of practice models (eg Burdett, 1998). However, it is important to accept that coaching does not come naturally to everyone, and that certain people will need extra support and time. This was observed by several of our case study companies:

The majority of participants have reported using the coaching skills back in the workplace and finding it useful. However, as with any new idea or change, a few participants have reported having difficulties applying the theory and knowledge back in the workplace. Some have accepted coaching more readily than others. They haven't noticed significant cultural differences in terms of participants' responses to coaching, but they do see individual differences depending on how open individuals are to new ideas and models.

Extract from Panasonic Europe case study, p. 278

While managers wouldn't be disciplined for not coaching (as the company appreciates that these skills don't come easily to everyone), there is an expectation that they will continue to drive to acquire and develop their coaching skills.

Extract from Perkins Shibaura Engines case study, p. 281

Most people start out in technical roles, and it is a significant shift for them to realise that as they become more senior, they must develop equally strong people management skills as well as having technical expertise.

Extract from Shell case study, p. 286

Managers who are used to the command-and-control form of management will often find it difficult to leave this predictable comfort zone and embrace coaching, with its longer timeframe and loss of direct control. There may also be pressure from peers and reports to 'sort out problems quickly' when dealing with a performance issue:

Nigel Briers, Change Manager at Perkins Shibaura Engines, says: 'This is the other side of the coin as people sometimes grumble that something is not being done about a person or issue. We know something is being done, but it takes time to produce results and people can get impatient.' When the coaching programme was first stepped up, there was an expectation that it would produce measurable performance improvement by the next quarter, but it is now recognised that three to four months is a reasonable timeline to see effective behavioural change.

Extract from Perkins Shibura Engines case study, p. 281

There was surprising agreement across our case study organisations that coaching often requires up to six months for results such as behaviour change to be achieved, and this is echoed in the academic literature. It is therefore not surprising that the short-term 'sticking-plaster' style of command-and-control may be very difficult for managers to ignore when faced with issues that need resolution within short time-scales.

A research project reported by Palmer (2003) based on a detailed study within one organisation identified that some managers do not respond to coach training as well as others and that it is possible to predict those who will not make such effective coaches. The balance between the time they talk rather than listen and the use of open rather than closed questions were particularly significant as predictors. This raises issues about the selection and deployment of training resources and was an area discussed by a few of our case study organisations, including Dixons:

> *Camilla Aitchison explains: 'You need people who won't bring their personal agenda to the table and who can detach themselves from their own situation to focus on the coachee's needs. We're looking for people who genuinely want to help other people to develop.' The vast majority of applicants are accepted on the programme, but occasionally someone does not have the requisite approach and it is not suitable for them.*

Extract from Dixons case study, p. 258

TO WHAT EXTENT ARE ORGANISATIONS TRAINING THEIR MANAGERS?

Of the different roles that the manager performs, Geber (1992) argues that of the coach is 'the most difficult one to perform'. Managers therefore need considerable training and support to learn the required skills. A study by the School of Coaching reported that most organisations will say 'Yes, our managers are coaching,' and 'Yes, we support it' (Kubicek, 2002). And yet it seems that many organisations are expecting their managers to coach with little training or ongoing support. The CIPD's 2004 training and development survey found that line managers are the most likely group to be delivering coaching in UK organisations, a third of respondents reporting that managers deliver 'a majority' of coaching, and a further quarter saying that line managers are responsible for delivering 'half' of the coaching activities (CIPD, 2004). However, worryingly, fewer than 20 per cent of respondents have 'all' or 'the majority' of their line managers trained to carry out coaching (see Table 13).

Table 13: | The proportion of line managers trained to coach

Responses from least to most	Percentage of respondents	Responses in rank order of proportion	Percentage of respondents
None	11	A minority	49
A minority	49	About half	16
About half	16	A majority	13
A majority	13	None	11
All	5	Don't know	6
Don't know	6	All	5

The survey also investigated the methods through which line managers are trained for coaching. Although 97 per cent believed that coaching was a necessary part of any manager's skillset, there is much less clarity about how managers should be prepared for this role, 73 per cent saying that coaching skills training is not compulsory. Line managers are most likely to receive training as part of a wider management training programme (54 per cent), although coaching skills workshops are used by just under half of respondents (48 per cent).

These findings are supported by other research studies. Kubicek (2002) found that two-fifths of companies (38 per cent) had an initiative in place to develop their line managers as coaches, but concerns were raised that on average the manager-coaches received only three days of training to develop their coaching skills. The training provided for manager-coaches was most commonly delivered by external or internal workshops, but 44 per cent spent less than two days on this, and 35 per cent two to five days. So even when training is provided, it tends to be offered in short workshops or as just one part of short management training programmes.

There appears to be a lack of specific training for managers on how to undertake coaching activities, indicating that many organisations are failing to make the necessary investment to ensure that manager-coaches have sufficient skills and support to complete their role effectively. In our research the case study organisations that showed the highest impact on performance (effective or very effective) were the ones that invested the most resources in training their manager-coaches. The most effective training programmes took place over several months (eg three to six), allowing participants plenty of opportunities for practice and reflection between workshops. An example of this is provided by our case study company, Boxwood:

> *There were five phases to the programme:*
>
> - *an initial briefing session that set the scene*
> - *a skills development workshop*
> - *a period to hone some of the skills learned*
> - *a follow-up workshop session*
> - *individual telephone coaching sessions.*
>
> *The main goal of this five-stage approach was to reinforce coaching skills and key learnings. Rather than having a one-off workshop and then participants going back to their day-to-day routines, the company wanted to make sure that the coaching programme acted as a catalyst for real behavioural change.*
>
> Except from Boxwood Group case study, p. 247

Where high effectiveness was identified but training was not extensive, the organisation tended to have a highly developed coaching culture. This meant that managers were likely to receive coaching on their newly developed skills in the workplace that helped to embed the new behaviours.

If we are expecting our managers to deliver effective coaching, it is essential that we train and equip them for their role. Many managers will need to learn new behaviours and/or change existing behaviours, and development programmes must therefore provide both training and ongoing support. We will now look in more detail at the analysis of the main features of the manager-coaching programmes used by organisations in our study to try to understand what effective training programmes look like.

COMPONENTS OF EFFECTIVE MANAGER-COACH TRAINING PROGRAMMES

The relatively restricted nature of the coaching agenda (ie not an open agenda) dealt with by manager-coaches does have implications for the level of training they require. Manager-coaches do not need the in-depth training that internal or external coaches require, but as with any form of learning, the greater the level of training and practice, the greater the level of skill your manager-coaches will have.

The elements required in a manager-coach programme are specific to the environment of each organisation, managers' previous experience of coaching and the coaching model the organisation is looking to embed. Programmes must also take into account the operational constraints of managers – eg the time commitments and the practicality of getting groups of people together, as the following quote illustrates:

> *This coaching course comprises five days of coach training in the Operational part of the business and three days in the Retail part of the business. The shorter length of the course in Retail reflects the difficulty in taking people away from their front-line jobs.*
>
> Extract from Nationwide case study, p. 269

Such operational constraints may require that novel learning environments are used – such as virtual classrooms – or that HR must come up with innovative ways of supporting manager-coaches when they return to the workplace so that they continue to develop their skills:

> *Following the workshop, participants undertake some post-course work. This takes place by phone and in virtual classrooms because many of the participants are geographically dispersed across Europe. Within six weeks of the workshop, participants must work in threes to undertake telephone-coaching sessions with each other. After this exercise, they take part in a virtual classroom to discuss what they have applied from the experience. Each of the participants presents their learning via online presentation software and talks through their experiences.*
>
> Extract from Panasonic Europe case study, p. 278

> *Shell has recently added a new online element to their coaching portfolio, reflecting a general move towards more online and blended learning in the organisation. The online coaching module is designed to support the other coaching programmes, helping participants to continue developing their coaching activities in the workplace. Participants are required to be in a coaching relationship as part of the programme, and it enables them to receive feedback on their skills as well as support from facilitators.*
>
> Extract from Shell case study, p. 286

Our review of the case study organisations' approach to training their managers allows us to identify some of the key components that are being used during training programmes. As mentioned earlier, the broad structure of manager-coach training is often similar to that of internal coaches (who are often managers), but is shorter, covers fewer techniques/models, and has less ongoing support and supervision mechanisms. We analysed the case study organisations that were using internal programmes to develop manager-coaches or people to work in broader internal coaching roles. From this, we can provide a list of the design features common to organisations' internal training programmes:

- introductory workshops
- assessment exercises
- intensive training days
- action learning sets or specific coaching assignments
- support for learners during training
- follow-through and reflection
- ongoing support for trainee-coaches.

Relatively few organisations used all of these components for manager-coach programmes. Instead, they chose a selection to form a programme that suited their needs and reflected the level of coaching expertise they required their managers to be able to deliver. Internal coach programmes tended to incorporate a greater number of these activities.

Introductory workshops

Many organisations kicked off their training programmes with an introductory workshop or meeting where the business case for coaching was made and the coaching model introduced. The most commonly-cited barriers to coaching were: a lack of understanding about what coaching is, a lack of belief that it can influence the bottom line, and the belief that it takes too much time. The initial meeting could be used to address these issues head-on and provide an opportunity for senior management buy-in to be made explicit:

> *A two-day launch was organised for the start of the coaching skills pilot programme, which was run by external consultants and members of Resourcing and Development. During the launch, they revisited themes from the leadership programme and aligned the coaching with the previous development activity. They introduced objectives for the coaching programme and set expectations for how the Selfridges coaching skills programme would work.*
>
> Extract from Selfridges case study, p. 283

> *The first day of the coaching programme is a business initiative day, which is run by internal trainers and external coaches to provide a consistent approach. ... The director for the business area also attends the day to sell the vision for coaching at Nationwide and to explain how coaching relates to raising performance in the business and culture change.*
>
> Extract from Nationwide coaching case study, p. 269

Assessment exercises

At some point before the actual training begins, many organisations encourage delegates to reflect on their development needs and current level of coaching skills. This can be via self-awareness exercises, 360-degree feedback, learning needs questionnaires or a variety of other assessment techniques and tools:

It's a nine-month programme that starts with the assessment of managers' current skills and development needs using 360-degree feedback.

Extract from Glenmorangie case study, p. 262

A week later, participants attend a second day, where they focus on building their self-awareness via a tool called 'Insights'. A few weeks later, there is a two-day coaching practice course. Prior to the course, all delegates complete a coaching behaviours analysis questionnaire. This is based on a set of coaching standards (levels 1–3) that have been developed at Nationwide. The questionnaire is used as a 360-degree feedback instrument, being given to participants' peers, manager and team members. Results are analysed to identify 'hot spots' in people's coaching capabilities, and this is used during the programme to highlight areas to develop managers' skills.

Extract from Nationwide case study, p. 269

Intensive training

The number of training days offered varied between two and five days. Some organisations split up these training days, allowing trainee-coaches to practise skills between the formal training days:

Between the fortnightly modules, participants are given 'homework', being expected to think through issues and practise their skills. For the duration of the coaching programme, each participant coaches one of the participants in the talent programme. They are expected to meet with their coachee at least once every two weeks and arrange conference calls between the contact sessions.

Extract from Selfridges case study, p. 283

Following the two-day course, participants have a period of six to eight weeks when they practise their coaching skills with their 'pet client'. After this, they have three separate input days where they review their learning, are introduced to new coaching models, techniques and ideas, and practise their skills. There is also an opportunity for them to raise issues they have been facing and to receive some coaching and advice on how to manage them. Each input day is separated by about six weeks, during which the coaches practise their new skills. The programme is designed to constantly increase the skills levels of coaches over the course of several months while allowing them to continually practise their skills.

Extract from United Utilities case study, p. 296

Some courses take place off-site to provide a learning environment without the normal distractions. During the training days, organisations offered a mix of theory, discussion and practice:

The programme comprises 30 per cent teaching, 50 per cent skills practice in threes and 20 per cent discussion.

Extract from Dixons case study, p. 258

During the half-day sessions, different coaching models and techniques are discussed and participants work in threes to practise their skills. The sessions are run as self-managed groups and are facilitated discussions rather than traditional training or instructional events. Coaching at

Selfridges is not designed as a rigid process or model – the company believes each person has to develop their own coaching style. The models and ground rules that are discussed are designed to help managers develop their own style and to give them a structure for their coaching conversations.

Extract from Selfridges case study, p. 283

All our case study organisations emphasised the importance of providing opportunities for observed coaching practice. This was considered essential to promoting behaviour change:

During the workshop, coaches practise the skills and techniques by co-coaching each other.

Extract from Surrey and Sussex Strategic Health Authority case study, p. 289

On the first day, the participants build on the theory covered in the virtual classroom and undertake a series of practical exercises to practise their coaching skills. During the second day they are divided into groups of four for more coaching skills practice. One person acts as coach, another as coachee, while the remaining two act as observers who note down comments and then coach the 'coach' on their coaching skills. All participants rotate through the different roles to practise their skills.

Extract from Panasonic Europe case study, p. 278

Action learning sets/specific coaching assignments

Some of the longer or more in-depth training programmes used 360-degree or learning needs questionnaires to design a mini-project, action learning task or specific coaching assignment for the individual to work on as a focus of his or her coaching practice over the coming months:

Participants are asked to come to the programme with some issues that they would like to receive coaching on. Management issues tend to be the common themes, or challenges they are experiencing at work. Participants work in threes – one person acts as coach, one person receives coaching, and the third acts as an observer. The observers are given a feedback checklist to assess the coach's coaching skills and are asked to use this to provide specific feedback. The observers are also expected to practise their own coaching skills when giving feedback to the 'coach'.

Extract from Tate Museums case study, p. 292

Coach training for managers at Nationwide has been introduced by relating it to specific business initiatives that managers are leading. An example of a business initiative is 'enhancing the member experience'. The aim is to frame coach training in practical applications within the business, rather than offering it as a stand-alone training activity.

Extract from Nationwide case study, p. 269

The coaching skills programme has acted as a bridge between the leadership development programme and a talent programme aimed at middle managers (level 4). Eleven participants in the leadership programme were selected to be trained as coaches for participants in the level 4 talent programme to support their ongoing development and promotion.

Extract from Selfridges case study, p. 283

Each participant chooses an improvement objective in line with the organisation's goals. 'It's all about improving the patient experience and improving access,' Head of Leadership and

Organisation Development Jonathan Harding said. ... Following on from the workshop, coaches take part in two action learning set events over the next six months. These are again facilitated by the external coaching company and provide an opportunity for the coaches to talk about their experiences and any issues that have arisen and to explore how they should be tackled.

Extract from Surrey and Sussex Strategic Health Authority case study, p. 289

Support for learners during training

Where coach training programmes took place over a series of workshops, a key feature of effective programmes were mechanisms that kept the motivation of learners high between sessions and which offered them opportunities to meet up with their peers, as well as to receive some coaching themselves:

Participants also meet once with other participants (in threes) in the coaching programme and the 'super coaches' between the formal modules. This means they have regular contact with other coaches every week for the whole six-month programme, both for support and to discuss issues they face. The six-month programme finishes with a full-day presentation from participants and a review of the programme and their learning.

Extract from Selfridges case study, p. 283

The coaches can also contact the external coaching company for ongoing support during the lifespan of the projects.

Extract from Surrey and Sussex Strategic Health Authority case study, p. 289

Follow-through and reflection

To end the coach-training programme, some organisations arranged follow-up sessions to reflect on the programme and to discuss progress or problems encountered. Some organisations also took this opportunity to provide an injection of new skills or information for continuing professional development purposes. This session was facilitated by either HR or an internal or external coach:

The two-day programme is followed by a confidential one-to-one session with the external coach. This allows participants to discuss issues that arise during the programme, as well as giving them an opportunity to receive coaching themselves (and it allows them to see the coaching approach in action again). A further half-day session for the whole group is organised by the L&D manager. During this session, they share and celebrate individual successes with coaching, identify areas that individuals need to continue developing, and work on some of these as a group.

Extract from Tate Museums case study, p. 292

The six-month programme finishes with a full-day presentation from participants and a review of the programme and their learning.

Extract from Selfridges case study, p. 283

Several organisations indicated that at the end of programmes they undertake an assessment of the coaching skills. This can be done by monitoring the outputs of projects/tasks or by direct observation of the coach:

The coaching behaviour questionnaire and insights tools are used to measure participants'
progress as coaches. Three months after the coach training, when individuals have been actively
coaching in the business, they repeat the questionnaires to analyse and evaluate changes in
coaches' behaviour and skills. Linking coaching with the results of the business initiative and
tracking the development of coaches' skills before and after the coaching allows them to
demonstrate that progress is being made.

Extract from Nationwide case study, p. 269

On the last day of the course, participants' coaching skills are assessed while they practise on a
'real-life coachee'. This enables coaches to practise their skills initially in a supportive
environment. And they continue coaching the coachee after the programme has finished. Dixons
wanted to provide internal certification for their coaches to recognise that they have reached a
certain level of coaching skills, so at the end of the course participants are given a certificate that
states they have been trained and are now accredited internal coaches.

Extract from Dixons case study, p. 258

It was clear in our case studies that where there was little training (less than two days) and no effective continuing support for development (no follow-through coaching or supervision), the perceived effectiveness of the manager-coaches was reduced. In these cases the effectiveness was described as 'patchy', relying on highly motivated individuals to continue coaching.

Ongoing support for trainee-coaches

Once employees have received their initial coach-training, behaviour change must be constantly reinforced if it is to be sustainable. The majority of our organisations had thought through and implemented mechanisms to support their trainee-coaches to continue using and building their coaching skills over time when they returned to the workplace. Peer-support networks were one way that organisations were using to provide support back in the workplace, while others had provided information and resources:

Everest has established a number of features to support the coaching process. These include
clear targets, strong support from senior management, sponsoring the signing-off of personal
learning plans, and the creation of the Everest Guide to Coaching which everyone receives. ...
Everest hopes that the Guide will provide a resource for coaches and coachees to use and also
sets expectations and guidelines about how coaching relationships should run.

Extract from Everest case study, p. 261

Other organisations provided regular events/sessions to continually build on their learning and develop their skills:

Master classes to help managers learn from those who have led service improvement elsewhere,
both inside and outside the NHS.

Extract from Surrey and Sussex Strategic Health Authority, p. 289

Some organisations went a step further and provided coaching support for trainee-coaches as they develop and embed new behaviours. In this way, they experience being coached while developing their own coaching skills:

Managers who are coaching are supported by a coaching champion. She has regular meetings with the coaches, observes them coaching their consultants and gives feedback on their performance. She is also the connection point with department managers and provides regular updates to the directors about progress.

Extract from KwikFit Financial Services case study, p. 268

Providing support for coaches after the initial training programme was frequently seen to be crucial for the sustainability of effective coaching practice. Many other wider organisational conditions for effective coach-training were identified by our case studies. For example, many respondents commented on the need for an organisational culture supportive of coaching as well as commitment and role modelling of senior managers. These form part of a wider discussion about the conditions for effective coaching in Chapter 9, but it is worthwhile noting briefly here that the most crucial factors identified by our case study organisations for the effectiveness of coach-training programmes were:

- buy-in, support and role-modelling by senior managers
- ongoing training and skills development
- effective support mechanisms
- a culture that is supportive of learning and development
- initiatives that were introduced for specific business reasons
- a commitment to measuring results
- HR practitioners being educated about coaching or trained as coaches themselves
- coaching being used to address specific issues, with boundaries being made clear.

HOW DOES INTERNAL COACH TRAINING DIFFER FROM THAT GIVEN TO MANAGER-COACHES?

What type of coaching services are internal coaches expected to deliver in the organisation? The answer to this question will determine the level of training that internal coaches should receive. The different roles and remits of internal coaches have implications for the range of competencies they will require, and this should form the basis of the design of their coach-training programme. Another area for consideration early on is the level of skills that already exist within the organisation because this will also impact on the training that is required. Many of our case studies proved that there was already considerable expertise within their own HR departments and senior managers. For example, many HR staff have an organisational psychology or professional HR accreditation that equips them with skills required for effective coaching.

Alongside the components of internal coach-training programmes discussed earlier, several generic requirements specific to internal coach-training programmes were identified by a number of our case study organisations:

- an organisational framework – a shared understanding by the internal coaches of their terms of reference, ethical framework and code of practice within the programme

- accreditation, evaluation and supervision of practice – the quality of provision must be monitored and supported to achieve the aims of the programme

- the internal coaches' services – these must be embedded in the organisational strategy for development, thereby providing the coaches with credibility and ensuring the sustainability of the provision.

Apart from these common design criteria, our case study organisations' training programmes for internal coaches often differed in length and content. Interestingly, some organisations expressed concern at the difficulty of accessing appropriate-level training for internal coaches:

We have had considerable difficulty in accessing training which can build on our current skills and allow us to develop without going fully into being executive coaches.

Sharon Green, Stephenson Harwood case study

In general, the training for internal coaches is more intensive than that given to manager-coaches (where two days' training was the norm), but shorter than that commonly undertaken by external coaches. Training ranged from a nine-month programme at postgraduate level involving a series of modules, practice and supervision, through to a five-day course:

Within the business, six HR practitioners have been trained as master practitioners. Master practitioners receive ten days' coach training rather than five and have access to 29 hours of e-learning CD-ROMs on coaching models, theory and techniques. Essentially, the master coaches learn a greater number of models and techniques and undertake more practice as part of their training.

Extract from Dixons case study, p. 258

BBC coaches are accredited through the BBC Coach Foundation Course. This is a modular programme with taught elements, observed practice sessions and assessed fieldwork ... The programme lasts for a period of four months and each trainee is mentored throughout by a coach mentor.

Quote from Aquilina, (2005)

HR work with their internal customers and are trained as coaches. They can then take further 'coaching excellence' modules leading to a postgraduate level award.

Neil Hounslow, Lloyds TSB

Although they are using external coaches for senior managers, the starting point for the coaching/mentoring programme as a whole was to create a supply of internal coaches trained in supervision who can deliver the training required to train coaches. In addition to the five-day core coaching programme, they provide a two-day training package exploring supervision models. This development is maintained through participation in an ongoing three-monthly continuous development group where the coaches meet with an external coach to review their experience and explore new frameworks. Through this organic growth of coaching it is envisaged that an 'infrastructure of coaching' will develop to facilitate the implementation of change and learning.

Extract from Norfolk, Suffolk and Cambridgeshire Strategic Health Authority case study, p. 273

All programmes contained an element of coaching practice either within the programme itself or by using a 'real' coachee from the organisation:

> *The coach-training programme at UU lasts for about nine months and involves a series of input modules. Before the course, each participant has to identify a coaching 'guinea pig' who they can practise their new coaching skills on – they are called their 'pet client' and are generally a colleague, rather than somebody in their direct team. ... Following the two-day course, participants have a period of six to eight weeks when they practise their coaching skills with their pet client.*

Extract from United Utilities case study, p. 296

Support and supervision is an ongoing provision in all the programmes where the newly trained internal coaches meet regularly with external or internal coaches. This took several forms, from formal supervision sessions to creating communities of practice:

> *Dixon's now has a community of 60 managers who have been trained as coaches. Via the Dixon's Training and Development website, this group can circulate stories, discuss what has gone well and what hasn't gone well and HR can set up key dates for people to come together if they are available to share best practice. These events are also an opportunity for people to keep their skills up to date and for T&D to make sure that the coaches activities are keeping true to what they were taught – they feel they have a responsibility to the coachee to check the quality of the skills and approach being used by coaches.*

Extract from Dixons case study, p. 258

> *After the programme, the external coaching company runs external supervision days for the internal coaches so that they can share learning and receive independent advice and coaching on difficult situations they experience. It is a minimum requirement to attend two supervision days every six months.*

Extract from United Utilities case study, p. 296

> *Coach/mentors within an ongoing relationship are required to undertake supervision by attending a 'supervision and continual development group' every three months or with an NSC supervisor by appointment. The NSC also runs an ongoing programme of development events.*

Extract from Norfolk, Suffolk and Cambridgeshire Strategic Health Authority case study, p. 273

> *This desire to have a convincing internal coaching operation also informed the supervision framework. This requires all internal coaches to have regular one-to-one supervision and attend shared learning sessions with other internal coaches. Further development is provided through quarterly workshops or short refresher courses.*

Quote from Aquilina, (2005)

In many cases, it is only by satisfactory completion of an agreed training programme that the coach is considered 'accredited' to work as an internal coach for the organisation:

> *Dixons wanted to provide internal certification for their coaches to recognise that they have reached a certain level of coaching skills, so at the end of the course participants are given a certificate that states they have been trained and are now accredited internal coaches.*

Extract from Dixons case study, p. 258

CONCLUSIONS

Organisations are training both manager- and internal coaches using different coaching models and techniques to deal with different issues and to operate at different levels of expertise. This variation between organisations' approaches to coach training means that it is difficult to come up with a specific formula to say how exactly manager- and internal coaches should be prepared for their role. What is clear is that such training must be fit for the purpose. Organisations must think through their expectations of their different coaching practitioners and consider how their activities will relate to other coaches operating within the organisation. A key feature to consider is the level and length of coach training and the model taught within that training. Often the most successful programmes for managers involve training them to use simple coaching models applied to specific issues over short timeframes. However, a worrying finding of the research is that coach training for managers is often limited to a few hours or just two or three days. Such short training programmes are unlikely to result in lasting behaviour change. However, some organisations have adopted more elaborate training programmes, backed by ongoing support and supervision. These programmes allow for more models, skills and assessment techniques to be learned but tend to be provided for internal coaches rather than manager-coaches because of the wider remit of their coaching role. Specific guidance should be given to all trainee-coaches about identifying the boundaries of their expertise and understanding where they can go for guidance and support.

9
Factors contributing to effective coaching

In the previous chapters, our review of the organisational case studies, academic papers and practitioner articles gave us a positive answer to our original question: does coaching work? But we have seen that there are some serious caveats to this. Coaching works, but only when several factors are present that combine to result in a positive climate for coaching. In this chapter we cut through the mass of data to provide a view of the main factors that can help or hinder the impact of coaching in organisational settings. Consideration of these factors can greatly enhance both the ease of initiating a coaching programme and its chances of delivering what is required.

WHAT ARE THE CONTRIBUTING FACTORS?

The factors arising from our review can be seen to fall under four main headings:

- coach attributes

- coachee attributes

- the organisational context for coaching

- the coaching process.

Obviously, there is a degree of overlap and interaction between these groupings, but they serve as a useful label for our discussion in this chapter. Figure 13 illustrates the interaction of these factors in influencing the outcomes of coaching.

We will take each of these areas in turn, look at the evidence for its inclusion, and refer to examples from our case studies to illustrate its effects.

Coach attributes

So, what does a good coach look like? In this section we review the personal attributes, skills and knowledge that effective coaches require. We also briefly discuss when to use different coaching practitioners and the importance of ensuring that coaches understand the wider organisational context.

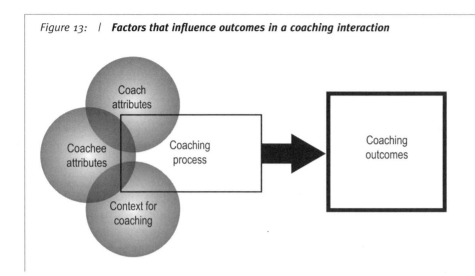

Figure 13: | ***Factors that influence outcomes in a coaching interaction***

There has been considerable debate about this issue: numerous researchers have tried to identify the critical attributes of an effective coach (Kilburg, 1996; Kilburg, 2001). The context for coaching is hugely important in defining this – coaches are likely to need different qualities depending on the specific individual, the problems being tackled and the organisational goals for coaching. Different types of coaches (eg manager-coach as against external coach) are also likely to need different levels of skills, knowledge and experience because they operate in very different contexts. But in spite of this, there are some common areas of competence that all coaches require.

Beyond looking for specific qualifications, experience and knowledge, it is important to look for coaches who have certain qualities or personal characteristics. During our research, the following three areas emerged as being critical coach attributes:

- *self-awareness* – Coaches must be able to separate out their own issues and focus on the coachee's agenda and needs. They must also recognise when their own issues are getting in the way of helping the coachee achieve his or her goals. The level of self-awareness would be expected to be broader and deeper the more complex the issues the coach is required to handle. This is particularly the case where supervision is part of the role.

- *core coaching competencies* – All coaches should have some basic coaching competencies, irrespective of the level they operate at. These include being able to listen actively, help clients define areas of concern, explore factors of influence, formulate new understanding, develop an intervention plan, and evaluate outcomes.

- *an understanding of the ethics and management of coaching relationships* – Coaches must have the ability to effectively contract and manage the coaching relationship. For external and internal coaches this will include specific contracting relationships and adequate knowledge of ethical codes of practice. For the external coach it is likely also to include being subject to an ethical code and disciplinary action through a professional body if necessary.

Other research studies have highlighted slightly different combinations of desirable coach attributes. Dingman (2004) categorises effective coach behaviour under three main headings:

- *Interpersonal skills*: empathy, encouragement, genuineness, authenticity, approachability, compassion, intelligence
- *Communication skills*: tact, listening/silence, questions, playful exchange
- *Instrumental support*: creativity, dealing with paradox, self-knowledge, positive regard, tolerance for intervention made, stimulation to think, feel and explore new ideas and behaviours, working on resistance to change.

Similarly, the CIPD guide *Coaching and Buying Coaching Services* (Jarvis, 2004) provides a list of coach attributes that commonly characterise effective coaches. These are outlined below.

The qualities and abilities of effective coaches
- the ability to be self-aware
- the ability to clearly and effectively communicate (verbally and non-verbally)
- the ability to build relationships
- the ability to flex their coaching approach
- the ability to listen and question
- the ability to design an effective coaching process
- the ability to assist goal development and setting, including giving feedback
- the ability to motivate
- the ability to encourage new perspectives
- the ability to assist sense-making
- the ability to identify significant patterns of thinking and behaving
- the ability to challenge and give feedback
- the ability to establish trust and respect
- the ability to establish rapport
- the ability to facilitate depth of understanding
- the ability to promote action
- the ability to build resiliency

The work of professional bodies

Uncovering core coaching competencies, skills and attributes is a rapidly developing area of practice and HR practitioners are well advised to follow the debates through professional bodies in this area. Groups such as the International Coach Federation have produced a list of coaching competencies, and the European Mentoring and Coaching Council (EMCC) has undertaken an international study looking at core competencies for coaching. The CIPD itself has developed competencies at the manager-coach and internal-coach level and co-operated with the EMCC on its project. Many training providers have also produced competency sets related to their own training programmes, or have them accredited by EMCC or others.

The coaching skills required of coaches are not universal. Coaches' skills and knowledge have to be fit for the purpose. For example, do they coach as part of their role as a manager, do they coach colleagues in technical skills, or are they operating as a full-time professional coach? It seems that, in line with the different coaching roles we have examined in the literature (manager-, internal and external coaches), different levels of coaching expertise are required. Accordingly, the EMCC has created three defined levels of practice and associated skills, although more may follow.

1   Fundamentals of coaching – appropriate to manager-coaches

2   Practitioner coaches – appropriate to internal coaches whose role is broader than manager-coaches

3   Master coaches – appropriate to external coaches.

We now review the skills and knowledge felt to be appropriate to different types of coaches working in organisations, starting with the manager-coach. These are based on the EMCC standards discussed earlier.

Manager-coach skills and knowledge

Manager-coaches do not need the breadth of expertise, knowledge and skills that external coaches do, but they must still have sufficient understanding of coaching theory and principles to operate within the limited context of their role in the organisation. They must also be competent in using coaching skills and models. The box below illustrates the skills and knowledge a manager-coach needs, but this also applies to internal technical coaches who only coach in a restricted range of situations.

Manager-coach skills and knowledge

Broadly speaking, manager-coaches should:

- have basic knowledge about coaching theory, principles and techniques
- understand at least one coaching model/approach and be able to use a small range of coaching concepts and techniques. This will enable manager-coaches to identify and choose appropriate courses of action
- understand the limitations of their knowledge base and practice and be able to recognise when to refer a client to coaches with more expertise
- be able to justify and evaluate their decisions about their approach to a task/problem

- be able to create a workable action plan leading to effective and appropriate action (by coach and client)
- be able to assess and reflect on their own coaching skills, leading to insights that improve personal and professional understanding and practice
- understand the importance of ethical practice or the use of a code of conduct (which may be limited to application in their own organisation)

For organisations considering designing or evaluating their manager-coach training programmes, the list above may prove to be useful to assess their programmes.

Skills and knowledge for internal (practitioner-level) and external (master-level) coaches

The difference between the skills and knowledge that internal and external coaches need does not necessarily relate to the level they operate at – both need to be able to operate at an advanced level. The difference relates to the breadth and depth of their understanding and application of coaching in many different situations and environments. Internal coaches will need to be able to work competently with a range of different people and in a wide variety of situations, but within *one* organisation. External coaches, on the other hand, require further skills and knowledge that lead to a specialism in a particular area of practice or, alternatively, they must be able to work across a wide range of people, organisations and sectors. Some may have a sufficient breadth of competence to supervise other coaches. It is also worth mentioning that because internal coaching is still relatively new, many newly-trained internal coaches will take time to build up their expertise and will not initially have the experience of external coaches. The skills and knowledge required of internal and external coaches build on those of the manager-coach, and are listed below.

Internal and external coach skills and knowledge

Broadly speaking, internal and external coaches should:
- use a broad range of coaching knowledge, theory, models and techniques
- explore and critically evaluate a wide range of options and decide between different approaches depending on client need
- undertake complex action planning that is likely to impact on the work of others
- be able to adapt their style and presentation to different audiences
- be able to operate within a range of contexts, often including leadership-level coaching
- be able to challenge and develop the practices and/or beliefs of others
- be able to self-appraise and reflect on their practice, leading to significant insights that have a lasting impact on their personal and professional understanding and practice
- have a strong ethical position that is fully understood and sensitively applied
- be able to balance and draw on their experiences of being coached and supervised for the benefit of their client

This list can be used when recruiting coaches to work with or in your organisation or to identify areas for further development or training for your internal coaches.

Because of the broader experience or specialist knowledge that external coaches must have, you should try to ascertain what they can offer your organisation above and beyond any internal expertise you have. This can be done by asking questions during the selection process to find out whether they:

- can demonstrate experience of working in multiple organisations and sectors, and with people at varying levels of seniority

- are familiar with, and able to draw on, knowledge and approaches from other relevant areas of practice that have particular relevance for their understanding and practice in coaching

- are able to discuss what learning and understanding they have gained from their breadth of practice and research

- are conceptually knowledgeable about a number of ways of working (eg individual, team, group coaching)

- are actively engaged in being supervised (in a non-managerial sense), so that personal and professional issues in coaching are open to continuing questioning, review and reconsideration

- are familiar with the full range of ethical and legal implications of coaching practice, including controversies and current issues such as equal opportunities and data protection.

As well as considering the positive qualities a coach should have, one negative attribute comes through strongly in practitioner publications as hampering the delivery of effective coaching (eg Saporito, 1996). This is the influence of the coach's own agenda. Specific mention is made of the coach who is too concerned with 'proving' his or her own model of practice even if it is not appropriate to the recruiting organisation's culture or development agenda. This is clearly something that HR practitioners should look out for when selecting coaches and monitoring coaching relationships in their organisation.

WHEN SHOULD WE USE DIFFERENT TYPES OF COACHES?

As well as the specific attributes of a coach, another factor that can impact on the success of coaching is whether the right type of coach is selected to work with an individual. Understanding when it is best to use manager-coaches, internal coaches and external coaches is crucial to the best use of resources and the effectiveness of coaching in meeting individual needs. Many of our case studies have available a selection of coaching practitioners, using different ones for different situations. Some examples are provided below:

Shell has opted for a blended approach, using a variety of practitioners to deliver their coaching activities. The default coach for an individual is the line manager, as all managers have a coaching element inherent in their roles and responsibilities ... But Shell also recognises that managers aren't always best equipped to coach (eg if technical skills coaching is required or if an individual needs a greater level of coaching expertise). ... Within the technical areas of the company the vast majority of formal coaching isn't delivered by the manager but by other coaches in the organisation who act as technical coaches or internal development coaches. ... Use of external coaches is largely linked to the executive coaching programme.

Extract from Shell case study, p. 286

External executive coaches are still used across UU for senior executives and in other instances when it is deemed appropriate. It is not seen as an either/or decision. Internal coaches are still relatively inexperienced compared to many external coaches. And the business is also conscious that internal coaches are taking on the coaching part of their role on top of their day jobs, so external coaches can help to relieve the demands on their time.

Extract from United Utilities case study, p. 296

Making good decisions about when to use different coaching practitioners can have a significant impact on how effective the coaching will be in addressing individual needs and the results that the organisation will get from its investment.

Organisational knowledge and understanding

A particular issue that was raised by some of our case study organisations was ensuring that coaches (particularly external coaches) fully understand the wider organisational context in which the coaching takes place. When a coach first begins to work with an organisation, time should be taken to explain the objectives and desired outcomes for the coaching, as well as to provide a good understanding of the broader organisational context. If the coach does not have this information, the lack of understanding of the culture, strategy and other initiatives in the organisation could result in the coaching failing to be appropriate in terms of the goals set and support given. The CIPD's guide *Coaching and Buying Coaching Services* (Jarvis, 2004) offers the following advice:

Prepare some background material on your organisation and a detailed brief for the coach.
During the meeting you could usefully consider covering:

- *organisation vision, mission, strategy, values, locations, products, customers, competitors and other important organisational issues*
- *strategy and context of why you're conducting coaching*
- *organisational objectives for the coaching initiative or programme*
- *how it fits into overall HR/training strategy and activities*
- *the coaching process and model, including the organisation's leadership and competency models ...*

The organisation should keep coaches abreast of key developments and changes in the organisation that may impact on the individual or the coaching intervention so that they can vary their coaching style and activities as necessary.

For maximum impact, organisations should seek to use or train coaches who have appropriate knowledge, skills and competencies to work with their clients. They should also seek to understand how best to use the range of different coaching practitioners to make the best use of their available resources.

COACHEE ATTRIBUTES

Equally, the attitude and approach of the coachee can impact on the effectiveness of coaching. Naturally, coaching works best when the individual is both a willing and an informed participant. This is because when people are learning things they have identified as important, relevant and beneficial to them, they have greater motivation to commit to making it happen. There are three main themes in the literature and case studies relating to coachee attributes that are felt to contribute to the success of coaching:

- coachee receptiveness to coaching and desire for behaviour change

- coachees being informed and educated about coaching

- types of coachee who may particularly benefit from coaching.

Coachee receptiveness to coaching and desire for behaviour change

Overwhelmingly, the published work and our case study respondents point to the willingness of the coachee to change their behaviour as a primary determinant of the success of coaching interactions. Interestingly, this is less well covered in the empirical research, although a few studies do exist.

> *Some have accepted coaching more readily than others. They haven't noticed significant cultural differences in terms of participants' responses to coaching, but they do see individual differences depending on how open individuals are to new ideas and models.*
>
> Extract from Panasonic Europe case study, p. 278

In a survey of her own clients from 16 years of practice, Wasylyshyn (2003) asked the question: 'What type of executives are most likely to benefit from coaching?' She observed that those people who have no performance issues and are genuinely interested in their own development are more likely to benefit from coaching. For those with significant performance problems, she advises performance management with perhaps the support of a coach or mentor.

The reverse side of the coin was investigated by Kilburg (2001), who looked at coachee attributes that can result in a negative outcome for a coaching intervention. These are: lack of motivation, unrealistic expectations and lack of follow-through, alongside the more obvious ones of psychopathology and severe interpersonal problems. Our research has also revealed that some people may not respond well to coaching – and there is a whole host of reasons why this may be the case, as outlined opposite.

In such cases, the problems are best dealt with by interventions other than coaching, either because the individual's attitude will interfere with the effectiveness of coaching or because he or she needs alternative specialist support. In many of these situations we are looking at the boundaries between coaching and therapy. Sometimes a clinical intervention will provide more appropriate support for the individual. The HR practitioner should try to identify these issues as early as possible.

Situations when coaching is unlikely to help

Coaching is not an appropriate solution when:

- *a person has psychological problems* – These individuals should be offered referral to appropriate specialist support, not coaching. Coaches do not generally have the depth of psychological training to deal with these issues nor the medical training to address any physiological components that may also be part of the problem (eg addiction, depression)
- *a person lacks self-insight or is not able to modify his or her behaviour from situation to situation* – In these cases, coaching will not be effective because the coach will not be able to overcome such strong resistance to change.
- *a person has a common developmental need* – In such a case the individual may not need an intervention as costly or intensive as coaching. A course or development programme may be an equally beneficial and more cost-effective solution
- *a person is resistant or closed to coaching* – Coaching works best when there is a receptive audience, so it is unlikely to be effective if the person is forced into it. Attempts should be made to understand why the person feels this way
- *a person sees coaching as a 'quick fix' and does not take responsibility for changing his or her behaviour* – Long-term successful behavioural change requires a great deal of effort and hard work to make it really happen
- *a person engages in socially inappropriate behaviour, eg sexual harassment* – The person will need long-term intensive counselling and may be subject to formal disciplinary processes. It is also in the best interests of employees to have professional counsellors available when addressing more deeply embedded behaviours

Coachees being informed and motivated about taking part in coaching

Coaching should never be forced on a person. If individuals are coerced into coaching, it will almost certainly fail. To be effective, the coachee should be willing, be informed and should accept responsibility for achieving his or her learning goals. The CIPD's *How do People Learn?* research report (Reynolds *et al*, 2002) found that:

> *The disposition and commitment of the learner – their motivation to learn – is one of the most critical factors influencing learning effectiveness. Under the right conditions, a strong disposition to learn, enhanced by solid experience and a positive attitude, can lead to exceptional performance.*

But being a coachee is not easy. In many cases, coachees do not know what to expect from coaching, or, even worse, may feel that it is being offered to them because of something they have done wrong. As Clutterbuck and Megginson (2005) comment:

> *Being a coachee takes courage, especially in an organisation in which admitting weakness is risky.*

When participants are sceptical, resistant or dismissive of coaching, it is important to try to understand, and if possible change, their attitude. In the past, coaching has often had negative connotations, being seen as a remedial activity. Time must therefore be spent explaining to individuals the purpose of coaching and on making sure they do not misinterpret why it is being offered. This is necessary for realistic expectations to be set and also to allay fears and start the initiative off on the right foot. These sentiments are frequently expressed by coaches writing in the field, and are illustrated by the quotes below which are taken from the CIPD book, *The Coach's Coach* (Hardingham, 2004).

> *The more coercion the coachee has felt in coming to coaching, the more carefully a coach will need to ensure that the permission is there and that it continues.*

> *'It is a mistake to think that everyone, all the time, wants to change, or wants to learn, or again, is open to learning from me.' [Quote from Mike Brearley]*

> *The very act of accepting a coach can threaten a coachee's belief that she is competent. She may have heard, or come to the view, 'Competent people don't need coaching.' She may know that in the past coaching has been offered to poor performers in her organisation.*

Before coaching gets under way, it helps if the individual is given information to prepare him or her for what will be happening. This still appears to be somewhat of a rarity in practice – only 28 per cent of respondents to the CIPD's 2006 learning and development survey reported that preparatory training/briefing for coachees was provided to a 'complete' or 'great' extent, and 22 per cent said that it was never provided at all. Being clear and supportive from the outset will motivate the individual and encourage him or her to 'own' the learning. If people understand and accept that coaching is there to help them achieve more from their work and career, they are more likely to commit to making it happen. This naturally can have a large impact on the success that is achieved from a coaching relationship.

Types of coachee who may particularly benefit from coaching

Some researchers have thrown the net wider and suggested that specific types of people may particularly benefit from coaching. Research has therefore examined the role of personality type, gender and other coachee characteristics. Two studies have attempted to find out whether there are specific personality types that benefit more than others from coaching. One study reported that the alpha male personality type may respond particularly well to coaching because 'their quintessential strengths are also what makes them so challenging, and often frustrating to work with' (Ludeman and Erlandson, 2004). The other study looked at 62 managers within a large engineering company who received coaching for at least six months from an external coaching firm (Dawdy, 2004). Although the research found that 90 per cent perceived the coaching as valuable, there was no difference in outcomes between different personality types. We can therefore conclude that at present there is no definitive evidence that coaching is especially suited to certain personality types.

Some researchers have examined the role of gender in the success of coaching and argued that traditional methods of leadership development can be overly geared towards male needs and learning requirements. According to Belenky *et al* (1986), female careers are more discontinuous (ie they happen in stages), as opposed to the linear male career progression model. It is argued that as a result women may require a variety of opportunities for learning (Vinnicombe and Singh, 2005). Coaching and mentoring are identified as contributing to such a portfolio approach. This argument is echoed in the case study for the Greater London Authority (GLA) where coaching was specifically provided to provide support for women's career development and progression:

> *The women's coaching programme doesn't involve a 'taught' element. Instead, it provides an appropriate framework and support for self-development and insight, while also building confidence and self-esteem. The GLA feels strongly that this is the most appropriate response for a diverse group of women who will be starting from different life-points, but who may also share universal issues. ... They believe that women, in particular, respond very positively to interventions that explicitly cater for their learning styles and career issues, which are often complex and hard to define.*

> Extract from the GLA case study, p. 264

Another area that is likely to play a role is the preferred learning style of the coachee. There is widespread agreement among researchers and practitioners that people have different characteristics, strengths and preferences in the way they learn (eg Cassidy, 2004; Kolb, 1999; Honey and Mumford, 1992). Some prefer to learn actively and interactively, while others function more introspectively and individually. These differences are usually referred to as learning styles. Some of our case study organisations raised this as an issue and pointed to the fact that coaching will not always be someone's favoured way of learning, and that this can impact on the results that are achieved:

> *One learning point from the programme was that coaching isn't necessarily everyone's learning style. Some people really flourish having a coach, others less so. A number of factors can play a role, including the choice of coach, the geography of the coaches and coachees, the personality match and preferred learning styles of the coachees.*

> Extract from Selfridges case study, p. 283

> *The key is selecting the right learners from a business point of view and people who are able to actively develop through this type of process.*

> Lynn Edmonds, Everest

But what does the research say? Unfortunately, there is limited specific research looking at the role of learning styles and success in coaching. However, earlier research by Lane (2000) found that matching employee development activities to individuals' preferred learning styles and career preferences was a critical factor.

Although some people may have a stronger preference for coaching as a form of development, it does not mean that coaching is necessarily 'wrong' for some individuals. Coaches should work to accommodate different learning styles during their coaching activities so as to appeal to the full spectrum of different learners. For example, using Honey and Mumford's classification (1992), coaches should try to use activities that reflect activist, reflector, pragmatist and theorist learning styles. Using an array of different learning experiences has long been felt to be the best way for people to learn in any case. As Reynolds (2004) argues in the CIPD's *Helping People Learn* research: 'Practising the full spectrum of learning styles not only improves learning outcomes, but also increases learner satisfaction and self-confidence.' We can therefore conclude that the research and experiences of our case study organisations do indicate that the learning style of coachees can impact on the effectiveness of coaching if the coach fails to take it into account.

Although there is little research that specifically examines coachee attributes that play a role in the effectiveness of coaching, it is fair to say that there is fairly common agreement on the types of issues an individual may wish to address which are best dealt with by coaching. The analysis of our case study organisations in Chapter 4 indicated that coaching is being used to address a series of different coachee issues, but the most common are listed in Table 14.

Table 14: | ***Issues that organisations are addressing through coaching***

	Percentage of respondents reporting using coaching for this purpose
Individual performance issues	89
Skills deficits	79
Transition issues (to a new role or area of work)	79
Career progression	75
Team issues	71
Transformation issues (major change initiatives)	71
Personal non-work issues	57
Work–life balance issues	50
Diversity/equality issues	25

Furthermore, it seems that there are certain individual issues that are commonly understood to be particularly appropriate for coaching. These are detailed below.

Situations in which coaching is an appropriate approach
- *Developing an individual's potential* – Sometimes an individual can be performing perfectly well, but could be even more successful with some assistance. In this situation, the coach is not helping the individual to 'fix' any particular problem, but instead will try to help motivate the individual to consider his or her future plans and the next steps in his or her job or career
- *Developing interpersonal skills* – Some individuals in the workplace are highly competent technical experts. But they may need to develop their interpersonal skills to ensure that they get the best results from those they manage or colleagues they work with. Coaches can help managers to better 'read' interpersonal situations and be more effective in their interactions with colleagues
- *Ensuring performance* – In some cases, new demands require a new understanding of what it takes to perform well. Coaching can help to develop an analysis of what helps and hinders performance in the new situation

- *Skills at developing others* – Some managers have difficulty supporting the development of their team members. Coaching can help managers develop junior colleagues more effectively by learning some coaching skills themselves
- *Developing in a transition to a new role* – As managers move from management or front-line positions to more senior levels, they often need assistance in gaining a more strategic perspective or understanding the demands of the new role. This may involve making decisions based on the best interests of the organisation as a whole, rather than those of their specific area of the business. Coaches can help managers to become more sensitive to wider organisational concerns and to understand opportunities and problems occurring across multiple business units
- *Being part of a transformational change* – Transformational changes often involve a challenge to deeply held beliefs and ways of seeing the world (mental models). Coaching can help that transformation

There appears to be a wide array of coachee attributes that can play a role in the impact of coaching. Drawing on all our data, it is reasonable to conclude that for coaching to work most effectively, coachees should:

- be willing participants in coaching

- be well-informed and well-educated about what coaching requires of them

- have a level of self-awareness – the ability to reflect and consider alternative points of view without becoming defensive and rejecting them without consideration

- lack serious psychological problems

- have the ability to give and receive feedback

- have learning preferences that are catered for by their coach

- have the ability to undertake an analysis of their own performance and explore factors that influence their own behaviour and help or hinder change

- have the ability to action plan and draw up a viable personal development plan that can be applied in the context in which they work

- have problems/issues that are suitable to be addressed by coaching

- have the ability to use a network of support for developing their skills and improving performance.

Where coachees lack these attributes (ie other than the first two items in the list), coaching may still be viable, although it may require a longer timeframe. The more the individual understands about the coaching process and is engaged with it, the easier it will be for the coach to work with him or her. To gain maximum impact, our research indicates that it is important to spend time preparing the coachee for his or her role in the coaching process by setting expectations and educating him or her about what it will involve.

THE ORGANISATIONAL CONTEXT FOR COACHING

Effective coaching will only take place when the organisational conditions are conducive to coaching. The context for coaching has a powerful influence on the results that are seen from a coaching programme, the organisation's culture playing a particularly important role.

Why is culture important?

An organisation's culture sets the tone for learning and hence has the potential to greatly affect the success of a coaching programme. Considerable research has been done to investigate the ways in which organisational culture influences the way people behave at work. For example, Argyris (1994) argues that the rules, rituals and assumptions that exist in an organisation define its culture and dictate how its employees behave. An organisational culture influences a whole host of perceptions in the organisation, including what activities are regarded as most important, what behaviour is expected, and what is perceived to be rewarded and recognised. It strongly affects people through a combination of personal relationships, group dynamics, cultural norms and beliefs, and social participation – all entwined with its systems and policies.

Reynolds (2004) argues that culture is hugely pervasive in affecting the outcomes of different learning interventions such as coaching:

> *Bureaucratic systems, perverse reward systems and a lack of understanding of the issues (all integral parts of the organisation's culture) dissipate the impacts further.*

This is supported by a number of our case study organisations who recognised that aspects of their organisational culture acted as a barrier to their coaching activities:

> *Other barriers include the nature of the remuneration and commission culture which rewards indvidual achievements and does not reward those that might help underperformers or good performers to improve further.*
>
> Stephen Williamson, Pertemps Recruitment Partnership

> *Barriers to coaching at Tate: 'a lack of understanding of coaching' and the benefits it can bring and 'a lack of time for coaching'.*
>
> Colin Coombs, Tate Museums

> *High workloads are the main barrier.*
>
> Ian Walker, Exeter City Council

A culture of learning recognises and promotes the value of learning, and this translates into positive attitudes and support for activities such as coaching. Kilburg (2001) concurs with this view and argues that without the support of the client's working environment, coaching efforts may have little bearing. This is further illustrated by the CIPD's 2004 training and development survey results, which found that 80 per cent of respondents agreed that 'Coaching will only work well in a culture that supports learning and development.' Aquilina (2005) writes:

> *The client–coach setting needs a sufficiently mature learning culture to embrace an internal model of coaching. An organisation must think through how coaching will fit in with the*

organisation's learning and development agenda, what the purpose of the internal coaching model is, and how it will align with existing learning activities.

In line with this, research has indicated that the development of coaching (and particularly a coaching culture) has found its most effective application in organisations where learning is already clearly established as a key business enabler (Wasylyshyn, 2003; Clutterbuck and Megginson, 2005). Aquilina (2005) suggests that this may be because the organisational context determines 'how coaching is positioned within the organisational learning agenda, the purpose of adopting coaching and the shape of the coaching framework'. She calls for organisations therefore to assess the organisational environment and bear this in mind when working to create an effective coaching model.

But what about a coaching culture?

Many practitioners and academics suggest that, ideally, a 'coaching climate' or 'coaching culture' should exist within an organisation. Sherman and Freas (2004) argue the case for a coaching culture in a *Harvard Business Review* article:

> *When you create a culture of coaching, the result may not be directly measurable in dollars. But we have yet to find a company that can't benefit from more candour, less denial, richer communication, conscious development of talent, and disciplined leaders, who show compassion for people.*

But what do we mean by a 'coaching culture'? Unsurprisingly, a number of definitions exist, including:

- 'a culture where people coach each other all the time as a natural part of meetings, reviews and one-to-one discussions of all kinds' (Hardingham, 2004)

- 'where coaching is the predominant style of managing and working together, and where a commitment to grow the organisation is embedded in a parallel commitment to grow the people in the organisation' (Clutterbuck and Megginson, 2005).

David Clutterbuck kindly provided some information about how to recognise a coaching culture or climate for the CIPD's guide *Coaching and Buying Coaching Services* (Jarvis, 2004). He said that 'You will know you have a coaching climate when:

- personal growth, team development and organisational learning are integrated and the links clearly understood

- people are able to engage in constructive and positive confrontation

- people welcome feedback (even at the top) and actively seek it

- coaching is seen as a responsibility of managers and their direct reports

- there is good understanding at all levels about what effective developers and developees do

- coaching is seen primarily as an opportunity rather than as a remedial intervention
- people are recognised and rewarded for their activity in sharing knowledge
- time for reflection is valued
- there are effective mechanisms for identifying and addressing barriers to learning
- people look first inside the organisation for their next job
- there are strong role models of good coaching practice.'

The extent to which an organisation has a coaching culture in place is likely to have an impact on the success of coaching in the organisation. David Clutterbuck and David Megginson (2005) have produced a new model that identifies six characteristics of a coaching culture:

1 Coaching is linked to business drivers.

2 Being a coachee is encouraged and supported.

3 Coach training is provided.

4 Coaching is rewarded and recognised.

5 A systemic perspective is adopted.

6 The move to coaching is managed.

The degree to which an organisation's culture conforms with these characteristics is likely to determine how supportive it will be of coaching activities. This in turn is likely to impact on the results that coaching delivers to the organisation and the individuals involved. Furthermore, Clutterbuck and Megginson (2005) also identify four stages on the journey to achieving a coaching culture which are described opposite. More detail about this model can be found in their book *Making Coaching Work: Creating a coaching culture* (2005).

The CIPD's 2006 learning and development survey attempted to assess how far organisations are progressing along the journey to a fully developed coaching culture (CIPD, 2006). Eighty per cent of respondents using coaching claim their organisation aspires to develop a coaching culture, and 75 per cent report investing time, resources and effort in achieving this aim. With regard to progress towards the development of a coaching culture, there are positive signs within the survey data. Coaching is no longer (if it ever was) associated with remedial action and is linked to 'some' or a 'great' extent to business goals in around 90 per cent of organisations. At the same time, there are still major problems (see Table 15 on page 176). Two-fifths of organisations do not include coaching in managers' formal job descriptions (41 per cent); only 13 per cent of organisations address the quality of coaching through some form of accreditation; less than half recognise and reward people for involvement in coaching activities (46 per cent); and only 10 per cent say they have to a great extent effective mechanisms for identifying and addressing barriers to coaching. It therefore seems that although some progress is being made, there remains a long way to go.

Stages in the journey to achieving a coaching culture

- *Nascent stage* – The organisation shows little or no commitment to creating a coaching culture. Coaching may take place in the organisation, but is highly inconsistent in both frequency and quality. Top managers present poor role models and coaching behaviours tend to be abandoned in the face of more urgent demands on managers' time

- *Tactical stage* – The organisation recognises the value of establishing a coaching culture, but there is little understanding of what that means, or what will be involved. Top management see the issue as primarily one for HR There are systems in place to train coaches but the links between these and other HR systems and processes are, at best, tenuous. There is broad understanding among individuals and managers of the potential benefits of coaching, but commitment to coaching as integral to management style is low

- *Strategic stage* – The organisation has expended considerable effort to educate managers and employees in the value of coaching and give people the competence to coach in a variety of situations. Managers are rewarded for coaching and top management set an example by coaching others and explaining to employees how coaching supports key business drivers. However, while the formal coaching process works well, the information process works less well. There are plans to integrate coaching with the wider portfolio of HR systems and, at a mechanical level, these largely work

- *Embedded stage* – People at all levels in the organisation are engaged in coaching, both formal and informal, with colleagues both within and across functions and levels; 360-degree feedback is used at all levels to provide insights into areas where the individual can benefit from coaching help. Coaching is so seamlessly built into the structure of HR systems that it occurs automatically. The skills of learning dialogue are sufficiently widespread that people are able to raise difficult or controversial issues, knowing that their motivations will be respected and that colleagues will see this as an opportunity to improve either personally or organisationally, or both

Naturally, if an organisation does not have a culture that is supportive of learning or coaching, it will present a series of barriers to effective coaching and the results that can be achieved. Many organisational cultures present significant barriers to the concept of coaching. In today's fast pace of organisational life, making time for reflection and learning is often difficult because of other more pressing business demands. This was strongly felt by our case study organisations. They identified a series of barriers that formed part of their organisational context or culture. These were discussed in Chapter 4 and fell into six major themes, which can be understood to be heavily interlinked:

- lack of understanding of the value of coaching

- coaching not seen as a priority for the business

- organisational culture not conducive to coaching

Table 15: | *Progress towards developing a coaching culture*

To what extent ...	Percentage of respondents answering		
	Completely, or to a large extent	To a small extent	Not at all
is coaching seen as a positive development opportunity rather than as a remedial intervention?	10	45	46
are coaching activities linked to business goals?	11	42	47
is being a coachee encouraged and supported?	8	38	54
are coaches provided with in-depth coaching training?	28	31	42
are senior managers overtly supportive and committed to coaching?	14	30	56
are coachees provided with preparatory training/briefing?	22	28	51
is coaching integrated into wider HR strategy and processes?	18	27	55
is the move towards more use of coaching actively managed?	23	26	51
are there strong role models for good coaching practice?	21	25	54
is coaching followed up with ongoing support or supervision?	28	23	49
is coaching a formal part of managers' job descriptions?	41	23	36
is time for reflection and self-development valued?	28	21	51
do line managers take coaching responsibility seriously?	12	21	67
does coaching happen at all levels in the organisation?	25	18	57
is coaching the predominant management style?	42	14	44
are coaches accredited, certified or licensed?	69	13	19
are people recognised and rewarded for their involvement in coaching?	54	11	35
are there effective mechanisms to identify and address barriers to coaching?	44	10	47

Source: CIPD (2006)

- resistance to coaching

- low levels of skills and experience in the organisation

- lack of time and resources.

This issue was also investigated in the CIPD survey, and a similar picture emerged (CIPD, 2006). Table 16 shows that competing business pressures form the main barrier to developing a coaching culture. This is followed by some of the more usual suspects – lack of expertise, lack of investment and poor senior management commitment. Another major challenge appears to be a lack of data and research to prove the value of coaching – this was selected by 42 per cent of respondents.

Table 16: | ***Barriers to developing a coaching culture***

Barriers	Percentage of respondents
Competing business pressures	66
Lack of internal skills and experience	52
Lack of investment and resources	48
Lack of senior management commitment	48
Lack of data to prove the value of coaching activities	42
Lack of belief in the value of coaching	34

Despite organisations' aspirations about, and investment in, coaching to date, a number of issues exist that are impacting on their likely chances of success. More forethought and resources are required if organisations' aspirations of developing coaching cultures are to be realised.

Other factors in the organisational context that play a role in the effectiveness of coaching

Many factors relating to the environment in which the coaching takes place were identified as having particular influence on the success of coaching in our research. Above all, the case study respondents were unanimous in thinking the buy-in and role modelling of senior managers was critical to the effective support of a coaching programme. The most successful coaching programmes identified in our case studies were driven predominantly from the top – ie by a senior or chief executive:

Senior management buy-in is essential.

Colin Coombs, Tate Museums

Decisions have to be supported from the top down.

Ian Walker, Exeter City Council

Investment and endorsement by senior executives is needed to ensure high visibility.

Roger Williams, United Utilities

Visible, genuine buy-in and modelling from senior members of the organisation and being able to demonstrate practical applications of coaching is vital.

Pamela Tilt and Ola Adams, Nationwide

In addition, many of our case study organisations identified other factors that were felt potentially to have an impact on the effectiveness of coaching activities. For the most part, these reflect the organisational requirements identified in the CIPD's 2004 training and development survey for the promotion of learning activities such as coaching:

- a learning culture

- committed and motivated managers who were rewarded for coaching

- adequate resources

- encouragement for learning

- an understanding of employee preferences

- senior management commitment

- clear strategic intent

- support for learning.

If organisations lack any of these components, they are likely to experience some problems gaining the maximum impact from their coaching activities.

Our case study organisations also reported a number of factors in the organisational context which can disrupt or undermine the impact of coaching. Illustrative quotes about these other factors include:

Senior executives have to be willing to make the necessary investment without 'cast-iron' guarantees or immediate payback.

Roger Williams, United Utilities

Receptivity of coachees can be a barrier.

Neil Hounslow, Lloyds TSB

Managers must take responsibility for coaching and developing their teams.

Karen Boanas, Canada Life

There is sometimes initial resistance to coaching as it sometimes can be seen as something only for underperformers.

Roger Williams, United Utilities

Lack of understanding of what coaching is may slow the process down rather than form a barrier.

Lynn Edmonds, Everest

The pressure of maintaining targets can mean that people don't want to try anything different in case it doesn't work.

Ola Adams and Pamela Tilt, Nationwide

Some new employees have not experienced a coaching style previously and have difficulty adapting to a new culture.

Nigel Briers, Perkins Shibaura Engines

Barriers? A belief that coaching is a 'nice to have'. The lack of understanding of some that there are no real benefits. Ensuring that the business is in the right place to embrace such a change in culture.

Camilla Aitchison, Dixons

'I don't have time' is a common comment.

Tracey Smith, KwikFit Financial Services

While we have successfully introduced coaching, we would say that there are potential barriers to its ongoing success – these include: funding – coaching needs to be properly funded and resourced to support the whole process.

Jackie Kernaghan, London School of Economics and Political Science

To provide the right context or 'climate' for coaching, organisations should seek to instil practices that provide coaches and coachees with the right mix of inspiration, incentive and support. At the heart of this challenge lies the need to understand the role of an organisation's culture, which often determines employee attitudes to learning and change. Organisations should regularly assess their organisational culture to ascertain whether it is presenting any barriers to their coaching activities. Barriers to coaching can result in coaching failing to deliver the results it was designed to produce. Another result can be that coaching delivers significant benefits to individual coachees but may not contribute strategically to the organisation, thus resulting in only a partial success. Understanding the organisational dynamics and climate that form the backdrop for coaching activities is vital for ensuring that good results are achieved.

THE COACHING PROCESS

A comprehensive study of the effectiveness of individual components of the coaching process has not yet been undertaken, but through review of the work published to date it is clear that we can already identify three elements of the coaching process that impact on the success of coaching:

- the coach–coachee relationship
- the duration and structure of coaching relationships
- an appropriate coaching definition, goals and model of practice for the organisation.

The coach–coachee relationship

In all the coaching models used by our case studies, and in the literature, there is clearly an emphasis on the initial stages of the process – specifically, contracting and relationship-forming (eg Kilburg, 2001). The reason for this is simple: the most consistently identified factor seen as contributing to the success of a coaching engagement is the 'fit' between coach and coachee and the quality of the relationship that is established between them. Hall *et al* (1999) argue: 'It is an art to match temperament and learning styles for coaches and clients.' This mirrors findings from a range of therapeutic engagements – the relationship between client and practitioner is the primary factor in a successful outcome. For example, Assay and Lambert (1999) examined the relative importance of key factors in therapeutic relationships and found that the largest contributing factor is the existence of a positive relationship.

For coaching, this is not only evident within the practitioner publications but has been explicitly tested in the research literature. In the survey of clients by Wasylyshyn (2003), the highest-scoring personal characteristic of an effective coach was being able to form a strong connection with the coachee. In a study looking at the influence of coaching with 360-degree feedback on leadership development, the correct 'matching' of the coach with the coachee was identified as essential by the participants (Thach, 2002).

One study has tried to go further and test how far the quality of the coaching relationship impacts on levels of self-efficacy and work-related attitudes such as job satisfaction, organisational commitment and work–life balance (Dingham, 2004). Overall, it was found that both the quality of the coaching and the process of being coached impacted on self-efficacy and, through that, on work-related outcomes. The results indicated that the quality of the relationship positively impacted on job satisfaction. However, in some instances there was a negative relationship with job satisfaction, which may indicate that coaching was being used to 'coach people out of their jobs'.

The importance of the coach–coachee relationship should not be underestimated. As Aquilina (2005) states,

> The coach–client relationship is crucial to the success of the coaching intervention. Building and sustaining this relationship is dependent on the skills of the coach, their empathy and authenticity and their ability to select appropriate interventions from the behavioural field.

Because of this, Kilburg (2001) emphasises the importance of being explicit about what a coaching relationship entails. He suggests that this may take the form of a coaching contract and should include understanding about how the client and coach will work together so as to accomplish the agreed goal.

The duration and structure of coaching relationships

The duration of the coaching relationship has attracted comment in a number of studies. Its length naturally depends on the organisational goals for coaching, the individual's specific needs and the breadth of issues to be covered. Naturally, setting time boundaries for coaching relationships that involve managers and internal coaches is more awkward as there is likely to be an ongoing relationship because of the existing managerial or collegial relationship that exists. However, many researchers have argued that it is important for all coaching relationships to set goals that are time-bound. This approach prevents the quasi-counselling pattern of regular fortnightly or weekly sessions running on until the individual wants it to end. When using external coaches, setting time boundaries helps to control costs and reduces the likelihood of the individual becoming dependent on the coach. Programme lengths of four to six months are considered appropriate, while durations of one year or more are thought to yield decreasing returns (Luthans and Peterson, 2003). Downey (1999) suggests the following structure: four sessions, followed by a six-month break, then a check-up session, with the option of reverting to further sessions if the need arises. Some studies have looked at a single coaching session to address the outputs of 360-degree feedback and have yielded good results (Luthans and Peterson, 2003; Smither *et al*, 2003).

To be most effective, the coaching sessions themselves should be frequent enough for momentum on the coaching goals to be maintained, but should also allow the individual enough time to undertake any agreed activities and to reflect on the previous session. The CIPD guide *Coaching and Buying Coaching Services* (Jarvis, 2004) suggests that 'fortnightly or monthly sessions may be a sensible approach.' There are different opinions about the actual length of a coaching session, but many coaches recommend one to two hours as being appropriate. Janice Caplan (2002) suggests:

> *Some points to bear in mind are that coaching can be intense, and an hour might well be as much as a learner can take. There are also some situations where learners need to work in a sustained fashion on issues that require a lot of thinking through, and these may require a longer session. On the other hand, some sessions may be more action-based and the coaching will be shorter.*

It therefore seems as though the length of a coaching session should be between one and two hours but should remain flexible to suit the particular issues that are being discussed that day.

There is also the question of how the coaching sessions themselves are structured. Although coaches tailor their coaching in different ways depending on the specific individuals' needs, many coaching relationships follow a relatively simple structure. Dingham (2004) compared a series of different coaching processes and identified six steps or stages in coaching that most researchers agree on:

1   formal contracting

2   relationship-building

3   assessment

4   getting feedback and reflecting

5   goal-setting

6   implementation and evaluation.

In a similar vein, the CIPD guide *Coaching and Buying Coaching Services* discusses the following elements that often form the basic structure for a coaching assignment:

● setting initial goals for the proposed coaching intervention

- pre-coaching diagnostic work (eg psychometrics, 360-degree feedback)

- providing the individual with feedback on any diagnostic work

- developing more specific action and learning plans, and discussion of a variety of approaches for improving job effectiveness

- regular coaching sessions to implement new approaches and review progress towards goals

- periodic follow-up and monitoring after the regular coaching sessions have ended.

Research indicates that the individual coaching sessions should have a fairly simple structure that allows flexibility while retaining a consistent approach. Some example questions which can form the framework for a single coaching session (Jarvis, 2004) are:

- How do you feel about your progress with the action points from the last session?

- What issues would you like to discuss in this session?

- What would you like to achieve?

- What factors are stopping you?

- What do you need to change to achieve your goal(s)?

- What are your action points to work on before the next session?

The research indicates that the structure and duration of coaching relationships can impact on their effectiveness. Because of this, the organisation should ensure that there is clarity about the length of and the way that coaching relationships should be broadly structured.

An appropriate coaching definition, goals, and model of practice for the organisation

It makes sense for organisations to seek their own definitions of coaching that work for their specific context. Having an agreed understanding about what coaching means in your organisation will assist both the buy-in and implementation of coaching. When choosing a definition to use, you will find that there is a huge number out there put forward by different researchers. Table 17 provides a list of some of the common definitions of coaching for you to consider.

When organisations have a framework for coaching with a clear definition (including an agreed purpose), they are more likely to be able to gain buy-in and support for coaching within the organisation because their approach will look well-thought-through and researched. This sort of clear approach also prevents ambiguity and confusion when trying to

Table 17: | **Example definitions of coaching**

Author(s)	Definition of coaching
Parsloe (1999)	*A process that enables learning and development to occur and thus performance to improve.*
Cavanagh and Grant (2005)	*A goal-directed, results-orientated, systematic process in which one person facilitates sustained change in another individual or group through fostering the self-directed learning and personal growth of the coachee.*
Whitmore (1996)	*Unlocking a person's potential to maximise their own performance.*
Jarvis (2004)	*Developing a person's skills and knowledge so that their job performance improves, hopefully leading to the achievement of organisational objectives. It targets high performance and improvement at work, although it may also have an impact on an individual's private life. It usually lasts for a short period and focuses on specific skills and goals.*
Kampa and White (2002)	*A formal, ongoing relationship between an individual or team having managerial authority and responsibility in an organisation and a consultant who possesses knowledge of behaviour change and organisational functioning. This relationship has a goal of creating measurable behaviour change in the individual or collection of individuals (the team) that results in increased individual and organisational performance and where change is brought about by or through giving direct behaviourally-based feedback, creating opportunities for change and demanding accountability.*
Starr (2003)	*A conversation, or series of conversations, one person has with another.*
Hall et al (1999)	*Meant to be a practical, goal-focused form of personal, one-on-one learning for busy executives and may be used to improve performance or executive behaviour, enhance a career or prevent derailment, and work through organisational issues or change initiatives. Essentially, coaches provide executives with feedback they would normally never get about personal, performance, career and organisational issues.*

communicate about coaching in the organisation. All of this combines to result in more effective coaching taking place.

Choosing an achievable but challenging focus for coaching relationships is essential. There is a huge literature about the impact and theory of goal-setting (eg Locke and Latham, 2002) which there is no time to review here, but broadly, the research indicates that when applied appropriately it is a powerful mechanism for improving performance. Goal-setting appears to work by providing a direction for our efforts, focusing our attention, promoting persistence and increasing our confidence. But although goal-setting is an easy concept to understand, its application needs more thought and planning than most people realise. One of the main problems is that not all coaches are aware of the principles of goal-setting and how to apply them effectively. Setting clear goals is essential for establishing expectations and providing a shared agenda between the coach and coachee. Without clear goals, coaching relationships are unlikely to have a focus, and this can damage the effectiveness of the relationship and the results it achieves.

When goals are set in coaching relationships they need to be:

- within the power of the coachee to influence
- aligned with the organisational goals for coaching
- appropriate to the coaching model used
- valued by the coachee
- supported by the coachee's manager.

Naturally, it is important to establish goals that are SMART:

- Specific – people know exactly what is expected
- Measurable – results can be evaluated
- Achievable – the goals are within people's capabilities
- Realistic – there is a good chance of success
- Time-bound – there are clear milestones of progress.

Emerging research from the Worldwide Association of Business Coaches examining the competencies of experienced coaching practitioners does indicate that careful structuring of goals and maintaining a focus on them is a core area for successful coaching activity (WABC, forthcoming).

Another factor that can impact on the success of coaching is the model of coaching that an organisation adopts. Many different coaching models, techniques and tools exist, and to date, the research literature does not indicate that one model is necessarily more effective than the others – success is more likely to be determined by the effective application of a coaching model than by its content. What is clear is that everyone involved in coaching should have a strong understanding of the coaching model being used in the organisation. Many commentators have also stated that often a simple model is the most effective (eg Parsloe, 1995; Caplan, 2003). And in line with this, many of our case study organisations advocated a goal-focused model of coaching as one that offers a simple but effective framework for coaching activities at the manager-coach level.

If people fail to have a strong understanding of the coaching model within the organisation, confusion can arise, and this is likely to result in poor coaching outcomes for the individual and the organisation. Because of this, organisations should spend time communicating and clarifying their model of coaching, both when training manager-coaches and other internal coaches and when working with external coaches.

SUMMARY

The research we have reviewed has clearly illustrated that the success of coaching initiatives depend on many factors which HR can positively influence. The behaviour of the coach and coachee are critical to success, and organisations should make sure that they are fully prepared for their roles in the process. Efforts should also be made to ensure that coaches and coachees are well matched and have a positive working relationship, because this has been shown to be a key determinant of the results that can be achieved. The organisational context can be a powerful influence on the effectiveness of coaching, the organisational culture in particular playing a crucial role in influencing attitudes towards coaching. Many of our case study organisations reported that the prevailing organisational culture can act as a barrier to coaching, and it is therefore worth spending time analysing your organisation's culture and the attitudes of key stakeholders to ensure that your investment in coaching yields maximum returns.

10

Getting an insider view: what do coaches have to say?

If we want to find out about how to make coaching work effectively in practice, surely one group who will have an important perspective are coaches themselves. External coaches work with a number of organisations of different sizes and sectors in response to a whole host of business issues. As a result they are likely to have useful insights into many of the issues that organisations face – particularly those who are starting out. For example, they are likely to have experienced working with companies with varying levels of support from stakeholders, where communication has been problematic, or seen situations where coaching has not delivered results. The diversity and breadth of their experiences are of value in understanding the case for coaching.

Furthermore, external coaches can also give us that elusive insider view. Their role sits directly within one-to-one coaching relationships, and as a result they can give us a view from the inside out about what factors can help and hinder the effectiveness of a coaching relationship. They also lack 'corporate blindspots' that prevent those within the organisation from having a clear view about the causes of problems that are occurring, and can also give an alternative perspective about how to approach the design, management or delivery of certain aspects of coaching. All in all, they are likely to be a valuable source of information about 'what not to do' as well as what works in practice.

Some may think it foolish to ask coaches about the value of coaching and how it works – 'Of course they are going to say it works: their livelihood depends on it.' But while coaches have their own agenda in proving that coaching works, they also understand that the future of the coaching profession is dependent on their ability to prove demonstrable value from their services. Coaches themselves therefore also have a stake in ensuring that organisations' practices and policies around the management and delivery of coaching are designed to work with, rather than against, the coaching interventions they deliver. In this way, coaches and HR have much to gain from talking and listening to each others' perspectives.

As part of this research project, a number of different external coaching providers (both individual coaching practitioners and coaching firms) were contacted about their views on the effective use of coaching in organisational settings. They were asked to respond to a series of specific questions designed to obtain their views about what organisations can do to get maximum value from their investment in coaching, and particularly what they felt were the most critical areas for HR involvement and focus. Questions we asked included:

- What is it that coaching uniquely offers organisations?

- In what situations does coaching work best?

- How does coaching work?

- What factors can bolster the success of coaching?

- What can HR do to support and promote coaching in the organisation?

- What measures and evaluation activities are currently being used by organisations? Should they do anything different?

Themes from the coaches' responses to these questions are discussed in this chapter. By analysing their questions we aim to unpick what it is that those who deliver coaching think will help organisations improve their management and delivery of coaching. Where possible we have included direct quotes from coaches that best illustrate the different sentiments expressed.

WHAT IS SO SPECIAL ABOUT COACHING?

Before getting into the detail of how to make coaching work, we took a step back to gain coaches' views about what it was that coaching offered – both to learners trying to develop their skills or change their behaviour, and also to organisations who are often the coach's client. Although a wide range of responses was given, the unique offer of coaching was described in five main ways, and these are described below.

Time-out in today's high-pressure world

Many coaches felt that the success of coaching is largely because of its relevance to the needs of a modern society and business world. Most people's working lives are now characterised by change and time pressure. People rarely have time to think about what they want from their career and work, and are even less likely to think about how to make improvements. Coaching provides an opportunity for individuals to take time out to reflect on their performance at work.

It provides an opportunity for a 'legitimised conversation' in an organisational environment that is constantly changing and where there is little time for reflection.

Margaret Chapman

Making changes to how you work nearly always requires changes in self-awareness, behaviour and ways of thinking. None of these will happen by chance – it requires time and commitment. This is what many coaches feel their services offer people – time to think about how they are feeling, what to do about unresolved issues and how to improve the way they handle situations they face.

It provides, as one of my clients observed, 'a psychological massage'. Enabling the client to really examine issues that perhaps are often neglected, or prefer not to be faced.

Margaret Chapman

Modern working life is also increasingly competitive and cut-throat. Acknowledging and discussing personal weaknesses is awkward and difficult, and many people fear being honest or asking for help in case it is viewed as not coping or being unable to deal with pressure.

The fact that development discussions are often connected to appraisal (and therefore performance and salary discussions) makes it an area that few people have honest conversations about.

> *Coaching has emerged as a response to something that is missing in our society at large. It offers an opportunity for a person to engage in a non-judgemental discussion about their deepest concerns and for these concerns to be fully heard.*
>
> Anji Marychurch

Beats training hands down

Unsurprisingly, coaches believed that their services offered a number of distinct advantages over more traditional forms of training. Unlike conventional training courses, coaching sessions require little time away from the organisation and can be integrated into peoples' busy schedules. And it also provides ongoing support to individuals as they learn, rather than expecting them to develop their skills by themselves.

> *A series of sessions enables the individual to experience a continuous development process which can reinforce new learning and behaviour. Between sessions, the individual can put this new learning into practice in the workplace.*
>
> Helen Pitcher

> *In some earlier research, I noted that despite the psychological research in the area of individual differences, HR developers were still assuming a 'sheep-dip' approach to people learning and development. I think the advent of coaching therefore acknowledges the need for diversity in the application of HRD strategies and that emotional, cognitive and behavioural shifts need to be supported via a one-to-one developmental relationship.*
>
> Margaret Chapman

A trusted confidant

Working relationships are rarely strong enough for truly honest discussions. And managers themselves would often be the first to say that they do not feel they have the skills and expertise to have in-depth coaching conversations. Coaching is felt to provide people with somebody to talk to confidentially and honestly about their performance at work.

> *The coaching process helps to hold up a mirror to the individual being coached. It provides a uniquely safe and supportive place to reflect and explore beliefs, values, attitudes, thoughts, behaviours and their consequences.*
>
> John O'Brien

> *Anecdotally, coaching succeeds because the learning takes place in the space in between two individuals and is centred on those characteristics in a relationship that is essential to facilitate change and development. These characteristics are empathy, trust, congruence and unconditional positive regard.*
>
> Margaret Chapman

Focus on the individual

A popular response to this question pointed out that coaching offers a tailored approach. Rather than making assumptions about individuals' needs and their current level of skills, coaching can be designed with a bespoke approach in mind.

The most successful training courses can be very helpful and will do something for everyone, but the chances are that they won't 'hit all the buttons for all the people'. The difference with coaching is that the learning for the individual is a 'tailored fit' and will involve the coach supporting the individual to discover their own ideas and implement appropriate improvements to their performance that will work for them.

Alison Williamson

Coaching takes account of the individual's current skills, the preferred method of learning, and is able to provide a tailored approach to the individual. It does not make assumptions or go at the speed of the group.

Noreen Tehrani

Regardless of the kind of coaching, one of the key and possibly unique facets of good coaching is that it is a methodology that by its very nature is focused on the needs and requirements of the individual. Good coaching is coachee-focused and is a highly flexible means of helping coachees reach their goals, placing the coachee at the centre of the change process and tailoring the coaching intervention to take account of his or her psychological needs, values, inter- and intra-personal skills and development needs.

Anthony Grant

Others also pointed out that coaching can be very motivating as people enjoy receiving one-to-one undivided attention and support.

Having single-minded and non-judgemental focus upon your own issues.

David Megginson

Coaching can also work because it motivates employees towards higher performance and makes them feel valued and appreciated. It demonstrates the organisation's commitment to the individual's success and personal growth.

Helen Pitcher

Business focus

By having both an organisational and individual agenda, coaching was felt to provide organisations with an opportunity to offer employees development that is truly aligned to business needs.

Part of the strength of coaching is believed to be the way that the organisation, the individual and the coach create a triangle focused on an agenda for the individual. All three work to ensure measurable and observable results are achieved.

Robin Linecarr

An important characteristic of coaching for the business community is that coaching is goal- and outcome-focused. It is something the organisation can offer individuals to help them examine and deal with any psychological barriers that are getting in the way of their performance. In this way, coaching helps ensure that the individual is contributing fully to the business.

> *Organisations are helped as coaching gets new executives up to speed in the shortest possible time after being recruited. It also helps individuals to develop and hone skills which have become dormant or are underdeveloped.*

Robin Linecarr

While coaches do have an axe to grind, in terms of selling the value of their services, their beliefs about the unique offer of coaching reflects the thoughts and beliefs of the HR community which have been expressed in case studies and quotes throughout this book. It is interesting (and pleasing) to see the commonality of beliefs expressed by different stakeholder groups.

HOW DOES COACHING WORK?

> *We actually don't know how coaching works – in a hard, scientific sense.*

Carol Braddick

Researchers are still grappling with the question of *how* coaching works, but despite this we thought it would be an interesting question to throw at the coaches we interviewed. Given that they are the 'experts' in this field, we thought it was useful to gain their views on what they believed were the main mechanisms by which coaching works. It is hoped that this will be useful to HR practitioners as initial ideas and techniques to use in their design of coach-training interventions.

Many coaches we interviewed felt that coaching works because it is based on a combination of different techniques that are used in conjunction to help individuals develop, learn and make sustainable changes to their behaviour.

> *Coaching accelerates learning and change by focusing on specific actions and behaviours that an individual wants to change. It does this through the process of structured exploration and discussion, which generates new perspectives or courses of action for the coachee to try out. While a number of different variables can affect the quality and effectiveness of coaching, the efficacy will always be heavily determined by the way in which different tools and techniques are used. And that is down to the coach.*

Anji Marychurch

Important coaching techniques regularly mentioned by the coaches include goal-setting, feedback, facilitating action planning and reflection.

> *Professional coaching works by helping the client to develop realistic and achievable goals. The coaching process focuses on trouble-shooting or enhancing performance or in some circumstances, on achieving the desired outcome. The mechanisms may vary depending upon the theory underpinning the approach taken by the individual coach.*

Stephen Palmer

> *Coaching works by creating cycles of feedback and reflection, stimulated by learning dialogue.*

David Clutterbuck

By working to change values and beliefs that inhibit performance, coaching produces long-term improvements in an individual's performance.

Paul Brankin

It is goal- and outcome-focused and examines those psychological barriers that often get in the way of performance.

Margaret Chapman

Essentially, coaching is a methodology for enhancing self-regulation and the process of goal attainment. Some of the key psychological mechanisms are psychological-mindedness, insight and the ability to self-regulate.

Anthony Grant

WHAT LESSONS CAN WE LEARN? WHAT CAN AN ORGANISATION DO TO FOSTER EFFECTIVE COACHING?

Best practices are emerging in this area, but like many sets of best practices, they are a mix of common sense and lessons learned.

Carol Braddick

Coaches are well placed to offer their views on what an organisation can do to support coaching initiatives so that they can have maximum impact. Although they do not have all the answers, the nature of their work across a wide variety of different organisations and situations offers them the opportunity to compare and contrast different approaches, ideologies, strategies and processes. An experienced coach who reflects on the successes and lessons learned from his or her coaching assignments can therefore provide useful insights into what works and what does not in supporting coaching processes.

Before we start it is important to say that we should not underestimate the difficulty of understanding how to gain maximum value from coaching activities. What works in one organisation will not always work in another, but there are likely to be some generalisations that we can draw on. The context and culture of the organisation (and attitudes of employees) will determine the exact strategy for how coaching should be introduced and developed.

While the factors that enhance the effectiveness of coaching are not yet fully understood, an analysis of the comments of the coaches we talked to highlighted some strong themes. There appears to be fairly widespread agreement about the factors that help to improve the likely success of coaching in organisational settings.

Full commitment from stakeholders

Coaching does not happen in a vacuum. For coaching to be really effective, it was believed that a number of stakeholders within the organisation had to be involved in the coaching programme.

Support from key stakeholders (line managers and HR) formalised by a coaching contract.

Helen Pitcher

The only part of coaching that can be outsourced is the one-to-one conversation between the coach and the client – what happens 'in the room'. Everything else takes place 'outside the room' and involves the commitment of all stakeholders (manager, co-workers, HR and coach) and broader organisation reinforcement through recognition of and non-financial reward for development and behaviour change.

Carol Braddick

And the extent of their involvement and level of commitment was strongly felt to influence results, particularly with regard to the support of senior management.

Overt support from a high-profile and respected internal sponsor.

David Clutterbuck

Commitment of the top level who 'walk the talk'.

Anji Marychurch

Manager support was also felt to be highly significant in supporting the impact of individual coaching relationships.

Support by the person's boss is nearly always necessary.

John O'Brien

A clear strategy and objectives

The coaches we interviewed all commented on the need for clarity around what coaching is being introduced to achieve. Without shared understanding of this across all stakeholders, it was felt that problems would arise because of differing expectations and assumptions. Communication around these issues was felt to be vital.

Encouraging the involvement of key stakeholders at the beginning of the coaching process and facilitating discussions to clearly define what the objectives (and benefits) are and what each of the stakeholders can do to help the individual achieve them. This should continue throughout the coaching.

Helen Pitcher

Clear business objectives towards which all coaching activity contributes.

Anji Marychurch

It was also felt that it was essential to have a clear view of the parameters for coaching including who was receiving it, how long it would last as well as what the process would look like.

Agreement on the messy issues of 'coaching for whom' and 'what type of coaching' is needed. With clear objectives, you'll know what impact you want coaching to deliver and can look at how to examine this impact.

Carol Braddick

The need for ongoing communication and regular reviews against set objectives was also regularly discussed.

Ongoing reviews of initial objectives throughout the coaching programme and the flexibility to respond to and incorporate new issues as they occur.

Helen Pitcher

Providing support

Coaches felt that organisations need to think through what support individuals need to continue developing their skills and how they can be encouraged to fully utilise them in the workplace.

HR should also consider what additional support including training or work experiences might support the coaching. While it is important to understand the needs of the organisation, it is pointless coaching someone and then not providing opportunities to consolidate new skills.

Helen Pitcher

A culture that supports learning and development

Many coaches reported that the existence of a culture that supports learning or is characterised by coaching is something that can really enhance the impact of coaching initiatives. This reflects previous CIPD research which noted that a culture that supports learning and development is the most important factor in helping people learn (CIPD, 2004).

The existence of a coaching culture in the organisation, or at the very least a climate that fosters the possibility of one being created.

Anji Marychurch

Communication

Effective communication was felt to be crucial by the coaches we interviewed. This is a wide, varied and ongoing role, and coaches felt that it encompassed building understanding about coaching in the organisation as well as ensuring that effective lines of communication are open within individual coaching relationships and across stakeholder groups.

Educate the workforce about the benefits of coaching to them and the organisation through seminars and company communications such as newsletters.

Stephen Palmer

Ensuring that the client has been given clear input/feedback by line managers/the organisation on areas for performance improvement.

Paul Brankin

Ongoing communication and support from key stakeholders throughout the programme.

Helen Pitcher

Hopefully HR practitioners can reflect on these comments to assess the extent that they are true of their own coaching activities. Any gaps may highlight areas for future focus when reviewing organisations' own learned lessons and deciding where to dedicate resources.

WHAT ARE THE MOST CRITICAL ACTIVITIES FOR HR?

When asked about the most critical areas for HR involvement, a variety of views emerged. Some coaches picked out specific areas of activity in which HR could improve its contribution, while others felt that the role of HR involved a raft of different activities.

> *I don't think there is any one, discrete activity that will have noticeably greater impact than all the other activities. Managing a whole set of factors effectively is the key.*
>
> Carol Braddick

So it seems that HR does not have a simple task ahead – most coaches believe they cannot simply focus on single processes or activities but instead should try to play an active role in a wide variety of different areas. Needless to say, the coaches we spoke to had strong opinions about particular areas in which HR should focus its efforts as well as about areas it should keep clear of. In terms of advice for HR, coaches feel that there are a number of areas in which HR can add value.

Recruiting coaches and setting standards of practice

HR is felt to have an important role in selecting high-quality coaches. Given the confusion in the coaching marketplace, HR must use a variety of selection techniques to help it identify who the 'good coaches' are.

> *Look for coaches who have their own coach or supervisor and who are engaged in ongoing professional development. Ask yourself the question 'How much does this coach believe in coaching if they don't have a coach themselves?' You might also question how the impartiality, skills and rigour of the coach are maintained over time if they are not involved in these processes.*
>
> Jamie McDonald

> *HR needs to evaluate the quality of coaches providing the services and then manage the activity.*
>
> Robin Linecarr

> *The coach needs to be highly skilled and well-trained, and have the right personal disposition and interpersonal skill set.*
>
> John O'Brien

But HR's role is not simply to hire good coaches; there are many other aspects to its role.

> *I would be wary of a response that oversimplifies the issues to 'just hire qualified, accredited coaches'.*
>
> Carol Braddick

Following selection, many coaches felt that HR needed to play an active role in setting standards for practice.

> *The coaching contract should clearly set out the length, content and objectives of the coaching programme and should be signed by each of the key stakeholders.*
>
> Helen Pitcher

> *Agreed standards of practice and core competencies for those engaged in coaching.*
>
> Anji Marychurch

A clearly defined code of practice and confidentiality agreement.

Helen Pitcher

However, although clear standards and contractual arrangements needed to be set, coaches also strongly believed that HR practitioners should not be too rigid or inflexible in their management of coaching.

HR should provide clarity and structure while retaining flexibility.

Anthony Grant

Managing the outcomes of coaching

Many coaches discussed the need to plan for and manage the aftermath of coaching. Many coaches recognised that coaching can sometimes result in significant changes to the performance and style of an individual, or an organisation more generally if a large-scale coaching programme is introduced. Because of this, coaches advised that coaching should be introduced gradually rather than with a big fanfare.

HR must ask themselves, 'Is the organisation ready for its leaders to change as a result of coaching? The individual who experiences coaching continues to interact with the company's culture, which may or may not be receptive to the changes made by the individual.

Carol Braddick

Start small and ensure that coaches and coachees are trained and supported via supervision or peer coaching.

Margaret Chapman

It is sometimes overlooked but setting the scene can be crucial for future success. Thus initially it is important for HR to promote the coaching culture.

Stephen Palmer

Sometimes it was felt that organisations failed to plan for the changes in individual behaviour, performance and expectations that coaching can create.

Many clients talk about feeling 'more confident' and 'more motivated' after a coaching programme. For HR teams the key issue is realising that a performance-enhancing period needs 'feeding' at the end of it to be of greatest benefit. The organisations that can provide flexibility and scope for the higher-performing individual to have a meaningful role to play have the potential to reap the investment in coaching many times over. Those organisations that cannot or will not adapt to accommodate and motivate an individual performing at a new level will ultimately miss out if the individual looks elsewhere to another employer who will.

Alison Williamson

Monitoring progress and evaluation

Without doubt one of the most common themes emerging from the coaches was a call for HR to make evaluation and measurement a priority.

To establish clear benchmarks, qualitative and quantitative to assess the impact of the coaching intervention.

Margaret Chapman

In order to learn lessons and make sure that practices are working as efficiently as possible, coaches thought HR should regularly monitor progress and seek high-level feedback without asking them to break confidentiality arrangements.

> *HR should look for opportunities for generic feedback to the organisation from the coaches providing the service.*
>
> Robin Linecarr

> *In our experience, the most critical area for HR involvement is working with the coach and the client to monitor progress in the coaching process in reference to the organisational goals for the coaching.*
>
> Paul Brankin

Getting the buy-in and involvement of stakeholders

Many coaches feel that HR cannot and should not try do it all by themselves. Although coaching can be supported and driven by HR, other stakeholders such as managers and leaders have important roles to play.

> *HR must facilitate the development of coaching by the line rather than making it an HR-focused activity.*
>
> David Megginson

> *HR should ensure that senior executives and directors actively participate in coaching themselves. 'This should be publicised in company communications.'*
>
> Stephen Palmer

MAKING DECISIONS ABOUT THE PARAMETERS FOR COACHING

Even if HR professionals are highly enthusiastic about the possibilities that coaching offers within their organisation, coaches felt that there is a real need for HR to ensure that it forms part of an overall learning and development strategy, only being used when it is really needed.

> *To ensure that coaching isn't seen and applied as a panacea. It may not work for everyone, in every context. It needs to be applied strategically, as with any other development/learning strategy.*
>
> Margaret Chapman

HR must also make decisions about when coaching is the most appropriate type of development for people.

> *Can needs be met by training, or is this something that is better achieved on an individual basis? I think it is important that the relative costs are considered. It is significantly cheaper to run a training course where the costs of the trainer are split between a number of people.*
>
> Noreen Tehrani

> *An effective initial assessment of the individual.*
>
> Helen Pitcher

There was a strong sentiment from the coaches that HR should not force coaching on people. It should be offered rather than prescribed. Many coaches commented on the importance of accepting that coaching is not everyone's learning style and that at some stages in people's lives they just are not open to coaching.

The contracting phase is critical and there is a need for a level of voluntarism and buy-in on the part of the coachee.

John O'Brien

It is a mistake to think that everyone, all the time, wants to change, or wants to learn, or again, is open to learning from me.

Mike Brearley

The more coercion the coachee has felt in coming to coaching, the more carefully a coach will need to ensure that the permission is there and that it continues.

Alison Hardingham

Playing a part in building an evidence-based profession

Finally, many coaches believed that HR also had a key role to play in entering the debate more fully about the effective use of coaching in business settings.

Case studies or action research to be shared via magazines, conferences, newsletters and forums. Not just by large corporations, but other environments and contexts.

Margaret Chapman

WHAT CAN COACHES TELL US ABOUT ORGANISATIONS' EVALUATION ACTIVITIES?

Coaches themselves are keen to develop the research base about the impact of coaching in business settings, and hence were very encouraging about HR making more efforts on evaluation and measurement. Coaches felt that HR buyers should have confidence in their position as the representative of the organisation's interests.

Organisations embarking on coaching programmes should not be afraid to ask 'What's in it for us?' Where accountabilities are clear and the individual can link improvements in their own performance to business improvements, these can be discussed and agreed as goals to achieve. At the most simple level, a manager could link reduction in turnover in their department or specific improvements in productivity to changes in their behaviour at work. Often it's just a question of raising the question, 'What changes can the business expect to see as a result of the individual demonstrating new behaviours?'

Alison Williamson

However, there were large differences in beliefs about the extent to which organisations should focus on evaluation and what level of evaluation was really necessary.

Clarity of purpose and an element of measurability of progress and success is key.

John O'Brien

It is crucial to measure coaching outcomes in terms set by individuals rather than by scheme organisers.

David Megginson

In our view the only useful measure is whether the coaching goals have been achieved.

Paul Brankin

What does current evaluation practice look like?

In terms of organisations' current evaluation and measurement practices, disappointingly many coaches commented that they are often not asked that much about measures and evaluation by the HR people who hire them. Frequent comments included 'We're not asked for much' or 'not a lot'. However, others felt that HR was asking more enquiring questions about the value of its services.

We are frequently asked to define the value of coaching and how coaching can contribute to the bottom line.

Helen Pitcher

Some coaches were critical of some of the approaches to evaluation that organisations currently took, feeling that they failed to give them the hard evidence they sought about the value of their activities

The data that coaches are asked for by HR is not always the most useful information for understanding the impact of coaching. And the evaluation may not be a useful exercise for the company or the coach. What we are asked for tends to be what is obtainable without creating any additional work or what fits into existing practices at most companies – feedback from the executive (formal and informal), feedback from stakeholders (formal and informal), both of which can cover examples of behaviour change and business results that may be perceived as being influenced by the coaching, but rarely proven as a direct result.

Carol Braddick

However, when the coaches were asked what they felt HR should be asking coaches for in terms of assistance with evaluation, the responses were remarkably consistent.

The best coaches determine clear intended outcomes of the intervention at the earliest stages and expect to be assessed against these. Wherever possible these measures relate to SMART goals, supplemented by softer, self-reported outcomes identified by the coachee.

David Clutterbuck

Clear contracting, clear goal-setting, proper review process mid-way and at the end of a coaching contract. They should also get feedback from coachees as to how the intervention has helped them to be more effective in their role and delivery.

John O'Brien

We need to go back to basics. What were the original objectives of introducing a coaching programme for the company? Often these are implicit and never properly explored and developed. They need to be explicit right at the beginning. Then you can consider whether the objectives have been achieved. The objectives may determine what measures are made and the type of evaluation.

Stephen Palmer

As part of the negotiation process, I agree with both the organisational sponsor and individual client what is to be achieved and how the parties will assess that the coaching programme has been a success.

Margaret Chapman

We also asked coaches what gets less focus at present in evaluation than it should – and some interesting responses emerged.

An honest discussion about evaluation – the company's motives for wanting to know the impact, underlying beliefs about investing in development, a hard look at what is meaningful to measure about coaching, the pros and cons of different approaches, and ways the company could get more from coaching without measuring. (Eg which would be more worthwhile: getting co-workers to do the follow-up that seems to have such a positive impact, or chasing surveys on coaching from executives?)

Carol Braddick

The challenges of evaluation

Coaches were sympathetic to the difficulties involved in evaluating the impact of coaching.

The monetary value of a coaching programme will vary from individual to individual, and, given that his or her performance will impact upon others in the organisation, it is often hard to evaluate. What we can do is measure and celebrate their successes and improved performance with key stakeholders in the organisation. Our problem is making this information public, given the terms of confidentiality agreements and the responsibility to our clients.

Helen Pitcher

Many coaches felt that HR practitioners seeking the holy grail of 'proof' that coaching works may well struggle to find it.

It will always be difficult to isolate the specific factors that have the most impact, as well as quantifying their unique impact.

Name withheld

Anthony Grant offered this advice on evaluation to the HR community:

One of the main problems organisations have in measuring outcomes in coaching is the lack of understanding about the different types of coaching. I delineate three types of coaching: skills, performance and development. Many organisations want to put a dollar figure on ROI for development coaching. However, this is extremely hard to do. Successful outcomes for development coaching are unlikely to be directly seen in terms of increased profitability. And even if the organisation's profit does increase, there will be a very tenuous causal link back to development coaching. Outcomes for development coaching should be measured in terms of employee engagement, cultural change or workplace climate (including aspects of perceived emotional labour).

On the other hand, a performance coaching engagement (for example, bringing a specific project in on time and to a very tight stretch schedule) can be measured in terms of dollar ROI. Similarly skills coaching can be measured in terms of 'Did they acquire and sustain the skill set or not?' Again a dollar-based ROI would not be hard to calculate.

Many well-publicised ROI studies, some of which cite ROI of 500+ per cent, use poorly-defined coaching interventions which are developmental in nature but claim to be able to make causal links between performance outcomes and developmental coaching which in my opinion are not often justified.

Coaching can be a highly effective intervention for creating and sustaining human and organisational change, and there is a growing body of research that supports this statement. But the coaching industry as a whole needs to develop more sophisticated ways of conceptualising outcomes and linking those outcomes to ROI. It's an exciting challenge for sure!

TO CONCLUDE

Much of the feedback and advice from coaches we received during this exercise reflects comments from other stakeholder groups that we have reported throughout this book. A consistent picture appears to be emerging about the factors that help and hinder coaching, as well as areas in which HR can add more value. Evaluation and measurement remain challenging areas for all the stakeholders in coaching. HR should work with coaches and researchers to try to develop workable approaches to evaluation and to build up the evidence based around what works and what doesn't in supporting coaching interventions.

All the coaches working with your organisation (internal, external and manager-coaches) are likely to be great sources of information about the issues that are acting as barriers to, and facilitators of, effective coaching practice within your organisation. The information provided here from the external coaches we interviewed is just the tip of the iceberg. You have got a whole host of experts sitting in your organisation right now who can help you improve your practices – just get out there and ask them for their views and feedback.

Part 3

Evaluating the results and building the case for coaching

11

A brief look at evaluation

Throughout this book, a running theme has been a call for HR practitioners to help build the evidence-base for coaching by evaluating their initiatives to assess the impact. However, many people often feel this is easier said than done. In this chapter we aim to try to persuade you one last time about the importance of evaluation, before providing some practical guidance about planning and carrying out evaluation activities.

HR practitioners are not the only people who are responsible and interested in evaluation. If senior managers want evidence of the value of HR activities such as coaching, then they must also ensure that they have the resources needed to make it happen – both in terms of HR time and money, as well as by encouraging other stakeholders such as managers to take part in evaluation activities. HR do, however, hold the responsibility for developing the procedures and ensuring that the process works – and this is where this chapter will hopefully help you.

A LAST-DITCH CHANCE TO PERSUADE YOU – WHY BOTHER WITH EVALUATION?

Evaluation is really more a way of thinking and working than a set of methods and practices. It involves continuously improving designs, responding to changing needs and situations, regularly reviewing costs and benefits, and of course reporting on progress.

It is one of those topics that while generally accepted as a good thing, is also viewed as quite a daunting prospect because it is thought to be difficult to do well. But at a simple level, evaluation is just a mechanism to help us improve quality and prove worth. Surely this is something to embrace, rather than avoid?

Evaluation does not improve the benefits of HR activities; it just allows you to put a number and description on them. By gathering information about the results and impact of coaching activities, you will be able to report progress to stakeholders and (hopefully) demonstrate that the investment is worthwhile. Without evaluation, it will be extremely difficult to prove the value of coaching. And in tough economic circumstances, this may mean that coaching will be vulnerable to budgets and resources being cut.

Evaluation is carried out for a wide range of reasons, but generally it aims to assess effectiveness, improve quality or justify an investment. Which of these are your main objectives? Evaluation should not just be an attempt to prove that coaching is working. The truth is that in some cases it may not be achieving the goals it was designed to for a variety of reasons. Information you gather from evaluation activities can significantly improve the effective management and delivery of coaching. Feedback to coaches will help them develop their skills and behaviours, and allow you to see whether they need additional training or support. It will also provide a mechanism to identify individual achievements from coaching so they can be celebrated and built upon. It is, however, important to accept that evaluating coaching activities will not always provide you with good news. Negative feedback is equally important because it can help to identify 'hot spots' and ways to improve future activities. It also gives you some reliable information to base changes on. Although pride may be slightly dented, learning from mistakes is just as crucial as evidencing successes, and it is certainly true that if you don't measure it, you can't manage it.

There are a variety of reasons people put forward for not taking evaluation seriously or failing to do it. One of them is the wrong assumption that time spent learning is always beneficial. Attending training courses or taking part in coaching sessions does not necessarily result in actual learning. Employees may enjoy them, but whether or not they result in sustainable learning and/or behaviour change is a completely different matter. Furthermore, investment in different types of employee development does not deliver equal paybacks, and evaluation can help to identify the best types of activities in which to invest money and resources. HR and the coaching activities they implement should not be given a blank cheque – coaching must be shown to be delivering against the objectives it was designed to achieve; otherwise, there is no reason to keep investing in it.

HR practitioners must stop fearing evaluation and make it their friend. For many HR practitioners it can help to raise their credibility. By demonstrating results and aligning their activities with the business, HR is showing how they can support their colleagues' activities. Evaluation is also a way of getting stakeholders (and sceptics) more closely involved and opens up opportunities to show how activities like coaching can play a role in improving performance. In short, it can be a way for HR to build relationships and credibility with people across the business.

We could keep going on – evaluation really can result in a whole range of benefits for HR. The box below provides some further information about the benefits that can be achieved.

The benefits of evaluating your coaching initiatives
- It can motivate people by highlighting an individual's performance improvement or heightened contribution.
- It acts as a basis for continuous improvement through which the skills and abilities of coaches can be improved.
- Positive data can help to persuade sceptics of the value of coaching.
- It allows you to justify the investment in coaching in your organisation.
- It can identify problems in the processes.
- It allows you to benchmark your activities with other organisations.
- Feedback from evaluation activities can help you to better integrate coaching activities with business needs and other HR activities.
- Data from evaluation activities can be used to benchmark the design and delivery of the activities against best practice.

- It provides an ongoing dialogue about the success of coaching between HR, coaches, coachees, and senior and line managers.
- It can help to build support for coaching within the organisation if positive results are seen.
- Negative results and feedback can help to shape and improve the design of future activities.
- It offers a way for individuals and organisations to learn to improve their use of coaching.

CURRENT APPROACHES TO EVALUATION

So what does the current picture look like? We thought it would be helpful to start by discussing how practitioners are approaching evaluation in the wider fields of learning and development, before looking more closely at coaching. A recent CIPD survey (CIPD, 2006) reveals that 91 per cent of respondents reported that they did evaluate learning, training and development activities in their organisation. At first glance, this appears to be a relatively high figure. However, closer examination reveals that a much smaller proportion (36 per cent) seek to capture the effect on the organisation's bottom line, with fewer still undertaking a 'return on investment' evaluation (18 per cent). It seems that the vast majority of organisations are relying on little more than anecdotal evidence or 'happy sheets' to measure effectiveness.

Other CIPD research has taken a close look at evaluation practices used specifically in coaching. Again, as shown in Table 18, the most common form of evaluation used in coaching is feedback from participants, indicating a strikingly similar picture.

Table 18: | *Evaluation practices used in coaching*

	Percentage of respondents using this practice
Feedback from participants	75
Appraisal systems	61
Feedback from coaches	44
Employee attitude surveys	41
Exit interviews	38
Assessment against objectives set at the start of a coaching initiative	37
Business performance indicators	29
360° feedback	25
Staff turnover rates	21
Other	6

Source: CIPD (2004)

There has never been greater pressure to measure the impact of HR activities, and coaching is unlikely to get away without being targeted – particularly when a number of people remain to be convinced by the research evidence available to date. Thirty-four per cent of respondents to the CIPD's 2006 learning and development survey think that 'lack of belief in the value of coaching' is a barrier to coaching activities, and 42 per cent believe that a 'lack of data to prove the value of coaching activities' is another major hindrance. Failing to evaluate coaching activities fully is unlikely to help this situation.

Some 57 per cent of respondents to the 2006 learning and development survey feel that there is now more emphasis on evaluation and proving the value of training than a few years previously. These findings suggest that while respondents may struggle with effective evaluation, organisations are not letting them off the hook. They continue to be pushed to provide evidence of the value they are delivering. Frustratingly, the overwhelming majority of respondents 'believe' that training and development delivers greater value to their organisation than they are able to demonstrate (80 per cent). But this value *must* be demonstrated if the commitment of stakeholders is to be secured or sustained. So the need to evaluate is not going to go away – HR has got to take the plunge and learn how to do it well. Yet how exactly should HR begin to approach this tricky area?

DESIGNING YOUR EVALUATION ACTIVITIES

Planning your approach and setting objectives

Many commentators (eg Bee and Bee, 2003) argue that evaluation should be considered and planned as early as possible – preferably at the point when you are undertaking the learning/business needs analysis and planning the implementation of the coaching initiative. Many problems and difficulties with evaluation arise because they have not been discussed at an early enough stage. Without early discussion about measurement and evaluation your stakeholders may have unrealistic expectations about what information or data they are going to receive. The earlier you can begin planning evaluation activities and setting expectations the better.

Evaluation is not just something that HR is interested in. You'll have a whole series of different people who have a vested interest in evaluation activities – typically, these include senior managers, line managers and participants in coaching activities, as well as any external coaching practitioners or training providers you may be working with. But it is the views of your internal stakeholders that really count, and they will all have different expectations as well as ideas about what types of evaluation activities will be the most useful. You may also want them to get involved in evaluation by taking part in activities and providing feedback. Getting them involved early on affords a good opportunity to find out about their interest areas, and if you want them to participate later down the line it can help to build their commitment to the project.

The first step is to consider why you are evaluating. Are you under pressure to provide evidence of the value of your activities, do you want to assess progress or gain information about how to improve activities, or are you trying to gather evidence to help build the business case for future activities? There is no point carrying out evaluation activities for the sake of it – it is only worth all your time and effort if the information is going to be used. A good starting point when planning evaluation is to think about the following questions:

- What information do your stakeholders want to know?
- What are your (HR) objectives in evaluating coaching initiatives?
- How will you use the evaluation results?

It is useful to look back at your original objectives in introducing the coaching initiative and use these to guide your objectives for evaluation. For example:

- Have the learning needs you identified been met? Or have the performance gaps been bridged?
- Have the business needs been fulfilled?

Being clear about the reasons you are undertaking evaluation will help to provide a focus for your activities.

There are probably a wide range of questions that you and your stakeholders would like to obtain information about. And your evaluation activities can take place at a number of different levels and with differing degrees of complexity. But unless you have got a bottomless pit of money and limitless time, it is likely that you will have to decide on some priority areas of interest because of the level of resources available to you. Consider:

- What are the most important things (ie the priorities) for your organisation to know about the coaching initiative you have implemented?
- What level of support is available from coaching stakeholders for evaluation? How much will they get involved?
- How much are you prepared to spend (resources, time, etc) on evaluation activities?
- Have you got the skills and expertise to undertake evaluation activities?
- What level of evaluation are you committed to measuring (using Kirkpatrick's levels of evaluation)?

Evaluation does, of course, cost money. And it takes time, commitment and expertise. HR practitioners must therefore be selective about when evaluation is really important. Pilot programmes are particularly worth evaluating in order to correct and improve the format before it is more widely implemented, and to decide whether it is worth a more major investment.

Evaluation in coaching is most commonly focused on outcomes (eg improvements in knowledge, skills, behaviours). However, you can also obtain a lot of interesting information from asking questions about *why* and *how* the outcomes came about. Without this kind of information it may be difficult to make good decisions about what adjustments or changes to your coaching activities are most appropriate. Think about how your evaluation activities can help you describe the outcomes of coaching, as well as how results were achieved. Overall, plan evaluation activities that are well scoped out, that are realistic given the resources you have, and that will give you the information you require. Evaluation should not be over-complicated, but it does require time, forethought and focus.

Scoping out your evaluating activities and deciding on criteria

Following setting your objectives for evaluation, there are several points to consider in designing the actual evaluation activities. A major part of the design is setting the scope and boundaries of your activities:

- type of coaching activities to be evaluated (eg coaching of graduates using a set of coaches from a specific provider, or coaching by managers within their teams)

- proportion of coaching activities that will be evaluated (are you going to attempt to gain data from everyone in your target group, or just a sample?)

- sources of input (coachees, their managers, their subordinates, HR professionals, coaches, peers, senior managers)

- timeline for evaluation of results (eg short, medium or long term)

- internal evaluators or use of third party.

The answers to these questions will help you to define the scope and parameters for your evaluation activities. Once you have decided upon your objectives for evaluation and set your parameters and boundaries, you can start to think about evaluation criteria. These will directly relate to your objectives and can include a wide range of different variables. Criteria can reflect participant satisfaction, degree of learning and individual behaviour change, impact on individual and performance, changes in business performance indicators, improvements in management information (eg turnover, absenteeism), improvement in cultural indicators, and so on. It is important to choose criteria which have a resonance for non-HR practitioners and key stakeholders if you want to hold their interest. Deciding upon your criteria for each of the objectives you have set will then move you forwards to thinking about which evaluation methods work best to provide you with the information you want.

Different evaluation methods

A vast number of different evaluation models and techniques exist in the literature – the most well-known being that of Donald Kirkpatrick (Kirkpatrick, 1967) who set out four levels at which learning interventions can be evaluated: reaction level, learning level, job behaviour level, and results level. We are not going to attempt to review them here because a whole host of articles and books is solely focused on this topic (eg Bee and Bee, 2003; Bramley, 2004). It is probably helpful to read through some of these prior to beginning your evaluation activities in order to grasp some of the basic information about this complex topic. An important consideration is to think through the level of evaluation data you want to gather, because this will influence the methods of evaluation you employ. Are you going to attempt multi-level evaluation activities to gain data that aligns with several of Kirkpatrick's levels of evaluation? If so, which ones are really important to your stakeholders?

As mentioned earlier, feedback from participants is the most common form of evaluation used in coaching. This is probably because it is one of the easiest ways to gather information. However, it is also very appropriate for an activity like coaching, in which ultimately the learner is the best person to comment on whether coaching has helped him or her achieve the goals set. This is particularly the case in the light of the confidentiality that often exists in coaching relationships. Getting feedback from participants in coaching or 'happy sheet' data should not be dismissed, even if does not prove that actual learning has taken place: it is often a quick and easy litmus test to gauge views, satisfaction and progress. However, most organisations want to know more about how well coaching is working than simply whether or not those who take part enjoy it and feel it is worthwhile. And that is where HR need to start looking at the higher-level criteria in line with Kirkpatrick's four-tier model of evaluation (Kirkpatrick, 1967). In particular, HR should look at methods to measure the degree of learning by the individual, the extent of behavioural change and performance enhancement, and the level of improvement in business unit effectiveness.

So what different methods are there to think about? The CIPD guide *Coaching and Buying Coaching Services* (Jarvis, 2004) suggested a number of different evaluation methods that might be considered. These are featured in Figure 14.

Identifying and collating different types of data is helpful in painting a rounded picture of results. This can be qualitative and quantitative, anecdotal or concrete, and positive or negative. Positive data can be used to ensure continuous investment in coaching, and negative data can be used to identify ways of improving practices. Some common methods that can be used independently or in combination to fulfil your evaluation objectives are outlined sequentially below.

Figure 14: | ***Evaluating coaching – some options***

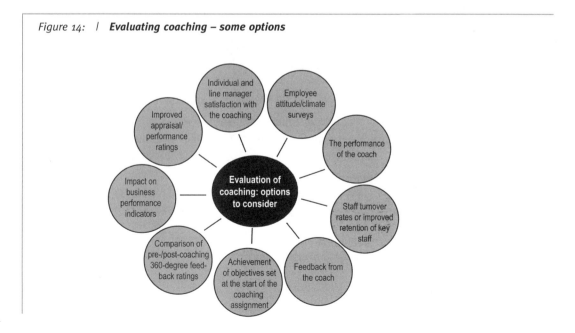

Progress checks

These are regular, qualitative updates that typically involve those people who are involved in the coaching activity and are best placed to observe progress. In the case of an executive coaching assignment this may be the individual, his or her manager and the coach. HR professionals may also participate in these discussions or have separate 'check-ins' with the stakeholders. These kinds of activities are good practice in monitoring coaching activities, but to contribute to more formal evaluation the information from these discussions should be tracked in some way. An example is to include a question such as 'How useful is the coaching?' in the discussion and record the responses you receive.

Discussions with stakeholders at the end of coaching interventions

These are a more comprehensive version of the progress check and involve a longer discussion about satisfaction with coaching activities and the results that have been experienced. In these discussions, the following questions may be useful:

- How effective has the coaching/training etc been in addressing the goals and changes we targeted?

- What has been most beneficial about the coaching intervention to you? To the business?

- Are there any specific business results that you think are attributable (directly or indirectly) to the coaching initiative?

Because of the qualitative nature of these discussions it is important to summarise the discussion in a way that links to the overall evaluation approach. For example, to close the discussion participants might be asked to rate different aspects of their coaching experience on a series of scales of 1 to 5 (1 not useful; 5 highly effective). But alongside this it is often very helpful for HR to gather stories and comments about performance improvements and measurable business savings which are believed to have stemmed from the coaching activities. Although they are subjective pieces of information, they can often be very persuasive and help to provide a more 'human' view of the impact of coaching activities.

Assessing the achievement of objectives set at the start of a coaching intervention

The very nature of the one-to-one coaching relationship lends itself to the establishment of clear objectives. And the extent to which these learning goals are met are surely a key measure of effectiveness. Achievement of individual objectives can be assessed via a number of different methods including stakeholder discussions and surveys. Assessing the achievement of wider organisational goals for coaching is also critical, but depending on the exact nature of the objectives a variety of different evaluation methods may have to be employed.

Pre- and post-intervention stakeholder input

This is often used to assess the impact of coaching because it offers the opportunity to measure progress and perceptions on competencies or performance ratings before *and* after an intervention. Data from 360-feedback activities is probably the most common type of information used in this type of evaluation activity. Because activities like 360-degree feedback can generate huge amounts of information, it can be helpful to focus on the behavioural changes that will have the greatest impact for the individual and the organisation.

Stakeholder surveys

These can be used to gather information from a larger number of sources than one-to-one interviews, particularly if an online survey is designed. They can be aimed at individuals who have received coaching or coach-training, their managers, peers or subordinates or other stakeholder groups. The challenge for HR in using surveys is ensuring a high response rate, particularly when many of the people you want to gain information from are likely to be extremely busy. One of the CIPD practical tools offers some example items that can be used in these types of survey (CIPD, 2005a):

> *Here are a few survey items that work well with a 5-point scale of degree of agreement*
> *(1 – I disagree strongly; 5 – I agree strongly):*
>
> ❏ *The coaching was helpful in accelerating achievements on the goals we agreed.*
> ❏ *The coaching has been helpful in making changes that are key to my success at work.*
> ❏ *I consider the coaching of value relative to the fees and time invested.*
> ❏ *Coaching has helped me become a better leader.*

These are just some examples, but hopefully they will give you some ideas for the types of questions/rating scales you could include in a survey.

Depending on your goals for evaluation, you can also consider a survey that delves into views on the processes used to manage and deliver the coaching initiative (eg to assess matching, quality of training providers, communication, etc). Feedback on processes may also be collected via interviews or focus groups. Whichever method you decide on, this activity is likely to yield useful information when trying to make improvements to your coaching programmes.

Tracking improvements in business indicators

While proving a direct link between coaching and changes in business indicators is difficult, it is still worth analysing this type of information. Although some people may argue that you cannot prove a causal link between coaching and these type of indicators because of other influencing factors that may have played a role, it can still help to provide some persuasive material to support your other evaluation data. Some examples of indicators to track include management information (such as staff turnover, retention of staff, absenteeism, etc), cultural indicators (eg information from culture or climate surveys), and specific business objectives that coaching interventions were designed to support.

ROI – return on investment

Return on investment calculations focusing on coaching activities are generally considered to be fairly difficult to do. And the complexity of the task will very much depend on the type of coaching intervention that has been implemented. The CIPD (2005a) offers the following advice for attempting this activity with regard to an executive coaching assignment:

1 Verify changes in behaviour and results through discussion with the client (the sponsoring manager may also be included in these steps)

2 Estimate the financial benefit of these changes

3 Judge the role of coaching in enabling the changes

4 Estimate the total financial benefit attributable to coaching

5 Estimate the cost of providing coaching

6 Calculate the return – ie the benefit (Step 4) relative to the cost (Step 5).

ROI evaluations are unfortunately rarely used because of the resource requirements and expertise that are needed.

Each of these different evaluation methods has pros and cons. Some of the common ones are shown in Table 19.

Table 19: | *The pros and cons of different evaluation methods*

Evaluation method	Pros	Cons
Progress checks	• A part of good practice in coaching relationships • Helps to identify issues that arise on an ongoing basis • Supports continuous emphasis on expectations and objectives of coaching activities	• HR needs to judge whether the initiative or coaching relationship has been successful and assign some type of label or rating that reflects the degree of success
Discussions with stakeholders at the end of coaching interventions	• A useful part of the coaching process regardless of whether HR uses the information in an evaluation exercise • Is considered good coaching practice	• Also requires HR to label the engagement as successful or not. However, this may be easier than in methods 1 and 3 because the discussion of success is more explicit.

Pre- and post-intervention stakeholder input	• A natural extension of familiar 360-degree feedback processes • Is easy to include multiple stakeholders: managers, peers and direct reports • Is easy to track changes in scores on competencies or performance ratings • Is also possible to aggregate scores across a number of different stakeholders or coaching relationships	• Other learnings and results may have been achieved in coaching that are not reflected in the questions asked or competencies assessed • No direct feedback on the coaches involved, who are assumed to be effective if the post-coaching scores show improvement
Surveys	• Consistent approach with less variability due to interpretation by HR • May be combined with stakeholder closing discussions: eg a discussion followed by a brief survey to formally record views • May be administered to individuals and their manager to note any discrepancies in views • Process surveys can provide feedback to target improvements in the management of coaching	• May be difficult for individuals and their managers to take the time to complete; puts HR in position of chasing completed surveys • A process survey may increase the number of questions to be answered • Surveys require a high number of participants to be able to draw firm conclusions
Tracking improvements in business performance indicators	• Is a business-focused activity that will resonate well with stakeholders • Utilises information that has often already been collected (eg management information), so avoids further costs	• It is hard to isolate the impact of a coaching intervention on business indicators such as productivity and turnover.
ROI	• Yields rich information on the range of results and individuals' views on the impact of coaching • Produces an output expressed in financial terms	• It is labour-intensive • It is a subjective estimate • It ignores long-term benefits or the value of preventing negative outcomes such as loss of a key employee

Some important considerations when choosing your methods for evaluation are to decide whether you are solely going to measure the results at the end of a coaching initiative, or try to get data before and afterwards in order to assess gains in performance or changes in behaviour. Measuring afterwards allows you to compare results against certain standards or targets, while measuring before and after allows you to measure how performance has improved in comparison with the start point.

Another thing to consider is whether or not you are going to try to compare groups of learners to build a 'control group' into your evaluation activities (ie those who did and did not take part in a particular coach-training programme). This can be quite difficult to organise due to the problem of finding equivalent groups of learners, but when it is used, the results achieved can be quite powerful and persuasive.

Decisions about the kinds of methods to employ will lead you to decide on a particular design for your evaluation activities. Evaluation can become extremely complex, and it is important not to make things overly complicated or unnecessarily time-consuming. Using a range of measures is likely to be the best option if you have sufficient resources. This is because a range can offer you complementary data and information (qualitative and quantitative) that will help you to assess the effectiveness of your coaching activities against a number of different criteria.

CHALLENGES INVOLVED WITH EVALUATION

Evaluating the impact of some coaching activities is made harder because of the difficulties presented by the confidential nature of coaching relationships. Confidentiality often prevents direct reporting by the coach, meaning that any feedback on the success of the coaching tends to be limited, non-specific or only provided if the individual is willing for information to be shared. This places considerable restrictions on the quality of data that can be gathered.

Another key challenge for evaluators is that the benefits of coaching are not always shown in financially measurable results – even if that is what some of your stakeholders are pushing you to focus on. The reality of an investment in coaching may be that the organisation cannot directly attribute all of the benefits of coaching to immediate performance improvements. The benefits may show up in a ripple effect – to another project or person, or some time down the road. Or they may simply be more subtle changes that take a while to show up (eg changes in confidence or other behaviours). As Sherman and Freas (2004) argue in a recent *Harvard Business Review* article:

> *When you create a culture of coaching, the result may not be directly measurable in dollars. But we have yet to find a company that can't benefit from more candour, less denial, richer communication, conscious development of talent, and disciplined leaders who show compassion for people.*

Setting expectations about the kind of data that will be gathered is crucial, and it is important to make stakeholders understand that evaluation of coaching has to involve a number of different data-capture methods to illustrate the breadth of results that can be obtained.

It may also take time to see the results from coaching interventions come through. Many of the case study organisations that we spoke to in our research said they felt it takes at least six months for the impact of coaching interventions to be truly felt in the organisation. This length of time means that an element of trust or 'leap of faith' from stakeholders is often required when investing in coaching activities.

HR may face a number of other barriers to their evaluation activities. Recent CIPD research looking at barriers to the evaluation of learning and development activities more generally, demonstrated that the most commonly-cited barriers to evaluation activities were a lack of resources to undertake lengthy evaluation exercises (76 per cent) and a lack of time (67 per cent) (CIPD, 2006). A little under two-thirds also cited difficulties in proving the impact on business performance indicators (60 per cent). And around a third said that another obstacle they faced was that other stakeholders in the organisation did not believe evaluation was worth spending time on (30 per cent). See Table 20.

Table 20: | *Main issues faced when trying to prove the effectiveness of learning, training and development activities*

Issues	Percentage of respondents
Lack of resources to undertake lengthy evaluation activities	76
Lack of time to undertake evaluation activities	67
Difficulty in proving the impact of training on business performance indicators	60
Lack of research evidence/ROI data to prove the value of training	44
Other stakeholders in the organisation don't think evaluation is worth spending time on	32
Lack of knowledge and understanding in the organisation about how to undertake evaluation	30

Source: CIPD (2006)

HR should try to assess the barriers they may face in evaluation early on, and undertake actions to try to counter their effect. But some of these challenges are unlikely to go away, so the best tactic is for HR to be aware of them and to educate their stakeholders about realistic approaches to evaluation.

ANALYSING EVALUATION DATA AND TAKING ACTION

Data on its own is meaningless. It must be converted into information before it can be used in the decision-making process.

Bee and Bee (1999)

Your evaluation activities may result in a great deal of data – the next challenge is analysing it and making sense of what it all means. Data analysis is a complex activity and something that requires a lot of expertise, so you may wish to read up on this or consult colleagues or external consultants who can help you with this part of the process. The different types of analysis will depend on the type of data you have collected (quantitative or qualitative) as well as your objectives for your evaluation activities (ie what you are trying to prove). It is generally wise to keep your analysis as simple as possible, and to focus on the objectives you set at the start of the process. You want your data analysis to provide you with some key messages and themes about the results that have been achieved from your coaching activities, but you also want to be able to communicate these to your stakeholders in simple and clear ways.

Presenting the results is the pinnacle of your evaluation activities. It is the stage that if done well will demonstrate to your stakeholders that you are committed to assessing and improving activities. You must think through who will be interested in the results, and how they would be most interested in receiving the information. The stakeholders in both your coaching efforts (and more specifically, your evaluation activities) are all likely to be interested in seeing the results. They have all contributed their time to the process so it is not only polite to provide them with the results but it is also important for future activities (when you may need their help again!) that they see that outcomes of their involvement are being discussed and used.

When providing information about evaluation activities it is important to keep messages simple and clear – do not bewilder people with excessive data or complex calculations. Bramley (2004) suggests providing:

- a statement of the purpose of the evaluation and how that affected the design
- a description of the methods used
- a summary of the findings, highlighting the achievement of objectives
- a summary of costs
- conclusions and recommendations.

Make sure your audience fully understands the results and is clear about the implications and next steps in the process.

So you have written a professional report, or given a clear presentation about the results – but what are you actually going to do next? In many ways, evaluation is only worthwhile if the findings are acted upon: collecting the data is only part of the process – stakeholders must receive and make decisions based on the information. Acting on evaluation information requires just as much commitment and energy as undertaking the evaluation itself. Timeliness is essential – if you are not careful, your glossy report could end up sitting on a shelf with no concrete actions happening as a result. Decide what next steps are going to be taken, consult with key stakeholders and then take action as quickly as possible. The cycle of setting objectives, planning, implementing and reviewing begins again. Design an action plan with targets and timescales, and get started.

CONCLUSIONS

Taking a realistic and pragmatic approach to evaluation is essential. Think about what resources you have available to you and do whatever you can given your circumstances. It is always better to do something than nothing, and some forms of evaluation are relatively cheap and simple to do – for example, collecting anecdotes from participants about how coaching has helped them in their jobs and asking managers to estimate a percentage improvement in their performance at work can provide useful data and need not take up too much time. Talking to your senior managers and setting expectations early on about what data you are going to collect is also important.

We should not make evaluation overly complicated. Many of our case studies talked about choosing a few measures that were particularly important for their organisations and then focusing on those. If you do not have enormous levels of resources, be selective and focus on a few key measures that are meaningful to your senior managers and the business. Often, some good personal stories about the impact of coaching, alongside some key metrics, will be just what your senior managers want to hear. Look for easy ways to gain high-quality data that do not involve too much extra work (eg using existing management information).

Hopefully, this chapter has helped to remove some of the mystery around evaluation and allowed you to see that it is not such a daunting task. Be realistic about what you can achieve, and do not try to over-complicate things – often simple approaches can provide good data that demonstrates your results. If you have still got lots of questions, seek support from colleagues or other more expert professionals: evaluation is a learning process and HR practitioners must try to learn as they go along the way.

Evaluation is often viewed as a cost or burden for HR practitioners. However, money spent on effective evaluation will ultimately result in less money being wasted on initiatives that are not delivering results or that need to be tweaked in order for them to work properly. It will also enable HR to ensure that money and resources are targeted at coaching activities that make the largest difference to organisational goals and that initiatives are delivered in the most cost-effective way. We must start to view evaluation as an investment – and one that if done well will reap dividends and more than cover its costs.

To end this chapter, Carol Colone has kindly given us permission to reproduce a case study she has written about her evaluation of a coaching programme within a global financial services company (Colone, 2005). It gives a great example of how HR researchers can take a pragmatic approach to evaluation and obtain evidence of the impact of their coaching activities. It demonstrates much of what has been discussed in this chapter – that with determination, planning and support from your stakeholders it is possible to undertake effective evaluation activities and demonstrate the value your coaching activities have been delivering.

CASE STUDY

Calculating the return on investment in executive coaching for a corporate staff function in a large global financial services company (Colone, 2005)

William M. is the executive vice president and division head of a large corporate staff function in one of the largest financial services institutions in the world. I am his senior Human Resources business partner. In late 2000, our company announced its decision to merge with another large financial services company. William was selected to head and integrate the two corporate staff functions into one. His goal was to create one high-performing team from the management groups of the two organisations. He wanted to accomplish this goal while also meeting his merger objective to reduce expense. His challenge was to retain the best people and continue developing future leaders for the company while downsizing the staff population. I believed that executive coaching was the least expensive development strategy to help him accomplish these aggressive goals. He agreed, and we embarked on what turned out to be, in the end, a three-year project.

In early 2001 I selected four executive coaches who would work with approximately 80 middle managers. William decided that a fifth coach, his executive coach, would work with his direct reports, the new management group, while he continued to work with her as well. I met with the coaches to brief them on the goals of the project and the process we wanted followed using 360-degree feedback on the managers' leadership competencies.

The coaches helped their clients focus on their key development opportunities based upon the clients' own self-assessment of how well they demonstrated the company's new leadership criteria. Each manager wrote his or her development plan with guidance from the executive coaches.

The senior team members were also directed to work with the December 2000 Merger Employee Climate Survey results to craft strategies and initiatives for improving the climate and the next employee climate survey scores. This project would provide them with opportunities for enhancing their leadership capabilities and measuring their success based upon changes in the climate survey scores year over year going forward.

At the end of three years, we had spent approximately $900,000 on executive coaching for 101 managers in this organisation, which equated to an investment of approximately $3,000 per person per year. From a purely financial perspective this was a large investment, and unprecedented in our company, in the development of managers in a staff function.

From the results that William and I had observed year over year, in accomplishment of the group's business goals to personal development of the individuals who had received coaching, and especially in the improvement in employee climate survey scores each year, we intuitively knew that the financial investment had produced great results. On the other hand, we wanted more tangible evidence of a positive return on this significant investment in management development.

Coincidently, I was also enrolled in the Beam Pines/Middlesex University Master's Program in Professional Development (Executive Coaching) and working on my research project and master's thesis. With William's sponsorship, I chose to determine how executive coaching affected the performance of the management team of this company from 2001 to 2003 as my research project. I was able to show the effects of executive coaching in terms of:

- what executive competencies the managers chose to work on developing as recorded in their development plans over the three-year period

- the employee climate survey results over the same period along with the results from the year 2000 as a baseline for comparison, measuring employees' responses to questions about values, partnership (teamwork), results, attitude and communication
- 360-degree feedback received by these managers over the three-year period measuring overall leadership effectiveness, values, partnership (teamwork), results, attitude and communication
- the effects executive coaching had on the performance of the management team in the managers' own words gathered from interviews with them.

But when I read 'Still, there are still nagging concerns about just how much coaching adds back to the bottom line' (Morgan, Harkins and Goldsmith, 2005), I decided that this research paper would not be complete in my mind unless I looked at other more tangible measures of return on investment that would reflect even more substantially on the effect that executive coaching had on the performance of this corporate staff function.

And when I found this: 'Employers are beginning to accept executive coaching as a strategic process and are measuring it [Return on Investment] with surprising results' (Patton, 2001), I decided to do more research. Quoting Steve Listansky, president, Success Dynamics and the Executive Coaching Institute, Concord, Mass., Patton (2001) suggests:

Remember these when measuring ROI for executive coaching:
1   Measure any result that is meaningful.
2   Recognise that not everything you measure will be objective like customer or employee satisfaction.
3   Clearly define the most important results an executive can actually influence or achieve.
4   Align your plans and outcomes for coaching with an executive's existing development plan.

Key ROI measurements are:
1   increase in profits, sales and gross margins
2   decrease in expenses
3   increase in customer and employee satisfaction
4   increase in employee retention
5   improvement in communication effectiveness
6   increase in leadership effectiveness
7   improvement in teamwork at all levels
8   improvement in processes such as product introduction cycle time or financial reporting.

From this, then, I posited that since this corporate staff function accumulated management information on a regular basis as a normal way of monitoring and controlling its business activities and of measuring performance, I could identify meaningful measures of executive coaching impact on this group of managers by studying and reflecting upon these measures. And since the executive coaching focused upon leadership capability and enhancing team performance, I determined that changes in significant performance measures could be directly linked to the work of the executive coaches with the managers of this organisation.

CASE STUDY continued

To confirm this thesis, I also interviewed 30 per cent of the managers who had received executive coaching during 2001 to 2003 to get their perspectives as to how coaching may have affected their performance and therefore the performance measures they used to monitor their business.

As a result, I also looked at employee retention, related decreases in expenses, and productivity, as well as climate survey results and improvement in 360-degree feedback scores as measurements that would demonstrate a clear and meaningful 'return on investment' in executive coaching for this organisation.

Here is what I found.

1 Retention

Figure 15: | *Retention v turnover rates of staff, 2000 to 2003*

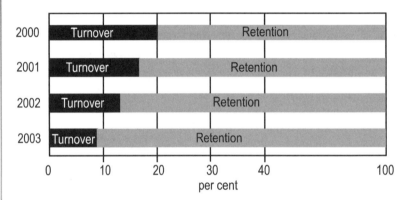

While turnover rates decreased from 20 per cent in 2000 to 8 per cent in 2003 (see Figure 15), virtually all of the group's 101 highest-performing employees stayed with the organisation.

Higher retention, from the perspective of a corporate function like this one translates to higher productivity from experienced and knowledgeable staff. Experienced employees do not need to learn the organisation's policies, procedures, work tools or get an orientation to the new culture that a new hire would require.

The intangible benefit derived from longer retention of the top performers of an organisation is the increased quality of work performed by the same increasingly more experienced people.

2 Decrease in expenses

The savings on executive recruiting fees generally required to source high-quality replacements to replace experienced employees for this group was substantial during the years 2000 to 2003. Conservative estimates for this organisation claim an expense saving of $540,000 per year in executive recruiting fees for the three years 2001, 2002 and 2003 for a total savings of approximately $1,620,000.

CASE STUDY continued

A comparison of this group's turnover to industry peer groups shows a markedly lower turnover rate than peers in each year except for 2001 (see Figure 16). A large portion of this population worked in New York City. Turnover in this lower-Manhattan-based group was higher than expected in 2001. A review of exit interview data for that year attributed the higher-than-expected turnover to the experiences of September 11, 2001.

Figure 16: / ***Turnover compared to top 25 industry peers (G25) and selected peer group's turnover rates***

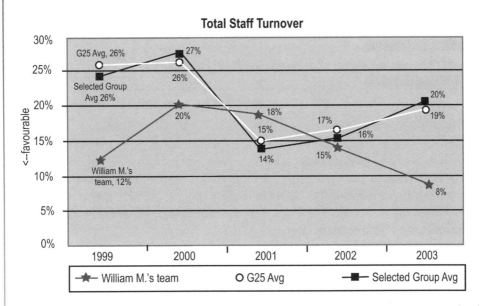

Another area in which savings were realised during this time period was executive, leadership and management development. We compared the cost of the 360-degree feedback coaching, averaging $3,000 per client, and the resulting impact on each individual manager's growth and development, to the cost of executive, leadership or management development training of between $4,000 and $20,000 and the return from the training, from both the individual recipient's perspective and his/her senior manager's perspective. We found that executive coaching as a development strategy was more cost-effective than training and had more impact on the executive's leadership behaviour and in influencing organisational change.

3 Productivity

Productivity for a corporate staff function such as this one can be measured in terms of the number of projects completed annually versus available resources (number of staff available) to complete those projects. William's group maintains a business plan database that records the number of projects begun, worked on and completed each year, and the number of hours charged to those projects, which translate into actual number of staff used to complete the

CASE STUDY continued

work. This team's productivity statistics for the years 2000 to 2003 are shown in relation to the actual headcount available to complete those projects in Figure 17.

*Figure 17: | **Productivity v resource statistics, 2000 to 2003***

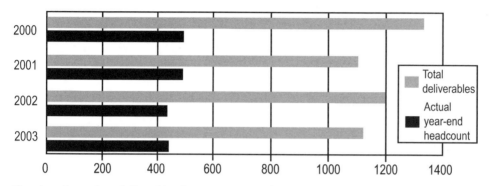

The drop in project deliverables between year-end 2000 and year-end 2001 was due to the impact of and disruption in activity due to the events of September 11, 2001 and the weeks thereafter. In 2002 productivity went up by 6 per cent even though headcount dropped by approximately 18 per cent. In 2003 productivity decreased by 5 per cent even though headcount increased by 1.2 per cent. The decrease in the number of projects over the four-year period was primarily due to changes in the scope of coverage following changes in the businesses supported by this corporate function.

In other words, while the number of projects either increased or remained stable in the period 2001 to 2003, the number of resources used to get the work done decreased, translating into higher productivity overall. This data provides tangible elements of the effect that executive coaching had on the performance on the senior management team of this corporate function during the period 2001 to 2003.

Although a high level of retention of top talent and productivity improvement are tangible measures of the return on investment in executive coaching for managers, the root cause of these positive results lies in the level of employee satisfaction with the organisation. So we looked at how employee satisfaction levels changed during this time period as well as indicated in the Employee Climate Survey results and in the 360-degree feedback to managers during the same time period.

4 Employee satisfaction – Climate Survey results

The attention the management team members placed on their own leadership development and on the continuous development of their team members garnered recognition from employees around the world in the form of their responses to the annual employee climate survey questions.

The response rates – ie the number of responders to the climate survey v the total population size of the group – rose in each of the three years 2001, 2002 and 2003 as compared to the baseline year of 2000. In 2003, 100 per cent of the population responded. See Figure 18.

Figure 18: | ***Employee Climate Survey participation rates, 2000 to 2003***

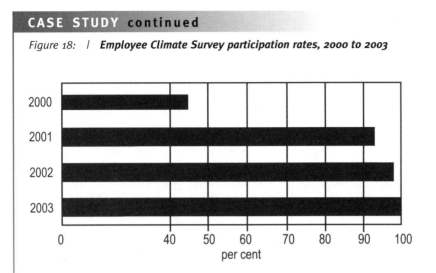

We looked at the Climate Survey trends, compared over the four-year period, 2000 to 2003, in employee responses to questions on commitment/retention, cooperation, execution/productivity, culture and leadership criteria. See Figure 19.

Figure 19: | ***Key Climate Index trends, 2000 to 2003***

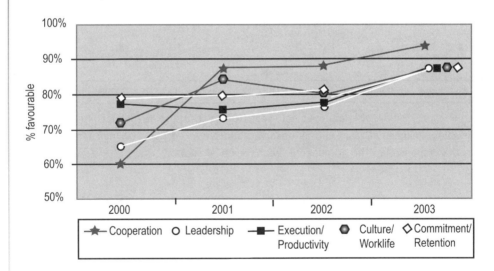

All key indices showed improvement over the three-year period from 2001 to 2003, and when also compared to the pre-merger benchmark year of 2000, the improvement in scores was even more pronounced. These survey results for all years were tested for statistical significance at (P = 0.05).

CASE STUDY continued

5 Employee satisfaction – 360-degree feedback to managers

To chart trends in 360-degree feedback, I plotted the scores or ratings over the three-year period, representing change or improvement over time, for the management team. Figure 20 shows the change in leadership behavior criteria scores over this period in the categories of values, partnership, results, attitude and communication.

Figure 20: | **360-degree feedback leadership behaviour criteria trends, 2001 to 2003**

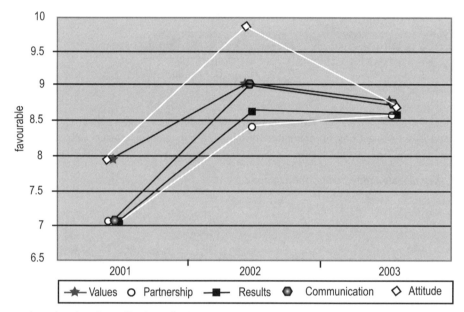

And again, the chart displays the improvement, year over year, in the key leadership criteria displayed by the management team and as observed and remarked upon by their staff members in the responses to the 360-degree feedback questions.

Conclusion

The return on investment in executive coaching in an organisation is measurable as long as the organisation maintains management information that can be compared over time. What is required of the researcher who is documenting this return is an understanding of the business and thoughtful reflection on how executive coaching has affected the people who do the work the data describes and how that data can be interpreted to demonstrate the return on the investment in executive coaching.

References

Patton, C. (2001) Rating the Returns, *Human Resource Executive*, vol. 15, no.5; 40-43

Morgan, H., Harkins, P. and Goldsmith, M. (2005) *The Art and Practice of Leadership Coaching – 50 top executive coaches reveal their secrets*, John Wiley

12

Making the case for coaching

In today's fast-paced organisations, even great proposals can fail to be implemented. Often this is not because they are flawed but because they never really get heard or seriously considered. This may be particularly the case for HR practitioners who frequently complain that they do not have the influence and standing at senior levels to secure attention and resources for their activities. Another related reason is that HR or training activities are sometimes dismissed by senior decision-makers as costs rather than investments.

Gaining the required resources and support for a coaching initiative requires HR to persuade a variety of stakeholders that it's a good idea. This means making a good case for the investment and selling it to the appropriate parties. Successful presentation of any business case requires careful planning and consideration. It takes time and effort, but it is necessary if you want your plans for coaching to become a reality.

It is important to remember that the other major group of people who frequently have to make the case for coaching are coaches themselves. Every time they pitch to a new client, they are likely to be faced by some people who are sceptical about what coaching can truly achieve. They will need to persuade these people about the benefits their coaching activities can deliver, and again this requires them to sell the business case for coaching. Although this chapter is mostly focused on helping HR practitioners, hopefully the information it contains will also be useful to those coaches who are looking for a bit more advice about making a successful case for coaching when they are seeking work.

WHAT ARE THE INGREDIENTS OF A SUCCESSFUL BUSINESS CASE?

It is hugely important to remember that making the case for coaching is not just a one-off effort – it should be an ongoing dialogue that reviews coaching activities and justifies the ongoing investment. Getting your senior managers to invest in coaching is only the first step – after that you will need to prove it is working by demonstrating what results it is delivering.

When you initially prepare the case for investing in coaching as an initiative, you will need to persuade sceptics and build support at senior levels. Preparation and forethought are vital. The more planning work you can do, the better – it really is a good investment of your time. There are a few key areas that it is worth considering in advance, which we now discuss in turn.

Understanding your stakeholders

You cannot present a case effectively if you do not know your audience. Do your homework and try to understand the perspective of your stakeholders. If you were in their shoes, what would your concerns and objections be? Why should they support your plans? Prepare your responses to their likely questions carefully, because it will help you to feel more confident.

Different stakeholders will have different agendas, and until you understand these you cannot assess what benefits will be relevant to each of them. The finance director, for example, may be concerned with cost savings or improved margins, while the operations manager may be more interested in improvements in staff retention or productivity.

A common mistake is telling the audience too much operational detail and falling short on the discussion of the business benefits. Although you are keen to tell them all about what the programme may look like, failing to focus on the business benefits will not help you to keep their attention or win support. Make sure your presentation highlights the outcomes rather than the inputs, and select benefits that will appeal to your audience.

Preparing your proposal and developing your strategy for coaching

Coaching is unlikely to be the only option that needs consideration. You must think through all the options so that you are truly sure that coaching offers the most cost-effective and appropriate solution. If after this analysis you decide that coaching is indeed the best solution, then part of selling the case to stakeholders is demonstrating that you have discussed and weighed up a number of options resulting in your recommendation of coaching as the best option.

It is highly likely that your stakeholders will want to know what evidence exists to demonstrate the value of coaching. You can use the literature reviewed in this book (and in other publications) for this purpose and demonstrate how your proposal is based on the best current thinking. The good news is that current research, although still a bit patchy in places, is painting a positive picture, despite a few caveats here and there – use this to your advantage when building support in your organisation. You can also use the case studies in this book to discuss how other similar organisations are using coaching to help them achieve their business goals.

One of the worrying findings from recent CIPD surveys was that two thirds of survey participants have no formal strategy for their coaching activities (CIPD, 2004). The benefit of having a strategy is that it provides a framework for discussion and implementation of coaching activities and also allows effective planning for the resources needed. When preparing your proposal to make the case for investing in coaching, you will need to develop an initial coaching strategy because you will find it extremely hard to gain interest and support for a vague or woolly proposal that has not been thought through. With regard to coaching, some of the initial things to consider are who will receive the coaching, when and why it will be offered, and who will be delivering it.

There is little doubt that almost everyone in your organisation – regardless of role – could potentially benefit from an additional investment such as coaching. Work is changing for everyone and everyone needs new skills just to stay in the game. However, when starting out, it is crucial to be selective by identifying and prioritising needs for coaching across your organisation. Equally, it is important to be clear when coaching is not an appropriate solution. Identifying the initial parameters for coaching will help you to develop your initial strategy for coaching and the key messages you need for your proposal. Presentation 1, provided later in this chapter, offers some questions for you to consider when planning the content of your proposal.

Deciding upon your key messages

Without a doubt, the most successful organisations we spoke to during our research had achieved strong buy-in for coaching by linking it with wider strategic goals and demonstrating how it can help managers and the business to achieve their targets. It seems that framing coaching in your specific business requirements, rather than simply introducing yet another new development initiative, really helps to build support for making an investment in this area. The main focus of your key messages should therefore be why an investment in coaching will support the organisation's strategic goals, and what benefits it will deliver. Other key messages should focus on the details of your coaching strategy, your suggestions for implementation, and the resources you require. Again, look at the slides in Presentation 1 later in this chapter for some prompting questions about what your key messages may be.

Remember that implementing a coaching initiative has costs as well as benefits, and it is the costs that will be the source of objections – whether these are in the form of disruption, resources or loss of control. When making your case it is important that your key messages clearly show that the benefits outweigh the costs.

Communication and building buy-in

Communication with stakeholders is an ongoing task. If you do win support and the resources needed, you will have to repeat the whole process – this time to secure the involvement and support of those who you need to help you with implementation. But firstly, you've got to get support for your initial proposal.

Once you know who your audience is and what messages you must get across, it is time to consider the most appropriate communication channels. This decision will be influenced by the culture and typical practices in your organisation, but think about a few alternative methods. Quite often a formal meeting will be the setting, but other more informal options are available. The more resistance you think you may face (eg perceptions that coaching is simply a fad or another fluffy HR initiative), the more important it is to try to influence stakeholders' views prior to a formal presentation or meeting so that you can build support early on. This gives stakeholders time to consider the proposal in advance, rather than being pushed into an on-the-spot decision

Delivering the case for coaching

No matter how much previous experience as a presenter you have, preparing and rehearsing is still important. First impressions do make a difference, and it is always worth taking time to check the detail. Check that your messages are clear and are appropriate to your audience. Another good idea is to think about possible objections or questions and to practise your responses. The more complex your proposal is, the more important it will be to provide handouts or reports to illustrate your rationale. At the end of this chapter we have provided you with some sample content for a series of slides that will help you design your own presentation – these can be shaped for your particular situation but will hopefully give you a canvas on which to build.

After you have given the initial presentation, the next challenge is to get your decision-makers to commit to a definite course of action. One technique for achieving this is to present not a single solution but a choice. This leaves the decision-makers feeling in control, and instead of forcing a cut-and-dried 'yes' or 'no' response to your proposal, you are increasing your chances of gaining support for part of your proposal even if it is not the full programme you would like to implement. One of your options should always be a fall-back position, perhaps asking for a pilot project rather than a whole company change, or a phased roll-out of a programme.

Don't sit back on your laurels

Winning support is no guarantee of retaining it. Ongoing communication is vital, and therefore providing regular progress updates, reporting quick wins and milestones to your stakeholders will help to maintain the momentum for the initiative. Keep communication and feedback channels open and deal with any problems that arise on a one-to-one basis as the project progresses.

EXAMPLE PRESENTATIONS FOR USE IN MAKING THE CASE FOR COACHING

To help practitioners make the case for coaching we have provided content for three different presentations that can be used:

- Presentation 1: Thinking through your proposal

- Presentation 2: Making the case for coaching – what does the research tell us?

- Presentation 3: Making the case for coaching – a proposal

These are designed to make you think through issues, to give you ideas, and for you to amend to fit your exact needs. You know your audience and so will be able to decide what you think will work best at persuading them. Are they fairly analytical and want to hear the evidence that supports your proposal, or will a top-level pitch work better?

Presentation 1: Thinking through your proposal

This presentation is for you to use internally within HR (or the coaching project team) in order to prepare your case for coaching effectively. It provides you with a number of questions that you will need to answer before you are able to present your coaching strategy. If you have a team working on the project, you can use this presentation as the basis for a discussion about the coaching strategy as well as to gather input and feedback. The information you gather will form the basis of your strategy and key messages.

1   Thinking through your proposal

2   Why coach?
- What is the attraction of coaching to our business? What will it help us achieve?
- How is coaching defined in relation to other development activities (eg mentoring, training etc)?
- How is coaching different, and why do we think it will help us?
- What evidence exists that coaching works?
- What are the experiences of other organisations who have implemented coaching (particularly our competitors)?

3   Options
- What other alternatives should be considered?
- The pros and cons of different options
- What does coaching offer that makes it the most appropriate solution?

4   How will coaching be used?
- Who is coaching going to be aimed at?
- What kind of issues will coaching address?
- What issues will coaching not be used to address?
- What benefits do we think it will deliver to the business?

5   Who will deliver the coaching?
- What type of coaching practitioners are needed to deliver the coaching?
- What level of skills and experience are required?
- The pros and cons of different coaching practitioners (internal, executive, manager, a combination?)
- Do we want to build up internal coaching capability or does using external resources make more sense?
- Do our managers have the time, skills and attitudes to be effective coaches?

6 **Cultural backdrop**
- Do we have an organisational culture that is supportive of learning and development?
- Will coaching 'fit' with the existing culture?
- What barriers exist to implementing a coaching initiative?
- Are we really willing to invest in changing the culture?

7 **Training coaches**
- Who will train our coaches? Internal/external providers?
- How will we select external coaches or training providers? What criteria?
- Are there exemplars of good coaching practice in the organisation already? Can they be used to support coach-training programmes?
- Do our managers have the basic level of good management/leadership skills, prior to training them as coaches?

8 **Supporting coaching initiatives**
- How will we support trainee coaches once they have learned the new skills?
- How will we safeguard their subordinates as they learn?
- What contingencies can we put in place?

9 **Evaluating and proving the impact of coaching**
- What benefits do we think coaching will deliver?
- What ROI are we expecting?
- What is the anticipated payback period?
- Is this realistic?
- How else could this money be spent?
- How are we going to measure the impact of coaching?
- Do we have sufficient resources and expertise to undertake evaluation activities?

10 **How will we implement?**
- A pilot programme to test what results can be achieved?
- A phased roll-out within the organisation?
- Who will drive the initiative? HR? A steering group from the business?
- Who will champion the initiative at senior management levels?
- How will communications be managed?

Presentation 2: Making the case for coaching – what does the research tell us?

This presentation will be useful to HR practitioners where stakeholders want to see an evidence-based approach that draws on research and latest thinking. It examines the research findings we reviewed in the central chapters of the book and condenses it into some simple slides that you can use as the basis of your discussion. Depending on the exact nature of your coaching activities, you can use the slides that are most relevant to you (eg if you are proposing a new manager-coach training programme, you probably will not need to use the slides relating to internal or executive coach). Explanations for each of the bullet points of the slides can be found in the relevant chapters of this book, and more/less information can be added if required.

1 **Making the case for coaching:**

What does the research tell us?

2 **UK organisations' use of coaching (CIPD, 2005)**

- Nine out of ten organisations use coaching by line managers
- Two out of three organisations use external coaches
- 84 per cent regard coaching by line managers as 'effective' or 'very effective'
- 92 per cent judge coaching by external practitioners to be effective.

A high level of use and belief in the power of coaching

3 **Beliefs about the power of coaching (CIPD, 2004)**

A high level of belief that it can deliver benefits to individuals and organisations

	% who agreed
Coaching can deliver benefits to both individuals and organisations	99
Coaching is an effective way to promote learning in organisations	96
Coaching and mentoring are key mechanisms for transferring learning from training courses back to the workplace	93
when coaching is managed effectively it can have a positive impact on an organisation's bottom line	92

4

> **What does the research evidence tell us about the impact and power of coaching in organisational settings?**
>
> - Manager-coaches
> - Internal coaches
> - External or executive coaches
> - Organisational conditions for effective coaching

---

5 ## Manager-coaches

> Of the different roles that the manager performs, the coach is 'the most difficult one to perform'
> (Geber, 1992)

- Large growth area – 88% of organisations train manager-coaches
- But not 'new'
- What is driving its popularity?
  - Culture change/business goals
  - Managers need to support development of their teams
  - Low levels of managerial skills
  - Cutting costs?
  - Reaching a wider audience

---

6 ## Manager-coaching

- How is it different?
  - Fairly narrow form of coaching
  - Managerial relationship is not one of equals
  - Coaching agenda restricted – focus on improving performance and technical skills
- Benefits of manager-coaches
- Limitations of manager-coaches
- Implications for skills and training

> Allows broader audience to receive coaching, but managers unlikely to have the same high level of skills as internal/external coaches

---

7 ## Manager-coaching: Does it work?

- 19% very effective; 65% effective (CIPD, 2005)
- Lack of research looking at impact on business performance, but a wealth of case studies
- Wageman (2001): Coaching and team design interact positively to impact on performance

> Limited research to draw on at this stage, but can review the experiences of other organisations

8   Results from case studies

The impact of manager coaching - 10 main areas:

- changes the culture or helps to embed a coaching culture
- improved management skills and capability
- behaviour change in the coaches
- benefits for the coachees as a result of receiving coaching
- greater employee engagement and commitment
- improvements to business indicators or results
- savings in HR time/costs
- achievment of external awards and recognition
- unexpected spin-offs
- accelerated talent development

9   Quotes from case studies

'The construction industry has traditionally been known for having a command-and-control management culture. What we've started through coaching is a more empowering and creative culture where people don't need to tell someone what to do or wait to be told themselves.'

'Coaching can have a very positive impact on individuals for whom traditional learning modes such as classroom teaching have very negative associations.'

'Feedback from the coachees is that managers have created better working relationships and were more effective in communicating with their teams – resulting in improved team results .'

10   'Business results were growing steadily and the staff survey results were improving so the programme must have been doing something right.'

'Feedback from participants' managers was positive – they noticed improvements in their performance and ability to manage their teams. And comparison of the initial and final 360-degree feedback results demonstrated real improvement in leadership and management competencies.'

'The organisation has identified clear performance differences between those who are coached and those who are not in terms of meeting targets and quickly addressing issues that arise.'

11   'Within just five months, the sales team had met their targets for the first time and within a year were continually surpassing them.'

'Through these efforts, the organisation has seen evidence of performance improvements. For example, product quality was improved by 19 per cent last year and sickness/absence was down from 7 per cent to an average 2.4 per cent.'

'Change is quicker as well as more focused as a result of the coaching interventions.'

12 'In the *Sunday Times* poll of 100 Best Companies To Work For we went from 78th to 42nd to 30th and we were voted Scotland's Learning Employer of the Year 2004 by Learndirect Scotland.'

'With this new approach to people management and development, we achieved an Investors in People award within 12 months and turned around their reputation from being a 'hire and fire' company to a company people actively seek to join. This represents a significant improvement in HR time and costs: 'We used to be hiring every week and I haven't had to recruit for the last four months.' Disciplinary events are much less common.'

13 ## Internal coaches

'A one-to-one development intervention supported by the organisation and provided by a colleague of those coached who is trusted to shape and deliver a program yielding individual professional growth' (Frisch, 2001)

- A relatively new form of coaching
- Often a mixture of HR professionals and managers with additional coach training
- Why are they popular? Build internal expertise, control costs, deliver coaching to more people, knowledge of the organisation, etc
- Roles of internal coaches: development, skills, business change, supporting other coaching initiatives, etc

14 ## Internal coaching: Does it work?

- All case study organisations believe it is effective
- Examples from research:
    - Olivero *et al* (1997): 22.4% increase in productivity after management training, but 88% increase after internal coaching
    - NHS Leadership Centre (Woolnough *et al*, 2004): 41% of coachees were promoted, compared to 15% of the non-coached group, and leadership skills and job satisfaction improved

15 ## Results from case studies

'Feedback from individuals is that they have never received anything like this before and are grateful for the support. Being picked out for "special attention" when the intention is clearly positive can be a driver for positive changes in behaviour.'

'We are seeing a number of results:
- re-engagement with role and organisation
- increased proactivity and capacity for addressing issues
- increased confidence
- greater awareness of management/leadership styles
- more effective management of challenging people
- greater awareness of career options and choices.'

16

> 'Coaching in conjunction with the process review teams has had a positive impact on the business in terms of cost reduction and business growth. It has also made staff more aware of and responsible for delivering the customer proposition.'

> 'Three of the original cohort of twelve on the programme were promoted within nine months, and five more are now working in broader work streams.'

> 'Coaching is having a positive impact on patient care. It has proved particularly valuable when challenging established practice and when problem-solving around service development.'

17

> 'Trained internal coaches acquire skills which are transferable to other development programmes providing an internal resource to support other initiatives. This has been a big and unexpected bonus for our organisation.'

But other unexpected results as well

> 'But there have been instances where coaching has resulted in people leaving the business because they have realised that they want a change.'

18
Issues to be aware of when using internal coaches

Issues	Implications
• Credibility	• Need for supervision
• Trust and confidentiality	• Thorough training
• Conflicts of interest	• Careful recruitment
• Fuzzy boundaries	• Regular review of activities
• 'Corporate blind spots' (de Haan and Burger, 2005)	
• Demand over capacity	

19
External or executive coaches

- Growing resource for UK businesses
- 4,000 professional coaches in the UK (FT)
- 64% of organisations use external coaches (CIPD, 2005)
- 69%: effective; 23%: very effective (CIPD, 2005)
- History:
  - Remedial 'rescue fantasy'
  - 'Coaching envy'
  - Huge growth area
  - But indications of a decline?

> Large-scale investments by UK organisations, but an increasing demand for evidence to verify its value and impact.

20 ## Executive coaching

- Organisations' reasons for using executive coaching (Carter, 2001; Horner, 2002)
- What is the role of an executive coach?
  - Free agenda coaching
  - Set agenda coaching by organisation
  - Skills, performance and development coaching (Cavanagh and Grant, 2005)
  - Support development of internal coaching capacity/ coaching culture
- How are executive coaches different from other coaches?

The different roles have implications for the skills executive coaches need

---

21 ## Executive coaching: Does it work?

- Dawdy (2004): 90% thought coaching was effective
- Free agenda coaching:
  - Wales (2003): improved self-awareness and confidence ➔ better communication skills ➔ improved behaviours
  - Laske (2004): improved mental-emotional growth
- In conjunction with other development activity:
  - Smither *et al* (2003): compared performance of coached and non-coached executives – improved 360° results
  - Thach (2002): overall percentage increase in leadership effectiveness 55% (phase 2) and 60% (phase 3)

22
- Return on investment
  - Right management consultants – 5.7% ROI
  - Philips (2005) – 221% ROI
- Colone (2005): Major international bank (case study)
  - Improved senior staff retention
  - Decreased recruitment costs
  - Decreased executive development costs
  - Productivity gains
  - Measuring ROI is possible, but requires thoughtful reflection by HR

---

23 ## Quotes from our case studies

> 'Coaching has enabled us to move from justifying our existence to becoming creators of value to our parent group and in two year-long phases, deliver significant shareholder value and both strategic and competitive advantage.'

> 'The company has seen visible improvements in how people relate to each other. Staff are more open about their plans in life and how they feel about their work. Rather than sitting on a plan or issue, people now come and discuss it with their manager.'

> 'With the help of the partner coaching company, X is further developing its high-performance and learning culture. When coaching is at the centre of an organisational culture, it improves morale and accelerates talent development. It helps us continue on our dramatic growth path.'

24 Issues to be aware of when using executive coaches

'We would like to have external coaches we can trust. However, we are often subjected to the hard sell and there is no current way to verify their qualifications or their competency....'

Existing issues
- Confusion in the marketplace
- Cost
- Recruitment difficulties
- Lack of internal knowledge

25 Conditions for effective coaching

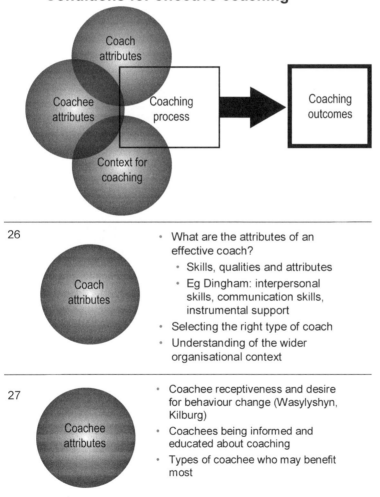

26
- What are the attributes of an effective coach?
  - Skills, qualities and attributes
  - Eg Dingham: interpersonal skills, communication skills, instrumental support
- Selecting the right type of coach
- Understanding of the wider organisational context

27
- Coachee receptiveness and desire for behaviour change (Wasylyshyn, Kilburg)
- Coachees being informed and educated about coaching
- Types of coachee who may benefit most

28

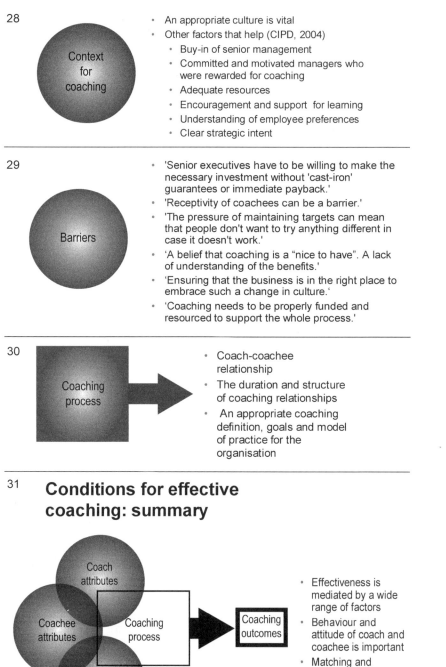

Context for coaching

- An appropriate culture is vital
- Other factors that help (CIPD, 2004)
    - Buy-in of senior management
    - Committed and motivated managers who were rewarded for coaching
    - Adequate resources
    - Encouragement and support for learning
    - Understanding of employee preferences
    - Clear strategic intent

29

Barriers

- 'Senior executives have to be willing to make the necessary investment without 'cast-iron' guarantees or immediate payback.'
- 'Receptivity of coachees can be a barrier.'
- 'The pressure of maintaining targets can mean that people don't want to try anything different in case it doesn't work.'
- 'A belief that coaching is a "nice to have". A lack of understanding of the benefits.'
- 'Ensuring that the business is in the right place to embrace such a change in culture.'
- 'Coaching needs to be properly funded and resourced to support the whole process.'

30

Coaching process

- Coach-coachee relationship
- The duration and structure of coaching relationships
- An appropriate coaching definition, goals and model of practice for the organisation

31 **Conditions for effective coaching: summary**

- Effectiveness is mediated by a wide range of factors
- Behaviour and attitude of coach and coachee is important
- Matching and ensuring a positive working relationship is critical
- Culture can often be a barrier

Coach attributes — Coachee attributes — Coaching process — Context for coaching — Coaching outcomes

32 ## Summary: Does coaching work?

- Research and case studies indicate that coaching can work
- But a number of contextual factors have to be in place
- Positive results seen from manager, internal and executive coaching
- But each type has issues to be taken into account
- Each organisation has to design its coaching activities to fit its particular culture and business circumstances

> Be cautious when interpreting the evidence – concerns remain about the robustness and design of some studies

---

Presentation 3: Making the case for coaching – a proposal

This short presentation contains some prompting slides that you can amend to produce your proposal presentation. It provides a simple framework for you to use, and allows you to insert the relevant information about your proposed coaching intervention. Depending on how much time you have to present your proposal (and the specific interests of your audience), you can add in as much content as you think fit, but remember your key messages and ensure that they are the focus of the presentation. Provide an opportunity at the end for questions.

1 ## Making the case for coaching:

A proposal

---

2 ## Why coaching?

- What is coaching? (*Provide your organisation's definition of coaching or one you think appropriate*)
- How it can help support our business:
    - X (*eg support culture change activities*)
    - Y (*eg improve staff turnover and retention*)
    - Z (*eg change the management style*)
- What are the risks of not implementing coaching?

---

3 ## What research evidence tells us

- The business benefits of coaching
    - Insert some relevant research evidence to support the type of coaching you intend to implement
    - Discuss competitors' use of coaching
    - Discuss benefits that can be achieved

4 Alternative options that have been considered

- Provide a list of alternative options (eg leadership development programme, bespoke Business School course, e-learning programme, training course)
- Provide a list of reasons for discounting them
- Provide reasons for why coaching is a better solution

5 Proposed coaching strategy

- Who? (*Coaching will initially be targeted at X employees - number, employee group*)
- When? (*Approximate timetable for coaching programme implementation*)
- Why? (*Review of business objectives and benefits it will bring*)
- How? (*Type of coaching that will be implemented - internal/manager/executive/combination*)
- What will it focus on? (*eg leadership behaviours, coaching skills for managers, free agenda, work-life balance, etc*)

6 Details of proposed coaching programme

- Provide details and exact parameters of coaching programme to be implemented
  - Eg Manager-coach programme (how many days' training, design of programme, who will deliver, who will attend, how learning will be sustained, etc)
  - Executive coach programme (criteria for providers, who will be eligible, how many sessions they will receive, whether agenda is open or set, arrangements for confidentiality, etc)

7 Resources required

- Costs of implementation (some examples):
  - Who will deliver the programme? (HR/external providers)
  - Physical resources (venues, support materials, etc)

- Other costs (some examples):
  - Senior management's/stakeholders' support and time
  - Participant time away from work
  - HR time and skills upgrading (do HR need further training?)

8   Assessing success

- Proposed methods for evaluation – some examples:
  - Setting relevant business objectives and assessing against them
  - Gaining participant feedback (and other stakeholders, eg managers, subordinates)
  - Monitoring changes in organisational culture and climate (eg employee satisfaction surveys)
  - Monitoring changes in individual performance or behaviour change (eg appraisal ratings, 360-degree feedback)
  - Monitoring changes in business KPIs or other targets (eg absence, turnover, recruitment costs, etc)
- Reporting to senior management (how will progress be reported, and in what format?)

9   Summary

- Summarise the key messages of your proposal focusing on the business benefits that can be achieved

10   Possible options

- Provide two or three options for your audience to consider
  - Eg Design and implement a pilot project to assess the value of the initiative
  - Eg Undertake further research in response to feedback/questions on the proposal before any major decisions are taken
  - Eg Take the proposal forward and develop a more detailed strategy and programme
  - Take no further action at the present time

SUMMARY

HR practitioners often have a tough time gaining resources and commitment to new initiatives, particularly if there are no 'true believers' or 'champions' of HR at senior levels in the business. Other business initiatives are often perceived to be a priority, and so it is essential for HR practitioners to spend time planning and thinking through how best to present their proposal so that they build maximum support. To make a successful case for coaching, think about which stakeholders you need to persuade, and take time to understand how your proposals will affect them. Build your business case using the research evidence available to you and frame it in the specific needs of your organisation. Keep your organisation's strategy in mind and focus the presentation on the business benefits that can be achieved, rather than on details of the operational processes. This will hold the attention of your stakeholders and build support. Consider approaching key stakeholders in advance of the presentation so that specific issues and concerns can be addressed. Decision-makers may react better if given a series of choices to consider rather than a 'yes' or 'no' decision. Give decision-makers a choice of alternatives, and prepare for questions or scepticism that you may face. Remember that if you secure approval for your proposal, there is still a long way to go – to maintain momentum, you will need to regularly communicate with your stakeholders to ensure that their support is sustained, and ultimately you will have to prove that the initiative is delivering the results it was designed to achieve.

Good luck!

Appendix
The case studies

Bovis Lend Lease: Establishing a coaching culture

Bovis Lend Lease is one of the world's leading companies in the project management and construction services industry. Landmark projects the company has been involved in include the Petronas Towers in Kuala Lumpur, Malaysia (currently one of the world's tallest buildings), the Sapporo Dome Stadium in Japan, Bluewater, Europe's largest retail and leisure development, and Disneyland, Paris. Today, the company has 7,500 employees in 93 offices worldwide.

Ever since Charles William Bovis founded the company in London in 1885, it has had a reputation for quality, innovation and commitment recognised by its large and loyal client-base throughout the UK. Customer service has always been fundamental to Bovis Lend Lease's success, but despite this, the company believed that there was room for improvement in building an even stronger customer service and leadership culture. In early 2001 Ross Gorbert, head of Learning and Development at Lend Lease Europe, started to look at ways he could create development programmes that would deliver genuine self-sustaining behaviour change in customer service and leadership. He explains:

> *Despite our perception that we offered customer service, in a competitive industry like ours, we knew we couldn't afford to become complacent. We wanted the key people in the business to think in terms of clients, not projects, and we also wanted them to examine how best they could further build profitable customer relationships and ensure that our thinking was focused with our customers.*

Building a stronger client focus

The first task for the external coaching company Bovis Lend Lease hired to work with them was to design a series of workshops to incorporate a greater customer service ethos and client focus among senior managers. The goal and vision was clear – to develop a client-centred organisation where people naturally focus on and think about their clients.

Initially targeting those in senior management, who would then go on to train and coach their subordinates, they ran Coaching for Business Success – Becoming More Client-Centric workshops for 150 individuals who were identified from the company's international talent pool, in groups of 18–25 people at a time. Five courses for European Global managers took place in the UK, three courses in the United States, and one in Australia. In addition, as a means of developing executives' interpersonal skills and to enhance their skills in developing profitable customer relationships, the external coaching company worked with Bovis Lend

Lease's Scottish region as part of a longer-term six-month coaching programme. Later, workshops and telephone coaching were also supplemented by 360-degree open feedback.

'Coaching managers to coach' and giving them the necessary tools to develop, empower and coach their own teams brought tangible results within Bovis Lend Lease. One of the attendees subsequently moved to head Bovis Lend Lease's Manchester office, where he applied the skills he had learned at a senior business level.

Further leadership and coaching initiatives

Following the success of the initial workshops, further work was planned to help develop the leadership skills and strategic thinking of senior business heads and European country managers. Again working with the external coaching provider, a module to form part of the company's Advanced Leadership programme was designed. The module consisted of an initial 360-degree leadership assessment, with group workshops supported by one-to-one executive coaching. A similar programme was also designed to form part of the Leading Business Transformation programme, which targeted more people within the organisation and took place over a six-month period. The external coaching company ran workshops that focused on enhancing personal leadership styles and helping employees fulfil their leadership potential.

The impact of coaching

The propagation of a coaching culture is gathering pace. Having provided managers with the skills and the mindset to 'coach' their own managers and staff, the result has been a proactive learning environment in which people think more for themselves and in which the customer remains at the forefront of the business.

Employees have also gained a great deal from the coaching programmes. Feedback from the workshops has been very positive and there has been a consistent increase in requests from employees who want to attend the programmes. From a business perspective as well, the programme is believed to have reaped dividends. Today, the client-centred approach applies to everyone within the company – not just to the traditional client-facing parts of the business but also to project managers who must always keep their customers' needs and strategic objectives closely in mind. Coaching is felt to have helped them provide a consistent and cohesive service worldwide as well as ensuring that the company is fully aligned with each customer's strategic goals. Ross Gorbert explains:

> *The construction industry has traditionally been known for having a command-and-control management culture. What we've started through coaching is a more empowering and creative culture where people don't need to wait to tell someone what to do or wait to be told themselves.*

Too often in the past the concept of executive coaching has been undermined by its 'touchy-feely' associations – it has not been considered a substitute for practical training courses, and has often been seen as a remedy to be applied to those who are poor performers. Bovis Lend Lease's experience has been quite the opposite – coaching has been a highly tangible, results-driven part of the organisation's development. Outstanding results have been achieved as a result of coaching the talent within the organisation. Ross Gorbert concludes:

CASE STUDY continued

We didn't set out to embed coaching in our culture, but as we created development programmes, including a coaching element, it has proved to be the most beneficial and most sustainable way of achieving behaviour change.

Information provided by Full Potential Group.

Boxwood Group: Coaching as a catalyst for behavioural change

Business performance improvement company the Boxwood Group is an organisation on the move. Having recently been positioned 11th on the *Sunday Times* Fast-Track 100 list following an average increase in sales of 168 per cent over each of the past three years, the company has over 80 employees and posted £10.7 million in annual revenues to the year ending March 2003.

Objectives and challenges

For all its successes in its seven-year history, it was important to Boxwood's senior management that the company continue to further enhance its client relationships. Vital to this was arming its people – particularly client-focusing consultants – with the tools they need to develop professionally and the motivation to deliver significant results which would be encouraged by transformational leadership. Furthermore, the company's impressive growth had brought with it the new challenges of being a bigger and more mature company. Jackie Hoare, Training Manager of Boxwood, says:

> *Despite our continued successes over the last few years, we knew we couldn't afford to be complacent both in our relations with each other internally and with our clients externally. When I arrived at the company in 2000, we had 24 people. By the start of 2004, this number had increased to more than 80. The demands on our people had changed and we needed the systems and processes to reflect this. We wanted to develop a greater learning and development culture throughout Boxwood and give senior management the tools to implement this. We also wanted to ensure that Boxwood was known for its capabilities in developing the human potential in client companies as well as its process-oriented approach. The result would be even stronger relationships with our clients.*

An internal survey backed the growing demand within Boxwood for greater focus on professional and personal development. It was at this stage that Boxwood started to look for an executive coaching and people development specialist company to partner. At the same time, Boxwood decided to implement a more rigorous performance development and review process. This aimed to provide greater clarity over individual employee competencies, development opportunities, development paths and the assignment of career coaches. To kick-start this programme, senior management had to acquire coaching skills which would allow them to take on the role of career coaches and ultimately help embed coaching within Boxwood's corporate culture. It was also hoped that coaching would provide managers with transformational leadership abilities, which was considered essential to a company looking to continue its dramatic growth.

The coaching programme

The external coaching company was brought on board in a substantial capacity after a series of discussions in the summer of 2004. Jackie explains:

> *The right personality fit and the ability to listen were the key criteria behind choosing our coaching provider. Rather than telling us from the outset what they could do for us, they listened, took on board our goals and challenged our thinking. It was this credibility and understanding of what we wanted to achieve which shone through in our early meetings.*

The goals of the coaching programme were:
- to progress a learning and development culture within Boxwood
- to provide managers with the skills to become competent coaching leaders capable of applying coaching principles and practices on a daily basis: this would lead to a peer coaching programme throughout the whole company, each senior manager being assigned the role of career coach
- to achieve enhanced employee commitment and understanding of their career development
- to improve and strengthen the relationship with Boxwood's clients, moving from a process-oriented approach to a people- and capability-oriented approach
- to encourage transformational leadership throughout the company.

Programme delivery

A five-month customised coaching programme was designed and delivered for Boxwood. All those in senior management, including the executive team, were participants in the programme – a total of 15 people. Boxwood's Managing Director, Chris Wakerley, was involved in every stage of the programme, emphasising buy-in from the very top:

> *Creating a high-performance environment where people feel challenged, excited and trusted requires the input and support of everyone. We see coaching as an essential ingredient for the development of our leaders and their team members. Through having a common understanding of an effective coaching style of leadership, we can continually transform our performance and ensure our whole team moves in the same direction.*

The coaching programme was led by an experienced coach from the external company who works internationally with senior leaders and teams. There were five phases to the programme:
- an initial briefing session that set the scene
- a skills development workshop
- a period to hone some of the skills learned
- a follow-up workshop session
- individual telephone coaching sessions.

The main goal of this five-stage approach was to reinforce coaching skills and key learnings. Rather than having a one-off workshop and then participants going back to their day-to-day routines, the company wanted to make sure that the coaching programme acted as a catalyst for real behavioural change. The concept of developing internal coaches within Boxwood was central to the programme. Each manager was required to take on the role of career coach as part of the new performance and development review process. Techniques deployed in training the managers included role-plays and the practical application of coaching tools and techniques in the workplace.

Outcomes and benefits

With the help of the partner coaching company, Boxwood is further developing its high-performance and learning culture. Although the corporate coaching programme only finished in December 2004, there is already an embryonic coaching culture within Boxwood. It is fuelled by the performance and development review process which has coaching at its heart. As Jackie Hoare explains, the introduction of career coaches outside of reporting lines has also resulted in greater cohesiveness within the company:

> *Through regular coaching sessions, many employees are communicating with people they previously had little contact with. It has really added to the sense of collaboration and behavioural change within the company. Rather than people working in isolation in their assigned service unit, today there is a greater awareness of what other people are doing and the challenges they face.*

The net result of the coaching programme to date is that more people at Boxwood feel they have a more structured career path and a clearer understanding of what they need to do to be successful. There is also greater evidence of transformational leadership throughout the company. It is intended that such behavioural change will be reinforced and validated through processes and robust measurement techniques, including employee engagement surveys and 360-degree feedback at individual and team levels.

Plans are under way to develop a second tier of coaches such that programme managers – clients' day-to-day points of contact – are provided with coaching skills that they can use with team members and clients alike. Jackie Hoare concludes:

> *More and more companies are realising that benefits from coaching can be substantial. When coaching is at the centre of an organisational culture, it can help improve morale and accelerate talent development. It can help Boxwood continue on its dramatic growth path. Leaders must realise that introducing a coaching culture is not simply a quick fix or something to delegate. It requires a willingness to really change behaviour over a substantial period of time. We're at the start of an exciting journey.*

Information provided by Full Potential Group.

BPB Paperboard: Coaching to support major organisational change

Two years ago, David Anderson, Managing Director for BPB Paperboard, introduced coaching as a means of encouraging his senior managers to think more laterally, develop a more open perspective and examine their interactions to see how working relationships could be improved. In the words of Les Morrison, Sales Manager, Global Paper Supply:

CASE STUDY continued

Coaching was provided to help to unite a disjointed team which functioned as a group of individuals but which needed to function as a single unit.

At the time, the company was experiencing a period of change. The Paperboard division had inconsistent performance levels and the UK manufacturing market was generally in decline because of competition and technology improvements led by the Far East, central Europe and America. The organisation undertook a major restructuring and culture change programme to meet the changing demands of the external business environment. The managing director specifically requested personal support via external coaching for the entire senior team throughout the change process and encouraged the development of coaching skills internally.

Why coaching?

Coaching was chosen over other training alternatives because team members were all starting from different places and had various skills, hang-ups, agendas and worries about the potential threat from change. 'We had to look at options because each team member needed something different,' says David Anderson.

Coaching is a very flexible breed of training, where the syllabus or agenda is informal and changes with the mood or circumstances of the moment. Formal training usually comprises listening to instruction and then attempting to put it into practice (if you can afterwards remember more than 10 per cent of what's been said). We 'lived' the coaching experience and hence could more readily adopt the changes we experienced.

The impact of coaching

Coaching at BPB is delivered as a mixture of individual coaching (face-to-face and by phone) by external coaches, alongside team days and mentoring. Murray Shearer, a BPB Paperboard senior manager who runs a paper mill in Scotland, says:

Coaching changed the team view of how our business was conducted. Initially, it made us look at ourselves and then at our interactions. It was a very effective process, particularly the one-to-one sessions, and the team definitely communicated and operated more effectively.

'Change occurred at a pace and level we hadn't envisaged,' says David Anderson. Initially, there was a resistance to openness and some suspicion about what outcomes were required. But this was overcome as individuals understood that they could drive outcomes rather than be victims of the change process.

Coaching helped the senior team to agree a common purpose, develop confidence as a team, identify how to recognise, modify and develop self-awareness and to better understand the team dynamic. Team members who were previously 'typecast' have moved on and up in the organisation. Others have seen a significant change in their roles. 'I have specifically noted a qualitative improvement in the team's acceptance of delegated tasks and am impressed by their contribution to the strategic restructure following the coaching sessions,' Anderson adds.

> *Coaching has enabled us to move from justifying our existence to becoming creators of value to our parent group and in two year-long phases deliver significant shareholder value and both strategic and competitive advantage. Our restructuring and the exploitation of unique market circumstances would not have happened without the coaching initiative. We are in the process of evaluating this, so my assessment thus far is based purely on my observations. But it is based on the fact that we have created tens of millions of pounds in shareholder value and improvements in safety and other key performance indicators measures on management performance.*

The impact on individuals

BPB Paperboard's Sales Manager, Les Morrison, says:

> *Coaching worked for me in the circumstances of major strategy changes and ongoing developments. But it may not work for others. Some claim coaching didn't help them, but we observed radical changes in behaviour in most participants during the coaching process – principally, people became more open, honest and better able to interact with their team.*

Initially, some people did not appreciate the subtle probing and intrusion into personal feelings and behaviour that the coaching necessitated. But it gradually became evident that dissection and examination of individual patterns of behaviour, emotional responses and reactions were valuable elements of decision-making in difficult circumstances.

What else changed along the way?

The coaching process was overshadowed by the decision to close the first paper mill. At this time the team expanded and the senior roles came under greater scrutiny. Coaching was used to facilitate the decision-making process and ensure that good choices were made. Two major changes were seen. The agenda items for meetings altered dramatically, the focus changing from past events to future actions, and the team began to function more autonomously. These are seen to be a direct result of the coaching input.

Challenges

The 'impenetrability' of some of the team participants was a hindrance. A further difficulty was that some participants' major personal issues got in the way of what they were trying to achieve. Anderson believes that for coaching to be effective, the management must believe it can lead to lasting and fundamental change: unless senior management and executives demonstrate honestly, openly and enthusiastically that they have bought into the process, it will not be successful.

Information provided by Richard Uglow, Managing Director, Enrichyou Ltd, and by David Anderson, Managing Director, BPB Paperboard

Canada Life: Using coaching to support business quality improvement and leadership development

Coaching in Canada Life is used in a variety of ways, but the two main applications are in supporting business quality improvement processes and as part of leadership development activities. Coaching is delivered by two internal coaches from the HR department who have the job title 'business consultant'.

Coaching to support business process review initiatives

Canada Life works with an external company to deliver two-day 'boot camp' business simulation programmes to help embed a process of continuous improvement within the business. During the programme, groups of employees work together to improve the customer experience by identifying ways to resolve ineffective business processes. After 'boot camp', employ-ees continue to work together in teams for a further 6–8 weeks, in some cases coming out of their business roles on a full- or part-time basis, to focus on applying the process of continuous improvement to their own processes. Process reviews take place across all areas of the business, including customer service, sales, finance, legal and HR.

Coaching is an integral part of the business process reviews. Each process review team has a clear mandate and an assigned internal coach who meets with them on a regular basis to coach them through a systematic process of continuous improvement which includes speaking to customers, gathering and analysing data, identifying root causes and implementing process improvements. Throughout the review the coach will support the team as they enter new territory, challenging corporate culture and cutting across divisional hierarchies to deliver processes that focus on customer and quality. Canada Life has been working to develop a measurement culture within the business, and therefore specific targets often form part of the business process review projects. This is particularly the case in service areas, where weekly and monthly customer service and productivity data is gathered. When a business process is identified for review, they identify baseline data about how productive and efficient the process is and use it to monitor improvements.

Evaluating coaching as part of business review processes

Due to the focus on measurement in the business, the internal coaches closely evaluate the progress of the business process reviews and the impact of coaching in helping the team achieve their targets. They generally use a 'gut feel' approach for assessing how well the coaching is working and evidence it by keeping a track of measures that reflect performance in the particular business area, as well as looking for signs that 'good management' is being practised. When the internal coaches coach the business performance review teams, they look at a variety of measures of success to assess the impact of the coaching intervention. Quantitative measures they consider include:

- quality improvement
- improvements in customer response times (cycle time improvements)
- improvements in feedback from customer surveys
- productivity improvement
- higher revenue and/or market share
- cost reduction.

The process review coaching is also assessed on a qualitative basis, the internal coach looking for evidence of:

- team commitment to tasks
- team involvement in and outside of meetings

- application/implementation of process steps
- grasping the opportunity to make change.

Coaching in conjunction with the process review teams has had a positive impact on the business in terms of cost reduction and business growth. It has also made staff more aware of and responsible for delivering the customer proposition. Linking coaching to business initiatives has been crucial for the credibility of coaching. Canada Life has been through a lot of change and the internal coaches realise that people can be sceptical and dismissive of new initiatives if they are not clearly linked to business needs.

Coaching for leadership development

Alongside coaching as part of the business process review initiatives, the internal coaches also coach individuals as part of leadership development activities. They coach leaders on general effectiveness and how best to deal with the challenges they face in their roles, as well as encouraging them to use coaching skills with their own teams. They additionally coach those leading transformation initiatives in the organisation to help them to lead and manage change effectively, considering the business goals as well as what is required from their staff in order for the goals to be delivered.

The internal coaches start by understanding what the coachee wants to achieve and how committed he or she is to achieving the goals. With commitment to move forward the coaches can work with the coachees as they identify what they need to do, by when, the options they have and the support they need. Each coach will keep a record of each session and use the notes at the start of the next session to review progress by asking the coachee to recall what he or she said he or she was going to progress between meetings. When the answer given matches the commitment he or she made at the last session and he or she has made progress, the coach can be confident that the coaching is having a positive effect. Once the goals have been established and outcomes identified further sessions are about finding out how it went, providing an opportunity for the coachees to feel good about their recent achievements, reflect on what they might have done differently and take time to plan the next steps away from their normal work enviroment. The results achieved by coaching in leadership development often depend on how supportive the individual's manager is about developing his or her report. Because managers' support is so important, the internal coaches always try to work with them to keep them engaged and involved in the coaching. These discussions also provide an opportunity to gain feedback on whether the manager has noticed changes in the individual's performance as a result of the coaching.

When coaching is used for leadership development within Canada Life, the evaluation measures used are different from those used in business process review coaching. Instead, they depend on the individual and his or her development needs. Examples of areas where coaches may look for qualitative data to assess the impact of coaching on improved management/leadership skills include:

- the number of team members with set objectives and development goals
- measuring improvements in staff satisfaction via the regular staff survey – the results are

analysed by the team, allowing HR to identify teams with poor results and to track improvements as a result of coaching
- capability – the number of staff going through capability procedures
- improvement in team members' job performance
- skills matrix – the percentage of key tasks covered by their team.

The majority of measures for leadership coaching at Canada Life are qualitative, and focus more on feedback, observation and a general sense of how the individual leader/manager is developing. The impact of coaching is assessed by internal coaches who observe whether the individual has made changes to his or her behaviour – has he or she taken the coaching on board, and has it made a difference? They look at:
- overall commitment to the business's objectives and the team
- regular team one-to-ones taking place and planned for the year
- clarity around objectives for the team
- ability to deal with their own manager and ensure clarity of expectations and influence
- measures in place for team performance and regular review of progress of the leader, team and individuals
- new starter/transfer/exit interviews providing positive feedback
- the manager reporting satisfaction with their progress and performance
- process improvement initiatives undertaken with positive results
- whether they turn up on time for coaching, are prepared for meetings and have followed up on actions from last meeting and put any learning points into practice
- their commitment to the coaching and whether they see the value and benefits it delivers.

Attitudes and barriers to coaching within Canada Life

Time pressures, the view that coaching is 'fluffy' and some managers resisting coaching are all issues the business consultants have had to deal with. Another significant barrier to coaching has been the culture in some parts of the business that is still heavily focused on tasks and targets and means that people do not always make time for coaching. The business consultants realise that demonstrating the benefits of coaching and gaining commitment of senior managers are key ways of overcoming these barriers.

Attitudes towards coaching at Canada Life are varied. Some groups are excited about the potential of coaching and others simply pay lip-service to it. Senior managers are now generally supportive of coaching because they have seen positive results coming through from coaching activities. They also realise that they need to develop skilled people and future leaders and value coaching as a means of doing this. Some managers have initially resisted the efforts to evaluate and measure progress, but this is soon overcome as they understand that it helps them to focus on what they want to achieve and allows them to demonstrate to their bosses how they have improved their team's performance and contributed to the business.

The internal coaches have noticed that coaching can inspire people and make them enthusiastic and more engaged in their work. Some individuals have blossomed as a result of coaching, having gained a greater appreciation of the influence and impact of their role. Managers have taken more ownership of their work and the customer processes they manage, moving away from always checking with their boss to actually presenting ideas and solutions instead. But there have also been instances where coaching has resulted in people leaving the business as they have realised that they want a change. In these instances, coaching is still considered to have had a positive impact. If people are not engaged in their work, they are unlikely to be performing effectively for the business.

Other coaching activities at Canada Life

Coaching skills and techniques are also used by the business consultants informally in a range of business settings, but these are often not labelled as coaching. Informally, coaching can develop individuals who are key to the business but who may feel threatened by formal coaching. This works in the form of 'catching up' by phone or in meetings on specific subjects, with a focus on reflecting with them on their experiences, specific areas of delivery, the impact of their actions and their plans going forward. Alongside this, other informal coaching activities are regularly undertaken by HR and managers. For example, members of HR coach more junior managers and supervisors on dealing with HR issues as a result of individual requests. And line managers coach their team members and help them to develop their skills and improve their performance.

Overall, coaching is considered to be an accessible, effective and efficient way to improve employee performance that can be aligned to meeting the needs of the business.

Information provided by Karen Boanas, Business Consultant

Courtenay HR: Coaching for performance improvements and to create an open working culture

Coaching at Courtenay HR started by accident. The company was developing a new product as part of its executive HR search and selection services – a development programme for HR professionals which included a coaching component. While identifying suitable coaches to deliver the coaching part of the programme, one of the coaches offered the managing director free coaching sessions as a trial. The MD confessed that he didn't take it that seriously. But after four sessions his perspective had completely changed. Coaching raised his self-awareness and made a huge difference to his management style and how he managed his work relationships.

Following the MD's own positive experience, coaching was offered to a senior search consultant who was feeling demotivated and at a crossroads in her professional and personal life. This was resulting in a number of things including tensions within the team. She, too, found the coaching hugely beneficial: it helped her separate work from personal issues and consider them individually, and her work relationships improved dramatically.

Although Courtenay HR is a small business, a coaching programme was introduced for all client-facing staff (12 people). The coaching programme comprises 6–8 sessions, generally over 12–15 months. In the first session, the individual sets an agenda and four or five goals with the coach. Although managers specify or encourage staff to focus on certain work-oriented objectives, the coachees are also encouraged to discuss any personal issues they are facing.

The decision to allow the individual to focus on both personal and work goals is seen as a crucial part of the success of the coaching initiative. As the MD explains:

It's inevitable that personal issues impact on people's working lives. You just can't separate work from life outside work – you must recognise and accept that you can't get away from the impact of people's personal lives on their ability to perform at work. If you limit coaching discussions to work issues/goals, you're limiting the potential outcomes of coaching.

The company currently uses two external coaches to deliver the coaching. The MD now sees a different coach from the original one he employed in order to prevent ethical concerns about his being both a coachee and the 'client' for the coaching services he is providing for his staff. The coaching sessions are fully confidential, although some non-specific feedback is provided by the coach with the permission of the coachees. Quarterly, the coach provides top-line feedback on the common messages coming through from the group of people being coached. This has proved to be a useful exercise for the leadership team.

Coaching has replaced other development interventions in the last few months. As a small business, they had struggled with sourcing effective training, finding that programmes did not hit the mark, were too generic or did not suit the style of the company. An example of this is a business development training programme that while seemingly a good course, failed to change people's behaviours when they got back to work and therefore did not have a lasting impact. The MD believes that coaching offers a more personal approach to skills development that is more effective because it is a deeper learning process.

The impact of coaching in Courtenay HR

Since the introduction of coaching in October 2004, the company has seen visible improvements in how people relate to each other in the business, as well as in their ability to discuss their personal development and career needs. Staff are more open about their plans in life and how they feel about their work. Rather than sitting on a plan or issue, people now come and discuss it with their manager. This means that the business gets early warning signals about potential problems before they get too serious and while there is an opportunity to take action to address them. And people are not scared of saying 'I might not be here in 12 months' time.'

One of the spin-offs has been that managers receiving coaching are beginning to use a coaching style of management themselves with administrative staff. While they are not formally receiving training in coaching skills, they are receiving tips from the coach on managing issues and communication in their teams. This is resulting in managers adopting some coaching skills in their day-to-day management style, which, again, is having positive effects.

The most significant change for the organisation is a raised awareness of people's different interpersonal styles and shortcomings when dealing with other people. People now give each other more time and try to understand the other person's perspective. There is a lot less conflict and fewer misunderstandings, which has created a healthier, more positive working climate.

To date, the behaviour changes resulting from coaching have largely been sustained, but it is still early days. Inevitably there are slips, but on balance, because coaching has altered the culture to one where things are talked through, backward steps are easier to address. Coaching has provided a point of reference for behaviour in the organisation and this can be used to bring things back on track.

Evaluating the impact of coaching

Coaching is felt to have helped people make leaps in their performance. These performance changes have not been formally evaluated or measured, partly because in a small business it is much easier to notice changes in behaviours and improvements in performance. Managers have certainly reported improvements in participants' performance and the success of coaching is widely discussed throughout the business.

Although higher-level evaluation has not taken place, the company is tracking achievement of the goals set at the start of the coaching programme (at both an individual and organisational level). This was something strongly encouraged by the coach, who sets goals with each individual, but who also set some goals with the client (the MD) for the whole coaching programme. Some of these programme goals related to the performance of the company but others were more qualitative in nature, relating to the culture and leadership style in the organisation. The coach tracks progress towards goals and meets with the MD on a quarterly basis to update him on progress.

Lessons learned about the use of coaching in business settings

The MD firmly believes that coaching is basically a big dose of reality for people and the businesses they work in. He feels that many organisations are not prepared for the outcomes that arise from coaching and do not know how to deal with them. For example, one coachee who made significant improvements in performance and managing relationships following coaching has reassessed the balance between her personal and career aspirations and she is now leaving the organisation. But the MD feels that despite the end result, coaching has provided a positive environment for such discussions. Instead of simply handing in the required notice, she has given six months' notice to allow the company time to find a replacement and ensure a smooth transfer of clients. This is extremely valuable in a small business.

In terms of lessons learned, the MD thinks the most important thing is to get the right coach. He says you need someone who will suit the company and the individuals working there, but who also has the right credentials. He feels it is a valuable investment to spend time seeing a number of coaches and to get feedback from people who have worked with them before. In particular, Courtenay HR found that industry experience was helpful. Both coaches employed by the company are ex-HR professionals and so they fully understand the context of the business.

The future of coaching at Courtenay HR is as yet unknown. The coaching programme is still only in its early stages, so the company will continue to monitor progress and look at next steps in a few months' time.

Information provided by Gareth Jones, Managing Director

Dixons Group: Building a network of senior internal coaches

Dixons Group's business goals are to provide effective and efficient service for customers, differentiating themselves from their competitors with their outstanding product knowledge and customer service. To achieve this, they realise they need managers and leaders who encourage high employee engagement and commitment. As Camilla Aitchison, Dixons Group's director of management development says:

> *You're not going to get high-quality customer service by applying the dictator model of leadership.*

One of Dixons' main business objectives is to change the culture in the business from a directive culture to one in which leaders/managers act as coaches. To make the shift, Dixons Group has implemented a coach-training programme in the business to build up a network of internal coaches. By building coaching skills, they intend to motivate employees to achieve high performance and encourage them to work out solutions for themselves, resulting in improved service for the customer.

Becoming an internal coach at Dixons Group

Coaching at Dixons began as a pilot in-house programme in summer 2004. Coach training was initially pitched at senior managers/junior directors who run large teams and have an influence across the business. After two pilot groups of 15 people had attended the coach training, the positive impact and feedback led to a long waiting list of people wanting to go on future programmes.

To become an internal coach at Dixons Group, individuals fill in a request form to apply for the programme. Applicants are invited to a one-hour interview to assess whether they have the right attitude and approach to helping others to develop and improve their performance. Camilla Aitchison explains:

> *You need people who won't bring their personal agenda to the table and who can detach themselves from their own situation to focus on the coachee's needs. We're looking for people who genuinely want to help other people to develop.*

The vast majority of applicants are accepted on the programme, but occasionally someone does not have the requisite approach and it is not suitable for them.

Dixons Group's coach training programme

Dixons is a highly pragmatic retail organisation and both the coaching programme and the coaching provider needed to suit their culture. They were looking for coaches who offer a structured, specific and pragmatic coaching programme that fitted the style of the business. Nine different coaches were interviewed and the successful candidate proposed a programme that met Dixons' needs and who generally seemed to demonstrate good chemistry with the Dixons Group culture.

The external coach works with two master coaching practitioners from training and development (T&D) to deliver a five-day in-house coaching programme. The programme comprises 30 per cent teaching, 50 per cent skills practice in threes, and 20 per cent discussion. During the programme they cover a number of different topics, including:

- recognising differences
- eliciting people's motivation to change
- building development plans
- building a high level of rapport
- NLP interventions around change.

The approach to coaching at Dixons is heavily based on NLP techniques, because the company believes it fits well with the needs of a sales/retail business and is aligned with the direction they want the Dixons culture to take. On the last day of the course, participants' coaching skills are assessed while they practise on a 'real-life coachee'. This enables coaches to practise their skills initially in a supportive environment. And they continue coaching the coachee after the programme has finished. Dixons wanted to provide internal certification for their coaches to recognise that they have reached a certain level of coaching skills, so at the end of the course participants are given a certificate that states they have been trained and are now accredited internal coaches.

Delivering coaching within Dixons Group

Once trained, coaches are expected to act as internal coaches within the business. The coaching is completed on top of their day jobs but is limited so that each coach has no more than two or three coachees at any one time. Receiving coaching is open to anyone in the company, but at the moment it tends to be head office staff at management levels.

Dixons runs a clearing house for coach–coachee matching via the training and development website. Individuals requesting coaching are matched up, by the T&D team, with coaches in training or those who have completed the programme. Because those in the team do not know everyone in the business on a personal basis, a form has been developed to elicit information about the individual's interests, issues and background. Individuals requesting coaching are asked to fill in this form to help with the matching process. To date, the matching process seems to be going well, the majority of coach–coachee relationships working successfully.

Transferring learning back to the workplace

Within the business, six HR practitioners have been trained as master practitioners. Master practitioners receive ten days' coach training rather than five and have access to 29 hours of e-learning CD-ROMs on coaching models, theory and techniques. Essentially, the master coaches learn a greater number of models and techniques and undertake more practice as part of their training. The master practitioners act as an internal resource, helping managers who are training as coaches and also advising and guiding trained coaches in the business as issues arise. The Dixons T&D team has also designed and produced a booklet incorporating information, tools and techniques for coaches to use after they have completed the coach training. This type of support provides coaches with some guidance materials to use when they are back at work.

Creating a community of coaches

Dixons now has a community of 60 managers who have been trained as coaches. Via the T&D website this group can circulate stories and discuss their learning and progress (both what has gone well and what has not). The T&D team also uses the website to set up events for coaches to come together to share best practice and keep their skills up to date. For T&D, these events provide an opportunity to ensure that coaches are staying true to what they were taught on the programme, because the team feels it has a responsibility to the coachees to check the quality of the skills and approach being used by the internal coaches.

Evaluating and learning as they progress

At the moment Dixons are undertaking some evaluation of their coaching activities, but are finding it difficult to establish quantifiable results. They have received some fantastic anecdotal stories by asking people about their experiences and what they have seen as a result of the coaching programme. These 'good news stories' are circulated to the coaching community for their learning.

A questionnaire is sent to the coaches after the training programme to assess how useful it was and what changes they have experienced since. These questionnaires are followed up with a telephone interview. Changes that have been reported include:

- Managers are better at selecting new team members.
- Managers are better at having conversations about issues, and problems are resolved more quickly.
- People are going home and having better relationships with their families.

As yet, they have not attempted to quantify the bottom-line impact of the coach training. But two other forms of positive feedback have been seen. Demand for the coaching programme is growing as a result of the positive feedback from previous participants, and there is now a waiting list of senior people booked to attend the course, including one managing director.

To build on the success of the internal coach programme, a two-day coaching module for middle managers is currently being developed that will form part of the management development programme. It is hoped that these managers will have experienced being coached by their managers and that this course will then cascade coaching skills down to the next level in the organisation. Coaching is shifting from being 'the in thing to do' to becoming a way of behaving and managing people at Dixons. This positive shift in the culture and management style is something they have seen develop over the last 18 months. Ultimately, they want coaching to become a 'hygiene factor' in the organisation – everyone has to coach.

Information provided by Camilla Aitchison, Director, Management Development

Everest: Supporting coaching through development of a guide to coaching

Everest has adopted coaching as a framework for supporting staff to develop key business results. Everest uses a range of different types of coaching, but the majority is delivered by an internal coach in the HR department. Coaching is also used in the business to support succession planning, to help individuals make the transition to new job roles and to enhance the career progression of key employees. While there is an emphasis on achieving performance improvements and key targets, coaching is also designed to develop employees' abilities, potential and self-awareness.

Supporting coaching in the business

Everest has established a number of features to support the coaching process. These include clear targets, strong support from senior management, sponsoring the signing-off of personal learning plans, and the creation of the *Everest Guide to Coaching* which everyone receives. This covers such areas as:

- What is coaching?
- What is a coach?
- How does it start?
- How often should it happen?
- What paperwork is involved?
- Who is involved in coaching?
- What if my coach gets stuck?
- Why is coaching successful?

The *Guide* has further information in the appendices covering progress review, reflection, personal learning plans, and an ethical code. Everest hopes that the *Guide* will provide a resource for coaches and coachees to use and also sets expectations and guidelines about how coaching relationships should run. The use of the *Guide to Coaching* backed by an explicit ethical code is a key feature of the support structure at Everest.

Everest have found that coaching works best when it is supported by other development initiatives, believing that this helps to make coaching 'a more well-rounded process'. As part of this, learners regularly work with buddies or join leadership forums alongside the coaching relationship.

Measuring effectiveness

There is a commitment to measuring the effectiveness of coaching through the success of those coached, and the idea of coaching as a journey for both the coach and the learner. So, while there is an emphasis on achieving goals and improving performance, coaching is also designed to help the individual measure and evaluate his or her own progress in terms of skills and behaviours.

Assessment of the success of coaching takes place via a number of different mechanisms. Triad meetings (coach, manager and individual) are held at regular points during the coaching to pinpoint progress, and feedback is sought from all these parties. Results from a 180-degree feedback exercise (provided as part of the CIPD coaching qualifications) has allowed them to benchmark their activities against those of other organisations. This has demonstrated that their 180-degree coaching results are just above the national average. Feedback from sponsors and line managers has been positive, and this has resulted in requests for more coaching for other people in the business.

Information provided by Lynn Davidson, Internal Management Development Consultant

Glenmorangie: Developing manager-coaches

Coaching had been carried out in Glenmorangie on an informal basis for a number of years, but two years ago the company ran an employee satisfaction survey which kick-started them into taking coaching more seriously. Training and Development Manager Morag Mathieson explains:

> *The survey identified that the employees did not feel that our managers had good interpersonal skills. We therefore formally instigated a new management development programme.*

As a result, the company embarked on designing a programme to quickly and efficiently upskill the 60 management staff employed at the plant.

The management development programme

The programme was developed through an external supplier and is delivered using a residential workshop and then followed up with several monthly action learning sessions at Glenmorangie's Broxburn plant. The focus of the programme is development of the managers' people skills, and central to it is their development as manager coaches. It is a nine-month programme that starts with the assessment of managers' current skills and development needs using 360-degree feedback.

> *This needs to be done in a supportive atmosphere, and a residential environment is perfect.*

The core of the programme is an action learning set where participants develop their coaching skills to tackle the real-life issues confronting them in their work. The T&D manager explains:

> *The whole delivery mode of the programme is coaching, so they are coached themselves and are expected to coach each other within the programme.*

The programme ends with another 360-degree feedback assessment that is used by the individual and the coach to design a development plan for the future. Following on from the programme, regular mini-360-degree assessments are undertaken with the manager and their team as part of an ongoing contribution to the development plan. As Morag explains:

> *It takes the learning from the broad brush of the Management Development Programme through to the specific aims of the individual in terms of their continuing work with their line manager and team.*

There are compulsory courses for people who have responsibility for a team, and every manager must attend them. This approach paved the way for managers taking part in the management development programme as they accepted that it was part of their role as a manager. Initially, the Training and Development team built the credibility of the programme by gaining the involvement and support of a selection of managers. Morag says,

> *We put our most challenging managers through first, and by the time the second group were going through, the programme was on a roll and hasn't looked back. It took about seven months before we saw real benefits of the programme and in the meantime we had to keep getting feedback from managers who were going through it to keep the faith and our belief that the design of the programme was good.*

Evaluating the impact of coaching

Glenmorangie has undertaken a range of initiatives to assess the impact of coaching over the last two years, including:

- analysis of the pre- and post-360-degree feedback results
- assessment of changes in the employee attitude survey
- the changing position in external polls such as the *Sunday Times* 100 Best Companies To Work For
- feedback from participants and their managers
- success with tackling the issues managers work on during the action learning sets.

Feedback from participants' managers was positive – they noticed improvements in their performance and ability to manage their teams. And comparison of the initial and final 360-degree feedback results demonstrated real improvement in leadership and management competencies. However, Glenmorangie does not feel that the 360 results alone are a reliable measure because other factors were also changing for the individuals. In many cases, those that they had reporting to them had changed and those that were the same had an increased familiarity with the process that sometimes led to their being more critical the second time around.

Glenmorangie has also experimented with some more innovative forms of evaluation. Morag says:

> *We have tried to assess whether managers behaved more competently through a variety of evaluation methods, but at the end of the day we realised that we could spend a lot of time and resources trying to measure something which we were evaluating informally all the time.*

Many people in the business did not see the need for formal evaluation because of the high visibility of the results of the programme. Morag explains:

> *The managers were reporting that they saw significant improvements in the way people were working and asked why we needed to evaluate any more than that. Business results were growing steadily and the staff survey results were improving, so the programme must have been doing something right. In the Sunday Times poll of 100 Best Companies To Work For we went from 78th to 42nd to 30th, and we were voted Scotland's Learning Employer of the Year 2004 by learndirect Scotland.*

Lessons learned, and progress

The programme itself has evolved over the last two years as the company has seen what has worked well or less well. For example, initially, participants focused on a specific project during the action learning sets, but it became clear that greater benefits could be achieved if they focused on a specific area of their current work – eg a current management or team issue they faced. This change helped to integrate and align the programme with managers' current workload.

As a result of the programme, managers are now more confident and willing to contribute to the provision of training themselves – for example, helping to deliver training courses in their area of specialism for employees. This brings them into contact with other employees and promotes the concept of coaching within the company. The culture of learning and coaching is continuing to evolve and managers are now coaching outside their core remit and direct reports.

> *Obviously there must be a bit of give and take, as the manager has a full work load, but it is a developing area. In the future, we are keen to use the expertise the managers have developed and identify them as champions of an area where they can act as internal coaches.*

Information provided by Morag Mathieson, HR Manager

The Greater London Authority: Coaching to support career development for women

The Greater London Authority (GLA) is the strategic body with the responsibility for delivering the elected mayor's vision for the capital city. It is made up of a directly elected mayor, a separately elected assembly and some 670 staff to help the mayor and assembly in their duties. In recent years, the GLA has undertaken a series of initiatives aimed at enhancing the career development and opportunities for female employees of the GLA. The mayor has consistently stated that his commitment to equality and diversity is one of the underpinning elements in his vision for London. Women are represented in many senior posts in the organisation, such as director of finance, executive director of services and within the mayor's office. However, despite setting targets for the proportion of women in the workforce and using progressive recruitment mechanisms, women remain underrepresented at senior grades, and staff turnover at middle and junior levels has been quite high.

Developing the programme

The women's coaching programme was created because it was felt that a number of women in less-well-paid jobs 'didn't quite know how to move on, where to go and what to do'. Two focus groups were held in May 2003, one for female employees from black and ethnic-minority groups and one for any female employees. Similar themes emerged from both groups. Some participants felt that the organisation had a male-oriented culture; some felt that the GLA insufficiently implemented its commitment to career development; and some felt they did not have adequate support from their line manager and, importantly, did not know how to address this constructively.

CASE STUDY continued

It was evident that a development programme for women must recognise that because the GLA is a small organisation with limited possibilities for upwards movement, career development and progression opportunities must involve lateral as well as vertical career steps. Accordingly, a specification for a contract to design and deliver an appropriate and innovative programme was prepared and submissions invited from consultants. A budget costing of £2,000 per participant was agreed at this stage. The GLA was open to different models of intervention, but the following points formed the core of the specification document:

- a sound demonstration of coaching as a development model or approach and, in particular, how it can be used to benefit women in organisations
- a strong awareness of diversity issues, especially those facing black and ethnic-minority women in the workplace
- understanding how the success of the scheme can be measured
- addressing key themes identified from the focus groups, including work–life balance, career direction and mobility, organisational culture, confidence and assertiveness
- an explanation of options for how the programme could be delivered, highlighting the time spent per client and the types of communication to be used, with a demonstration of flexibility and responsiveness to changing needs also being desirable
- advice on encouraging buy-in from line managers, including an explanation of their role in supporting the programme.

The programme in practice

The successful consultancy designed and delivered a programme that gave each participant 12 hours of individual coaching, a detailed workbook to complete, and participation in three workshops. Each workshop lasted for a full day, and explored the following topics:

- clarifying career and life goals, and developing strategies to implement them successfully
- gaining greater understanding of individual styles, and how others perceive this
- reviewing approaches to personal and professional development
- building strategies for balancing work and home responsibilities
- encouraging networking, and drawing on mentors for support
- growing self-confidence in own abilities, and considering how to maximise opportunities in the workplace.

Additionally, there were three planned meetings of action learning sets over the duration of the programme, although sets often met more frequently in their own time. The coaching programme lasts for six months. The first programme, with 16 participants, began in autumn 2003; the second, with 12 participants, began in autumn 2004. There is a transparent nomination and selection procedure. Interested participants discuss taking part during their annual performance review and their line manager must present a business case for their participation, which must be supported by the director. Nominations then go forward to a selection panel. To date, there have been twice as many nominees as places and one key task is to give supportive feedback to the unsuccessful applicants.

CASE STUDY continued

The impact of the programme

So far, the programme has been highly successful. Some individuals have benefited in terms of immediate advancement – ie they have secured better jobs inside or outside the GLA. Equally important, though, have been the softer outcomes. Participants feel more positive and confident about their future and their ability to manage the challenges that lie ahead. This resulted, for example, in some applying for jobs that they would not previously have considered. Among the feedback received were the following statements:

- 'Helped me to clarify and prioritise – made me realise that the goals I had previously set myself were in fact not my goals but someone else's. Made me focus and re-evaluate.'
- 'Has resulted in a change in my working hours so I can balance home and work. Would not have done this before the programme – the programme has helped me to re-assess my lifestyle.'
- 'I'm achieving career goals as I am talking to my line manager more.'
- 'Made me think back to what I always wanted, the values I hold.'
- 'Within the group I did not feel alone, I could see a link with us all. We all learnt something from each other.'
- '360-degree feedback was good. I was scared at first, and the negative feedback was hurtful. However, as a result, my behaviours have changed.'

The effect in the organisation has also been very positive. Line managers have commented on the improved contribution from participants, and improved performance feeds back into the whole organisation. The scheme has also been highlighted in the mayor's annual report to Londoners as a tangible demonstration of the GLA's commitment to gender equality. In turn, this reflects well on the GLA's ambition to be an exemplar employer. In the next few months, the GLA intends to embed the approach used in the programme into the organisation. One way of achieving this is by training six volunteers from each group to work as facilitators for the action learning groups. This starts to build a critical mass of useful expertise within the organisation, after the programme has finished.

The women's coaching programme does not involve a 'taught' element. Instead, it provides an appropriate framework and support for self-development and insight, while also building confidence and self-esteem. The GLA feels strongly that this is the most appropriate response for a diverse group of women who will be starting from different life-points, but who may also share universal issues. They reject conventional thinking about women-only programmes, which often start from the premise that they have skills and experience deficiencies. Instead, they believe that women, in particular, respond very positively to interventions that explicitly cater for their learning styles and career issues, which are often complex and hard to define. This is why the GLA programme is so powerful. The mixture of activities are both challenging and supportive, and are felt to offer the best of individual and group learning.

Information provided by Angela Goldberg, former Learning and Development Manager at the GLA, now a Consultant at GatenbySanderson

High & Mighty: Collaboration with an external funding body to design business effectiveness coaching

High & Mighty (H&M) is a family-run business which has evolved from a traditional, somewhat matriarchal management style towards the development of a learning culture. As the company has developed, the management structure has flattened considerably and communication pathways have been expanded to assist the flow of information to staff. The management style expected of its managers is a coaching style and the HR department is available to deliver informal coaching and support for managers.

Coaching in the retail sector

The retail sector has traditionally employed some people who may not have attained their full potential in education. Coaching is felt to be particularly helpful in supporting staff from this background in developing their skills. As Nicky Hillier, H&M's Personnel Manager, points out:

> Coaching can have a very positive impact on individuals for whom traditional learning modes such as classroom teaching has very negative associations. It is possible to spot and develop the potential of employees and hence their contribution to the organisation through coaching.

Coaching is considered to have worked well for the company in this situation and Nicky illustrates her view by describing the development of a return-to-work employee whose personal development plan a few years ago included 'learn to send an email' and who is now responsible for the payroll of the company.

The company had used external coaches in the past but had concerns that externally provided coaching failed to focus sufficiently on the needs of the business. As Nicky has noted: 'There can be an issue about who is the client.'

Manager coaching and coaching by HR therefore remain the main ways for coaching to be delivered. No formal training is given to the managers to develop their coaching skills, although the HR department regularly coaches managers on an individual basis to help them improve the coaching skills they use with their teams. Each employee has an individual learning plan linked to the annual assessment process. Managers use coaching techniques to help employees achieve their plan.

Coaching is now accepted as 'the way we do things around here'. The company has gained Investors in People status but is also the only retail company to have been awarded the Matrix standard. Nicky Hillier believes that achieving the standard has helped to improve employee engagement because they were part of the accreditation process and so feel ownership of the process.

Taking part in a Learning and Skills Council-funded pilot programme

The positive climate and attitude towards coaching that exists in the business makes it unsurprising that the business was enthusiastic when offered the chance to pilot a specialised coaching programme designed to specifically address business issues in the retail sector. Jo Davies of SkillSmartRetail in collaboration with SEEDA had secured funding from the Learning and Skills Council to look at in-depth personal development in the retail sector. The pilot programme was designed and funded because of problems with training in the retail sector – eg low take-up, resource issues and a perceived lack of relevance. The aim of the coaching programme is personal development that is also linked directly with business outcomes, and focuses on business development because this is felt to be important in the retail sector. So, in collaboration with an external coaching provider, a programme called Business Fitness Coaching was designed.

Programme structure

The programme begins with a group day where managers are encouraged to think about their personal development. Then they undertake a one-to-one coaching programme to build on this work. The link to business effectiveness is maintained by the managers doing 'homework' after each session in which they have to action the learning through a work-based 'mini-project'. This project must be part of their business responsibilities and can include development of their soft skills – eg development of staff. The pilot programme also had a specific aim of assisting small businesses where there are limited career opportunities. In these cases, the coaching helps to identify the individuals' skills and talents that can be more widely used within the organisation, while also widening the employees' involvement.

Impact of the programme

Assessment of the impact of the coaching is built into the design of the programme. The individuals choose their development areas to link with the business effectiveness projects. It is hoped that the impact of the programme can be more directly measured. By linking the programme to the business, senior management can identify the impact quickly and reinvest any savings/gains in their employees' development.

H&M is using this coaching programme within a wider change programme and expects that the interim assessment report will be published soon. If successful – and early indications are that it is having an impact – the coaching programme will be offered within the retail sector more widely.

Information provided by Nicky Hillier, Personnel Manager

KwikFit Financial Services: Developing managers through coaching

Coaching has become a key feature of the development of managers at KwikFit Financial Services. The company believes that coaching forms an important part of a manager's skill set, to be used when people have specific development needs but also to encourage high performance from all staff. KwikFit Financial Services sees this as critical to ensuring high levels of customer service. Managers coach their line reports and receive both coach training and supervision from the training and recruitment manager. She completed an external coaching qualification supported by the business.

Managers who are coaching are supported by a coaching champion. She has regular meetings with the coaches, observes them coaching their consultants and gives feedback on their performance. She is also the connection point with department managers and provides regular updates for the directors about progress.

The organisation has identified clear performance differences between those who are coached and those who are not, in terms of meeting targets and quickly addressing issues that arise. These positive results have led to greater use of coaching in the business. Originally, individuals could choose their own goals for coaching, but a decision was taken to include additional department goals/targets. When measuring the impact of coaching, KwikFit generally looks at the managers' performance and focuses on issues such as attendance and quality. For example, when sales productivity had noticeably declined in a given area, individuals being coached were set achievement targets. Individuals were coached to help them achieve these targets, and productivity increased as a result.

Coaching has also been used to assist culture change issues. KwikFit Financial Services surveyed their employees and asked: 'How can we make this a fantastic place to work?' Specific projects were set up as a result of the responses they received, and coaching was used to help generate the changes. KwikFit Financial Services firmly believes that coaching has helped to change their culture.

Key features of the coaching process at Kwikfit Financial Services include:
- workshops to give managers coaching and training skills
- support for coaches by a coach champion
- buy-in from senior management
- setting specific targets for behaviour change
- a detailed method of change analysis to identify factors which help and hinder progress
- follow-up, and measurement
- coaching on both positive and negative behaviour.

Information provided by Tracey Smith, Recruitment and Training Manager

Nationwide: Aligning a coaching programme with business goals

Coaching at Nationwide has formed a significant part of the business's five-year strategy to develop leadership skills and build an empowered learning culture that maximises employee performance and job satisfaction while also delivering better member experience and value.

Nationwide's Group Training and Development department developed an integrated 'HR system' that was not just about training or learning but encompassed how the performance of an organisation is increased and all the people parts are fully integrated.

The coaching project aimed to shift the coaching focus from result-oriented outputs to people- and behaviour-based inputs, driving positive change in customer satisfaction/commitment and business performance with associated efficiency savings.

The overall aim was to demonstrate to managers the effectiveness of coaching as a key leadership skill when applied to their business area. Managers will then have the key skills and are more easily able to apply them back in the workplace.

One tool that has been developed is the prescribed standard Nationwide expect of a coach, and this has proved an effective framework for all roles.

The design of the programme included the evaluation strategy from the outset, aiming to focus on the changes in the coaching behaviours of the delegates, as judged by their coachees, as well as supporting the business to measure the success of their specific business initiative.

The development of the coaching training material has been a partnership of both Nationwide's internal training resources and external training providers. Using dedicated trainers has led to an increased skill level, consistency and commitment for these trainers, and has led to an easing of scheduling pressures when trying to book in events for specific divisions. Having a mix of external training providers has enabled the programme to achieve a level of consistency and specialist knowledge, also easing scheduling pressures.

Drivers for introducing coaching at Nationwide

Nationwide's Chief Executive, Philip Williamson, had a specific vision to deliver coaching to all areas of Nationwide.

> *To build an empowered employee-centric learning and development culture, led by inspirational leaders, which unleashes the potential of our employees and as a result maximises our employee and member experience and enables us to deliver greater member value through leveraged profit end efficiency.*

Nationwide's cultural programme, PRIDE, was introduced in February 2002 to align all employee behaviours. Philip Williamson, Nationwide's Chief Executive, confirmed at that time that 'Everyone will receive all the necessary coaching required to make PRIDE a success.' Evidence showed that this could not be fully achieved through existing thinking and business practices. New habits had to be formed, which was why Nationwide felt that coaching must be core in their range of capabilities.

From research carried out with an external company, Nationwide knew that employees wanted their managers to help them raise the bar of performance. This research also highlighted that people tended to be more satisfied and committed when they felt that they worked in an environment that supported their development and performance. There was a varying level of support following learning activity, to fully transfer the learning into the workplace, and this has been substantiated within many evaluation reports. Given the research, Nationwide wanted to find a way of changing the role of manager from 'tell' to 'show'.

Relating coaching to the business

Coaching for managers at Nationwide has been introduced by relating it to specific business initiatives that managers are leading. An example of a business initiative is 'enhancing the member experience'. The aim is to frame coaching in practical applications within the business, rather than offering it as a stand-alone training activity. This approach also allows them to evaluate how successful coaching has been in supporting managers to deliver business initiatives by putting it into context with their business goals.

Nationwide sees coaching as the natural way that they continually raise the bar of performance that leads to customer commitment and increased business success.

The coaching programme at Nationwide

Nationwide has developed a tailored coaching programme, being rolled out to all divisions across Nationwide, in each case delivering the coaching tools that would support their teams to achieve a key business initiative, specified by them. The trainers delivering the programme acted as coaches throughout the programme, acting as role models to the delegates when exploring the coaching models.

During the courses, managers are coached to develop their own coaching skills. The trainers delivering the programme act as coaches throughout the programme, acting as role models to the delegates when exploring the coaching models. This method allows participants to learn and develop their coaching skills while receiving coaching themselves.

The start of the programme encourages delegates to explore how coaching can support the business initiative and identify the behaviours needed to achieve success. High-level support from a senior manager or director at this early stage is seen as key to selling the vision for coaching at Nationwide and to explain how coaching relates to raising performance in the business and culture change.

Also included in the programme is a focus on building delegates' self-awareness via a tool called 'Insights', and by completing a feedback tool called a Coaching Behaviours Analysis Questionnaire. The latter is a questionnaire based on the set of coaching standards that have been developed at Nationwide. The questionnaire is used as a 360-degree feedback instrument, being given to delegates' peers, manager and team members. Results are analysed to identify 'hot spots' in people's coaching capabilities, and this is used during the programme to highlight areas to develop managers' skills. Following this, a range of different coaching models and techniques are then introduced and discussed. There follows the practical application of these models and techniques, the delegates practising using them in the context of their specific business initiative.

Reviews are in place to assess progress and provide focus at specific times following the course. The delegates are encouraged to evaluate the successes they have seen so far, as well as what has not gone so well. They discuss and evaluate the progress of the business initiative against the key measures, and then action plan the next steps.

Nationwide has undertaken a major roll-out of coaching – so far, 3,500 delegate-days' training have been delivered across Nationwide. The coaching programme at Nationwide is expected to take five years to fully implement, and Nationwide are about half-way through this programme.

Evaluating coaching at Nationwide

Planning the evaluation of coaching begins at an early stage. When a business initiative has been identified where coaching can be applied, the manager discusses what success will look like. This information is used to agree key goals/measures for them to focus on during the coaching. They also discuss what behaviours need to be improved in the team to achieve the goals of the business initiative.

The coaching behaviour questionnaire and insights tools are used to measure participants' progress as coaches. Delegates are encouraged to repeat the questionnaire when they have been actively coaching back in the workplace to analyse and evaluate changes in their coaching behaviour and skills. Linking coaching with the results of the business initiative and tracking the development of coaches' skills before and after the coaching allows them to demonstrate that progress is being made.

Nationwide also uses a validation questionnaire following the coaching programme to assess participants' satisfaction with the programme. It establishes whether delegates' objectives were met by the course and how satisfied they were with the programme. A consistent rating of 89 per cent satisfaction has been received so far.

An online survey called Back Web has also been undertaken three to six months after the coaching programme. The survey randomly surveys a cross-section of delegates, their team members and managers. This provides feedback on the coaching skills of the delegates. The Back Web survey results have shown that coachees saw an improvement in the way they were coached. Feedback from the coachees is that managers have created better working relationships and were more effective in communicating with their teams – resulting in improved team results.The coaches' line managers reported a change in behaviour following the coaching training in terms of improved attitudes and behaviours.

Overall, the feedback from the different survey instruments has been extremely positive and a real shift in behaviours and attitudes has been seen.

Other evaluation results so far have been exciting and very encouraging:

- Benchmarked with other financial organisations, Nationwide came top – responses to 11 questions were the highest, to 13 second-highest, and to 6 third-highest.
- There are improvements in key questionnaire responses in Nationwide's employee viewpoint survey. For example: the response to 'There are sufficient opportunities for me to improve my skills in my current job' improved by 2 per cent. The response to 'I feel I am treated with respect and fairness in my job' improved by 10 per cent.
- Evaluation also shows that 71 per cent of Area Managers and 93 per cent of Senior Branch Managers say that the member experience has been enhanced in their entire branches.
- Samples of individual behavioural comments from operational managers include 'It has changed my life! I am now managing my team very differently', 'I can see the changes in the behaviours of the delegates that have already been on the programme, and I want to go on my courses earlier', and 'I feel I have moved on as a person. It has had a very positive impact on me and how I will interact with my team in the future.'

The development and delivery of the coaching programmes, influencing key stakeholders and raising the profile of coaching as a key leadership skill across Nationwide has demonstrated the value of Group Training and Development department to the business by contributing to Nationwide's corporate goals of retaining business, members and employees.

Barriers to coaching

The advent of mortgage regulation has given a boost to support for coaching in the Operations part of the Nationwide business. The new regulations dictate that all staff must have regular one-to-one meetings with their managers, and coaching provides a specific method to frame the discussions. As part of the regulations, the manager's line manager must observe the manager doing the one-to-ones and then provide him or her with feedback on his or her skills. This is seen as a great opportunity to embed coaching into the organisation at different levels.

Some thoughts from trainers on the rollout so far:

- *'The extent to which delegates are engaged and brought in to the process seems to be dependent on many factors, but the key one in my view is whether the business area has dedicated an accountable person to project manage and oversee – therefore leading to clear and timely communication, a clear business initiative and clear ownership by the business area rather than Training and Development.'*
- *'The most successful business areas throughout the roll-out have been those that invested the time to communicate effectively with their people. X department have been a great example of this. They allocated a project manager and the communication has been very clear, and most importantly, they've taken ownership for the roll-out and the success of the Business Initiative.'*
- *'The challenges faced include poor communication, lack of presence on the Business Initiative day from Senior Management and negativity on the days.'*

Information provided by Pamela Tilt, Development Consultant, Operations Training, Group Training and Development

Norfolk, Suffolk and Cambridgeshire Strategic Health Authority

There is a plethora of leadership programmes, modernisation programmes and development initiatives in the NHS aimed at developing employee skills to improve the patient experience. Coaching and mentoring are seen as the glue that cements and embeds these initiatives into long-lasting sustainable change and to avoid a fragmented approach.

The Norfolk, Suffolk and Cambridgeshire (NSC) Strategic Health Authority understands that it needs to build coaching and mentoring capability and capacity within the organisation to support these initiatives. Considerable effort has been expended to establish a comprehensive and consistent approach to coaching/mentoring across the NSC, which will act as infrastructure for achieving sustained change. This is known as the universal integrated framework model.

How is coaching/mentoring defined at the NSC?

Within the universal integrated framework model (UIF), coaching/mentoring is defined broadly as 'help given by one person to another in making significant transitions in knowledge, work or thinking to aid personal development, career planning or performance improvement and leadership' (derived from Megginson and Clutterbuck, 1995).

For the NSC, coaching and mentoring are on a continuum linking personal development with performance improvement. Both activities are crucial to ensuring that programmes of development are transferred to work-based practice. And both involve a goal-centred process, are underpinned by the same skills sets, and should result in action. However, mentoring is seen as a personal-development-centred approach, primarily embracing career issues and personal development, whereas coaching is more performance-centred. The SHA believes that portraying coaching and mentoring as being on a continuum ensures that they remain at the core of the organisation's agenda for leadership development and organisational improvement, rather than being seen as isolated initiatives.

Different streams of coaching/mentoring

Coaching and mentoring are being used in a whole range of different ways throughout the SHA. As a result, a series of programmes has been developed to improve skills within the organisation in coaching/mentoring:

- local programmes – aimed at line managers to improve their coaching skills
- five-day co-coaching programme – aimed at Modernisation Associates whose remit is to support radical reform and leadership development in health and social care. By the end of the programme, participants should be able to support leaders in implementing radical change using a coaching approach and have acquired mentoring skills
- five-day black and minority ethnic (BME) leadership programme – aimed at BME leaders and leaders from partner organisations who want to mentor others and are interested in joining the BME mentoring leaders group. By the end of the programme, participants should be able to mentor and coach BME staff and other leaders
- two-day supervision training – exploring different supervision models and recognising the different tools available to support supervision process.
- continuous development group – quarterly meetings facilitated by an external coach to help mentor/coaches review and learn from their experience and to look at new tactics.

The SHA also supports and aligns its coaching activities with wider NHS initiatives for coaching/mentoring such as the Mentoring Forum in East England, national networks – eg for BME staff – and by supplying mentors and coaches for the National Management Development Programme and the wider global mentoring initiative.

How the NSC is strengthening coaching capabilities in the organisation

The SHA recognised that to meet the demand, mentoring/coaching capability and capacity needed to be strengthened. This is being done through a selection of initiatives:

- establishing a universal framework to ensure a shared understanding of the benefits of coaching/mentoring and that all activities and practices are aligned within one universal framework across the NHS and with partners
- addressing issues of quality and effectiveness by establishing more rigorous processes for supervision, accreditation and evaluation. The SHA is developing an accreditation system for in-house programmes that supports the universal framework. A menu of programmes is

available for different levels of skill attainment which in the future will lead to qualifications through an education provider. They are working towards greater clarity of roles of external and internal resources in mentoring/coaching by clearly articulated standards and systems for quality management for internal and external providers

- embedding coaching and mentoring in the organisation's culture to assure its sustainability over time. To achieve this, the NSC is mapping out where coaching and mentoring fits into other developmental provisions. It has also strengthened the links with any congruent HR/development processes including the inclusion of mentoring/coaching participation in job descriptions. Alongside this, it is creating an infrastructure to roll out mentoring and coaching locally but with access to resources and support through virtual and mixed economies of mentors and coaches.

Who are the NSC mentors/coaches?

External coaches and internal managers can be mentors and coaches in the NSC. The NSC believes that a mixed economy of internal and external coaching providers ensures choice and value for money. There is a demand for the external coaches/mentors of senior executives to assure confidentiality and support for those in the most challenging and demanding positions. The NHS Leadership Centre produced a list of external coaches accredited by them and the NSC selects external coaches from this pool.

The NSC's initial challenge was to create a critical mass of coach/mentors trained to the right level to provide access to mentoring and coaching. They created a supply of coaches/mentors trained in supervision who could support those trained in their mentoring/coaching undertakings. This would allow them to pilot the infrastructure and build up their numbers of coach/mentors so they could grow coach and mentor capacity organically in line with demand.

Accrediting its coaches

External coaches employed by the NSC must work to its model of coaching/mentoring and undertake supervision to ensure accountability within the framework. They must also be 'accredited', which requires that they undertake a short induction session to ensure that they understand and comply with the framework, to evidence supervision, and to ensure that they contribute to process review and evaluation. Accreditation is felt to be important in a high-quality coaching/mentoring service. By clarifying the competency requirements for coaches/mentors, the SHA can rely on greater consistency and quality. Accreditation is believed to enable the NHS to buy better coaching and mentoring services, achieve value for money, incorporate coaches/mentors into systems of accountability and evaluation, and offer internal coaches/mentors a meaningful development route with external recognition.

Internal mentors and coaches are accredited at various levels of competency, from basic skills training to advanced-level training. The different types of coaching/mentoring – such as BME mentoring, co-coaching and coaching as a manager – are all supported through accredited development options. Coach/mentors within an ongoing relationship are required to undertake supervision by attending a 'supervision and continual development group' every three months or with an NSC supervisor by appointment. The NSC also runs an ongoing programme of development events. NSC supervisors have two days of training to equip them to take on this role, and can only do this training if they have already completed the other five-day programme and have a significant level of mentoring and coaching experience.

Evaluating and ensuring best practice

A set of tools has been developed to help coach/mentors review and learn from their own experience on an ongoing basis, but which also feeds into an evaluation process of coach and mentor activity. The Coaching Skills Review Tool provides a culturally sensitive way to collect quantitative measures on coach/mentor performance and to review coachee/mentee experience through a 360-degree adaptation and a self-review questionnaire, feeding data into a general database which can be exported for analysis. The tool is based on the Goleman model of emotional intelligence (with an additional cultural competency), as well as specific skills and personal qualities. These have found to be effective predictors of mentoring and coaching success in NSC. Mentors and coachees input to evaluation at a range of agreed points in the relationship.

This online tool looks at performance ratings for the coach/mentor given by a coachee/mentee compared with self-assessment and competence ratings as coach. The database is used by local co-ordinators to inform development planning and review the impact of coach mentoring over time. Measures that are tracked include:

- promotion of the coachee/mentee
- an assigned rating of the effectiveness of the coach/mentor
- supplementary information such as:
  - 360-degree peer and coachee/mentee ratings against coach/mentor self-ratings
  - type of training as coach/mentor
  - link between emotional intelligence and general rating of competence
  - links between elements and predictors of success.

Qualitative feedback is also sought to feed into the ongoing development and group supervision of coaches/mentors. An example of comments gained from the coaches about the impact of coaching is,

> *Coaching has a profound impact on people. It recognises that the best people to improve a service are the people providing the service. A sense of empowerment enhances the ability to achieve what we wish to achieve. If this drive is somehow connected to planning or delivering patient care, the impact is extremely powerful.*
>
> clinician on BME coaching/mentoring programme

In terms of results from the different programmes, evaluation is still ongoing, but some of the findings to date are as follows. Three of the original cohort of 12 on the BME coach/mentoring programme were promoted within nine months, and five more have stated that they are now working in broader work streams, two further individuals stating that they are 'personally developing in unexpected ways'. Reviews of another cohort of pairings will take place later in the year.

Training the participants as mentees/coachees as well as for their role as mentor/coach brings particular advantages to coachee/mentees.They report higher satisfaction and benefits from the whole process, and increased wider role activity (an early indicator of readiness for promotion). Training also increases the likelihood of a successful coaching/mentoring relaitonship – they are more likely to solve relationship problems within the first six months. Those trained as mentor/coaches as well as being coachees/mentees report more benefits and greater empowerment. Mentors/coaches working with this cohort are more likely to describe the experience as 'mutually developmental'.

In terms of coach/mentor qualities and behaviours that are predictors of successsful relationships, NSC discovered that the following elements were key to effective mentoring and coaching:

- *'Mentor/coach is really interested in what happens to me.'*
- *'Mentor/coach has contact with me between meetings – eg by email.'*
- *Mentor/coach keeps meeting appointments.'*

Additionally, elements of the relationship were described as most useful over the long term but were not always obvious in the short term. These came from challenges about the bigger picture or from the assimilation of situations from different angles. Typical problems were linked to getting trapped within the 'culture of task review and improvement', parallelling meetings with line mangers and missing the opportunity to move beyond the targets that bind people in their everyday work.

Supervision was highly rated by attendees as very effective in helping them improve their performance, and some Chief Executives described it as useful for helping them introduce generic skill sets into their everyday work.

Addenbrooke's hospital in NSC has addressed the issue of linking mentoring and coaching to improving the patient experince. Staff there report as follows:

Coaching has particularly been embraced by the Service Improvement and Human Resources Directorates at Addenbrooke's. The benefits have been at two levels: at the individual level coaching has helped reduce self-limiting beliefs, and at the team level coaching has helped teams to work through issues affecting patient care.

The GROW model of coaching is used by the Service Improvement Team (Resource for Change) and is advocated by them to teams in other Directorates. Coaching is having a positive impact on patient care. It has proved particularly valuable when challenging established practice and when problem-solving around service development. One example where coaching has helped is in identifying and escalating issues preventing provision of a streamlined service to patients. They noted that success required that:

- *Leadership is a priority for the organisation.*

- *Coaching is linked to leadership.*
- *There were champions for coaching in the organisation.*
- *The champions had access to senior managers across the organisation.*
- *The champions demonstrated the benefits of coaching relevant to individual stakeholders.*
- *The champions were supported in terms of having time to learn and further develop skills, as well as time for supervision.*
- *Administrative support is available.*
- *Training support is available.*
- *There is a means of communicating coaching developments to Trust staff.*
- *Staff are interested enough to volunteer to be coaches or coaches.*
- *A plan exists to support coaches through supervision (eg action learning or one-to-one supervision).*
- *Previous experiences are used to improve future practices.*

Developing a coaching and mentoring culture

The development of a coaching and mentoring culture is a challenge for the NSC but it believes it is necessary if the other initiatives are to be sustained. Various activities have been designed to help achieve this. These include ensuring that coaching and mentoring is at the heart of the leadership strategy and that an infrastructure is built around it.

Information provided by Sara Ireland, previously Workforce Manager Psychologist, Leadership in the NSC, and currently a Mentoring and Coaching Advisor for a range of organisations

Panasonic Europe: Using a blended learning approach to developing coaching skills

Panasonic was established in Japan in 1918 and since then has grown to be one of the top global electronic companies. As global competition has grown, there has been more and more pressure on management to achieve their targets and grow sales year on year. To achieve these targets it was felt important that managers not only focus on the targets themselves but also on how to achieve them by getting the best from their people. Katrine Smith, training manager, Panasonic Europe, believes

A stronger coaching culture is vital to achieving greater focus on leadership and people development within the business. As a result we have been working to develop a coaching style of management, believing that it helps people to take more ownership for their work, supports personal development and encourages people to come up with solutions to issues they face. In this way, coaching will have an impact on bottom line success as well as supporting the personal development of their staff.

Training at Panasonic in the past has predominantly focused on developing business skills and knowledge, people management receiving less attention. As the company has become more globalised, it has recognised that it needs to focus more on training future leaders in aspects of people development and management. All of this has led to a change of emphasis in the design of training and development courses and initiatives.

Coaching is considered to be one of a number of tools that can be used for management and leadership development. In Panasonic, coaching skills modules have been incorporated into various leadership development courses, and a stand-alone coaching skills programme has been developed.

Coaching workshops for managers

Stand-alone coaching skills workshops have been run for managers and, to date, 40 managers have participated. These focused workshops aim to give managers practical coaching skills and techniques, and the opportunity to put them into practice in a 'safe' environment. Before attendance at the workshops the managers take part in a $2\frac{1}{2}$-hour virtual classroom session that covers coaching theory and background as well as the wider business context. The virtual classroom is interactive, comprising instructor-led sessions interspersed with participative question sessions. Participants log in to software through their computer and call in on their telephones. People can ask questions by phone and can respond to questions by typing into the software. The virtual classroom is a useful tool in preparing participants to get in the right frame of mind before the workshop. After the virtual classroom, participants attend a two-day workshop to practise and apply the skills and theory.

During the workshop participants undertake a series of practical exercises and role-plays to develop their coaching skills. During the role-plays, one person acts as coach, another as coachee, while the remaining two act as observers who note down comments and then coach the 'coach' on his or her coaching skills. All participants rotate through the different roles to practise their skills. Following the workshop, participants undertake some post-course work. This takes place by phone and in virtual classrooms because many of the participants are geographically dispersed across Europe. Within six weeks of the workshop, participants must work in threes to undertake telephone-coaching sessions with each other. After this exercise, they take part in a virtual classroom to discuss what they have applied from the experience. Each of the participants presents his or her learning via online presentation software and talks through his or her experiences.

Coaching within leadership programmes

Panasonic Europe offers a series of leadership development programmes for managers across its many companies in Europe. The programmes are modular and are typically a week in length, and the importance of coaching and some basic coaching skills are introduced. For example, as part of a 360-degree feedback process participants are asked to coach each other about their results.

Executive coaching

Although the workshops and leadership programmes are designed to create a coaching mindset amongst line managers in the business, Panasonic is also encouraging its senior leaders to consider executive coaching as an effective tool in their own personal development. Aimed at harnessing personal leadership development, executive coaching – provided through an external supplier– can focus on some key areas:

- enhancing personal presence and influence
- improving risk-taking and decision-making
- boosting creativity and collaboration during times of change.

The coachees set the agenda but agree business-based goals at the outset with HR and their managing director. External rather than internal coaches are thought to be the best solution for coaching at senior levels due to trust and confidence issues. Panasonic has chosen to work with a company that has a European base so that it can use the same company to source coaches from across Europe.

Phil Cox, Manager, Pan-European HR, explains:

> *The creation of an 'executive coaching culture' is likely to be gradual, and the focus of the programme in the first year is to simply raise awareness of the bottom-line benefits of executive coaching amongst the most influential leaders in the organisation, who are likely to become 'early adopters' of coaching services.*

Panasonic has used a number of communication channels to continually reiterate the potential impact and importance of executive coaching on the organisation, and is hopeful that these activities will lead to a 'snowball effect' as word-of-mouth success stories spread amongst the leadership group. The programme is still in its early stages, so the organisation will have to wait and see how popular it becomes and whether participants find it a useful form of development.

Feedback and evaluation of coaching activities at Panasonic

Feedback after the coaching skills programme has been very good, but the evaluation is based upon immediate feedback from evaluation sheets. The post-course virtual classroom provides a good arena for evaluation when participants discuss how they have or have not been able to practise their coaching skills and what did or did not work in the workshop. The majority of participants have reported using the coaching skills back in the workplace and finding it useful. However, as with any new idea or change, a few participants have reported having difficulties applying the theory and knowledge back in the workplace. Some have accepted coaching more readily than others. Those in charge have not noticed significant cultural differences in terms of participants' responses to coaching, but they do see individual differences depending on how open individuals are to new ideas and models.

Evaluation takes place for the wider management/leadership programmes, but it does not specifically focus on coaching skills and so it does not provide specific data. As more people are involved in the whole coaching process, the training team will contact them to evaluate how useful the programme was and to gain a better understanding of what worked and what did not.

Senior managers/leaders support for coaching

The move towards a coaching style of management is gradual. Firstly, managers have to understand what coaching is and how its use can actually have a benefit on the bottom line of the business. Some managers are unfamiliar with coaching and are wary, whereas others find it difficult to step back from being directive in the management of their teams.

The positive response from MDs and HR directors, however, in nominating participants onto programmes with a large element of coaching content, suggests that – slowly – this is increasingly seen as an effective part of the development toolkit available to Panasonic leaders.

Information provided by Katrine Smith, Training Manager, and Anjna Rughani, Training Supervisor

Perkins Shibaura Engines Ltd: Developing managers as coaches for culture change and business improvements

Perkins Shibaura engines is a world leader in the design, manufacture and sale of sub-75hp diesel engines. Organisationally, the company has a very flat structure and this is reflected by the company's culture, where everyone uses first names and wears the same working dress. Even office space is open-plan and there are no traditional supervisory levels such as foreman but working team leaders. Perkins Shibaura Engines has developed a continuum of coaching skills development – from taught basic skills developed at the firm's own training school, through to close supervision at the bench and peer coaching and development through 'professional friends'. The team coach is an integral part of this continuum.

Coaching is felt to be a critical mechanism for keeping employees' skills updated in line with the fast pace of the business environment. As Change Manager Nigel Briers explains:

> *The rate of change in the industry means that employees can't be continually retrained, so they are coached to understand the elements of change and move with them.*

This move to 'just in time' learning is part of the organisation's interest in encouraging lifelong learning and continual support for employee development from managers and peers – ie 'the guy standing next to you on the line'. Nigel explains:

> *We have a value and behaviours culture here which is explicit and mimics that of the family – just as you would expect support from your parents and brothers and sisters, so you can expect support from your leaders and peers at work.*

Training managers as coaches

Managers were initially trained by a coaching skills programme delivered by an external provider, but now that has been incorporated into general leadership modules that are run within the company. For example, the NVQ level 3 programme has a module called Coaching your Poor Performers. Alongside attending coaching skills training programmes, managers are also coached by their own managers, so all managers are continually developing their skills. Although managers would not be disciplined for not coaching (because the company appreciates that these skills do not come easily to everyone), there is an expectation that they will continue to drive to acquire and develop their coaching skills.

A significant number of the company's leaders come from military backgrounds, and some of them have initially found it difficult to adapt to this style of coaching culture, being used to having status and not expecting to have their decisions challenged. Nigel says:

They find this approach to coaching very different. Within the services, the job of the leader is to get everyone up to a required standard, but within industry it's about continually improving the standards for everyone.

Benefits to the organisation

The organisational culture is predominantly one of coaching and Nigel is clear that coaching has to have the right environment for benefits to accrue. Buy-in from senior management and a company-wide approach are felt to be critical. The benefits in terms of individual performance are clear. Nigel explains:

Once coaching skills are developed by the manager, an appreciation of the reportees' unique skills follow and teamwork flourishes where everyone is learning within the team.

But the company has also found additional benefits at the organisational level.

For example, motivation and learning is maintained within the flat organisational structure by lateral movement of employees within the company. The use of 360-degree coaching makes it possible to identify how employees' skills can be best used within different areas of the company. A good example of this was provided by the recent construction of a new factory. The employees employed in building the engines were also part of the team building the new factory. They were able to work with the manufacturing engineers to point out what their needs were within the design, thereby forestalling costly last-minute operational changes. Coaching is also used to help identify less visible skills in the workforce. The view is taken that when people are recruited into the company, not all of their potential skills and contributions are evident, and it is through coaching that they will become apparent.

Developing internal coaching capability

The company does not use external coaches to coach individuals. Where there is a need that cannot be met by internal resources, it uses external consultants to provide internal people with new knowledge or techniques. Following on from this, someone from the company will take responsibility for the area and incorporate it within company culture. As Nigel explains:

Embedding coaching into the culture is what makes it stick. We expect that even if our leaders change, coaching is so embedded within the culture and the benefits are so obvious that it will continue.

Evaluation of coaching

The company has made attempts to measure the impact of coaching using a range of business measures. Some examples include product quality measured in parts per million (PPM), sickness absence measured by number of days lost from work, and the performance management process measured by percentage ratings. Through these efforts, the organisation has seen evidence of performance improvements. For example, product quality was improved by 19 per cent last year and sickness/absence was down from 7 per cent to an average 2.4 per cent. They also measure employee performance against the company values and behaviours and have found that coaching has helped to embed the values into their culture.

The company also monitors other indirect measures, such as the type of issues being raised in the works association, views from 'opinion pulse checks' and 'talkback sessions', as well as the results of the employee opinion survey which provide a measure of employee satisfaction. Perkins Shibaura Engines reports that these mechanisms have increased two-way communication and brought improvements in employee engagement scores and in the employee opinion survey. The feedback is that the employees enjoy the coaching culture: they feel their ideas are valued and their efforts are appreciated. As one employee noted:

In my previous jobs, the only time I had been in an office was when they were going to let me go. Here I was in the office and someone was trying to help me – I kept waiting for the punch-line, but it didn't come.

The company tries to promote coaching in areas of the business where it believes it can have a large impact. For example, when an increase in sickness absence was identified in one part of the business, the company believed it was because employees were being challenged with too much change and felt their views were not being considered. As a result, the company responded by encouraging specific types of coaching to be delivered. As Nigel explains:

If people are unhappy, they start not coming in. When this happens, we coach around the principle of continuing to attend work even in the difficult times.

Managing expectations

The company has found that there are sometimes difficulties when both managers and reportees expect and want changes within a shorter time-scale than coaching can deliver. Nigel says:

This is the other side of the coin, as people sometimes grumble that something is not being done about a person or issue. We know something is being done, but it takes time to produce results and people can get impatient.

When the coaching programme was first stepped up, there was an expectation that it would produce measurable performance improvement by the next quarter, but it is now recognised that three to four months is a reasonable timeline to see effective behavioural change.

Information provided by Nigel Briers, Change Manager

Selfridges: A coaching skills programme for senior managers

Selfridges has recently completed a six-month coaching programme aimed at developing coaching skills in the business. The coaching project stemmed from a leadership development programme for the mid-senior management population (level 5) that identified a need for coaching skills to be developed within the business. The coaching programme at Selfridges has mostly been driven by the Resourcing and Development (R&D) team, but with support from some of the directors. To support the coaching initiative, three members of the R&D team were trained as 'super coaches' so that they could help to run the coaching workshops and help the participants throughout the coaching programme.

The coaching skills programme has acted as a bridge between the leadership development programme and a talent programme aimed at middle managers (level 4). Eleven participants in the leadership programme were selected to be trained as coaches for participants in the level 4 talent programme to support their ongoing development and promotion. As well as coaching the individuals from the talent programme, it was hoped that managers would also act as coaches for their own teams and in the organisation more generally. The selection of the participants in the coaching pilot programme was fairly subjective. The R&D team identified the people who they thought had excelled on the leadership programme and had the potential to be the best coaches. These people were approached (with their managers) about taking part and, from this, 11 people volunteered to take part in the programme.

Details of the coaching pilot programme

A two-day launch was organised for the start of the coaching skills pilot programme, which was run by external consultants (thenew.org) and members of R&D. During the launch, they revisited themes from the leadership programme and aligned the coaching with the previous development activity. They introduced objectives for the coaching programme and set expectations for how the Selfridges coaching skills programme would work. After the launch, participants met every two weeks to attend a half-day module facilitated by external consultants and the 'super coaches' from R&D. The topics covered in the half-day sessions included:

- communication and speaking (this was the focus of the leadership programme)
- metaphor, stories and anecdotes
- communication, listening and language
- outcomes, goals and results
- courage, challenges and letting go
- review session.

During the half-day sessions, different coaching models and techniques are discussed and participants work in threes to practise their skills. The sessions are run as self-managed groups and are facilitated discussions rather than traditional training or instructional events. Coaching at Selfridges is not designed as a rigid process or model – the company believes each person has to develop his or her own coaching style. The models and ground rules that are discussed are designed to help managers develop their own style and to give them a structure for their coaching conversations.

Between the fortnightly modules, participants are given 'homework', being expected to think through issues and practise their skills. For the duration of the coaching programme, each participant coaches one of the participants in the talent programme. They are expected to meet with their coachee at least once every two weeks and arrange conference calls between the contact sessions. Participants also meet once with other participants (in threes) in the coaching programme and the 'super coaches' between the formal modules. This means they have regular contact with other coaches every week for the whole six-month programme, both for support and to discuss issues they face. The six-month programme finishes with a full-day presentation from participants and a review of the programme and their learning.

Evaluation – did coaching have an impact?

The managers who took part in the coaching programme gave very positive feedback, believing it helped them develop their coaching and management skills. Behavioural change was observed in the coaches by their managers and peers in terms of their confidence, resilience and leadership skills, as well as their improved coaching skills. The coaches are now involved in formal and informal coaching relationships across the business, being recognised as people with strong coaching/development skills.

To date, Selfridges has not collected quantitative evaluation data about the coaching pilot but is in the process of collecting anecdotal information. Benefits have been reported by the coachees as a result of receiving the coaching. These include improved relationships, promotion, greater responsibility and new roles. Promotion of the talent programme coachees is the hardest demonstration of the impact of coaching, but it is difficult to attribute this solely to the coaching. Of the nine coachees who received coaching for the duration of the pilot programme, three have been promoted and another has made a sideways move that is likely to lead to a promotion in the next few months. Overall, there is a strong belief on the part of the participants in the programme and members of R&D that a coaching approach to management will confer significant benefits on the business.

Lessons learned from the coaching pilot

Selfridges is looking at mapping out a new coaching programme this year, and as part of this, wants to be clearer with the objectives for the programme and to link them more closely with business strategy.

Selfridges would also like to improve the selection of the individuals being trained as coaches because it thinks its previous approach was too subjective. Next time, the organisers intend to undertake a more rigorous and open process asking all participants in the leadership programme whether they would like to participate and then selecting participants based on their coaching experience and skills. They are also keen to ensure a good geographical spread of coaches so that coaching can be offered to managers in all their business locations.

Another area Selfridges would like to improve is assessing and measuring the development of participants' coaching skills. At the start of the future programmes, the organisers will assess participants' starting level of coaching skills and repeat the assessment half-way through the programme (at the four-month stage) and then on a regular basis as a continuous measure of skill development. They will also collect stories of the benefits of coaching to gain information more formally about what has happened as a result of the coaching in terms of the performance and development of the individual coachees. These stories will be used with senior managers to persuade them of the impact of coaching and to convince them that it is a worthwhile investment.

Feedback from coachees, although mostly positive, was mixed. One learning point from the programme was that coaching is not necessarily everyone's learning style. Some people really flourish having a coach; others less so. A number of factors can play a role, including the choice of coach, the geography of the coaches and coachees, the personality match and preferred learning styles of the coachees. Interestingly, those coaching relationships that achieved success early on are still going strong, whereas those whose relationship was weaker have all but given up. Selfridges has realised that careful matching and assessing individual learning preferences will help to identify how to make coaching relationships work most effectively.

The future of coaching at Selfridges

Since the programme started, Selfridges has experienced significant organisational changes as a result of a takeover. While at first it was business as usual, in recent months a new strategic direction has been taken and the R&D team realise that it will be essential for future coaching efforts to be aligned with the new business direction and strategy. They also realise that they need to gain the support of the new directors and senior managers who were not involved in the initial programme, because there have been some difficulties getting their buy-in and encouraging them to release people for training. If Selfridges decides to continue with its coaching efforts as a way of supporting the organisational changes, R&D will work to get full sign-off from the new senior team, satisfying their needs and expectations about what coaching can deliver to the business as well as building visible buy-in and support for coaching at a senior level.

Information provided by Stuart Haden, Management Development Manager, Selfridges & Co.

Shell: A blended approach to coaching

Although you can argue that coaching has always taken place at Shell (ie one-on-one development discussions), the trigger for taking coaching more seriously was a benchmarking study done in 1999. This indicated that Shell was not fully maximising the potential of coaching in the business and was therefore not gaining as much value from its activities. This triggered a greater investment in coaching, and since then the company has been working on implementing a range of programmes to develop coaching skills in the business.

The use of different types of coaching at Shell

Shell has opted for a blended approach, using a variety of practitioners to deliver its coaching activities. The default coach for an individual is his or her line manager because all managers have a coaching element inherent in their roles and responsibilities. Coaching by managers generally takes place as part of ongoing discussions about development and performance. But Shell also recognises that managers are not always best equipped to coach (eg if technical skills coaching is required, or if an individual needs a greater level of coaching expertise). Within the technical areas of the company the vast majority of formal coaching is not delivered by the manager but by other coaches in the organisation who act as technical coaches or internal development coaches. Many of the internal coaches at Shell are HR professionals who are trained to deliver leadership coaching in the organisation. Technical coaches are technical experts trained to develop their coaching expertise so that they can act as effective technical coaches. If someone requires coaching to improve technical skills, he or she agrees with the manager to approach a local expert in that subject to receive some coaching. Within such a large company, the solutions to technical coaching vary. In some parts of the organisation people are identified to act as full-time technical coaches (eg in business areas where there are lots of graduates who need coaching), whereas in other parts technical coaching forms a part of people's general job roles.

The use of external coaches is largely linked to the executive coaching programme. Shell has arrangements with a selection of external providers. When people in leadership positions are looking for a coach, individual needs are assessed and then individuals are put in touch with a suitable coach following a discussion with their manager. Executives often welcome the added value of an external perspective that an external coach brings and the coaching may also be seen to be more confidential. Overall, although a combination of practitioners are involved in delivering coaching within Shell, the vast majority of coaching is undertaken internally.

Description of coaching programmes

A series of coaching programmes has been delivered at Shell for several years now. One is a two-day coaching workshop open to all employees. Shell believes that people at all levels in the organisation can use coaching skills to improve their work relationships – it is not something solely for managers. The workshop is based on a programme developed by an external coaching company but is tailored to suit the culture and context of Shell. It is designed to introduce coaching to participants and provide them with an understanding of the basic principles and skills. Shell has found that it can be useful for whole teams to go through this programme so that they share a common view about coaching and can use it to work on team issues.

Other programmes are aimed at internal coaches who undertake technical skills coaching or who coach leaders as part of their role. The most recently developed coaching skills programmes are aimed specifically at HR managers – both junior and senior – recognising that they play a special coaching role with leaders and on management teams. Coaching is also built into other development programmes run at Shell because it is an element of the leadership competency framework. So people get exposure to coach training via these programmes and receive further follow-up coaching in the workplace. Programmes for senior executives also include action learning assisted by a coach. If people want to develop their coaching skills in more depth than the internal programmes offer, they can discuss attending external programmes with their line manager.

Shell has recently added a new online element to their coaching portfolio, reflecting a general move towards more online and blended learning in the organisation. The online coaching module is designed to support the other coaching programmes, helping participants to continue developing their coaching activities in the workplace. Participants are required to be in a coaching relationship as part of the programme, and it enables them to receive feedback on their skills as well as support from facilitators.

Attitudes to coaching by line and senior managers

Generally, there is little resistance to coaching in the business. People recognise that coaching works and survey evidence has helped to demonstrate the benefits. Questions tend to focus on how to do it better, rather than why to do it at all. This has been encouraged by the Chief Executive championing coaching in his discussions and presentations, which has helped to drive it into the business. He has publicly stated that he coaches his own team, expects them to be coaching their teams, and so on, through the organisation. Overall, there is a general acceptance at senior levels that coaching is important and effective.

However, despite this, the quality of coaching by line managers is felt to be patchy. Some managers have not attended coaching programmes, while others simply do not dedicate enough time to the coaching part of their role. The reasons for this are thought to partly stem from Shell's history as a very technical business where traditionally technical training has received more attention than softer skills training. Most people start out in technical roles and it is a significant shift for them to realise that as they become more senior, they must develop equally strong people management skills as well as having technical expertise. Another contributing factor may be that although coaching is one of the leadership competencies at Shell, it is one of many skills that managers have to exhibit, and this may result in managers failing to prioritise it. Shell realise that to improve managers' coaching skills and activities, coaching has to be recognised as a key tool to achieve business goals and given the necessary priority when it comes to role descriptions, tasks and targets and therefore performance appraisal and development. The company believes that as a result, more staff will be motivated to improve their coaching skills through real practice in the workplace.

Attempting to evaluate satisfaction and the impact of coaching

High-level evaluation of coaching is felt to be difficult because of all the other factors that are likely to affect business results. So Shell has focused on identifying changes in competence, behaviour and culture as well as gaining feedback from people about the benefits they have seen from coaching

Shell carries out a variety of qualitative web-based surveys to assess attitudes towards and experiences of coaching in terms of staff satisfaction with the quality and quantity of coaching they receive. A random sample of staff throughout the organisation are asked how regularly they receive coaching, whether they have personally benefited from coaching, and whether they believe coaching has resulted in benefits for the company. In addition, more targeted surveying of specific populations (eg graduates) is carried out to gain more in-depth data. Both internal and external coaches are questioned about the benefits they have personally gained from being trained as coaches as well as what positive results they have seen emerge from their coaching relaitonships. Alongside the survey evidence, Shell also collects and shares 'success stories' in which coaching has led to a quantifiable business improvement.

All the survey evidence to date indicates perceived benefits to coaches, coachees and the business. It indicates that staff are generally satisfied with the coaching they receive, but it is unclear whether this reflects the quality of the technical coaching from internal coaches, or manager coaching which is generally of a more varied quality. The most common benefits reported from those who have received coaching are that they are able to do their jobs better and have greater confidence in their abilities. Interviews with senior leaders indicate a positive behavioural impact and improved ease of dealing with change.

Shell also carries out a bi-annual organisation-wide employee attitude survey that contains some questions related to coaching. Some are specific – for example: Do you think you are being coached effectively by your supervisor or line manager? – while others are broader: Do you think you're getting the development opportunities you need? The results of the employee attitude survey are used to evaluate satisfaction and the quality of coaching in the business.The latest results demonstrate that a majority of employees think they receive effective coaching, with a slight increase on the results two years before. The survey data indicate that most new people in the organisation do receive a high level of effective coaching but that those who have been employed for a number of years receive much less. As a result of this feedback, Shell now wants to ensure that coaching is being used more continuously for people's development throughout their career.

Shell has recently begun to attempt to correlate coaching with improved competence via a new online competence-based development system. Individuals record their level of competence via an online tool (levels: awareness/knowledge/skill/mastery) in a range of competencies that have been defined for the Shell business. Depending on the individual's level of competence, assessment takes place either by self-assessment or by assessors who carry out assessment discussions to confirm that people actually have the level of skills they claim to have. In the future, the data this tool can provide should identify improvements in competence for coaches before and after coach-training programmes, as well as improvements in those receiving coaching for development. This will help to demonstrate the impact of coach training in developing people's competence as coaches, as well as demonstrating how coaching can support the improvement of other competencies and skills. The system is very new, so unfortunately it is too soon to quote data, but later this year Shell hopes to have this information available.

Information provided by Lester Desmond, Coaching and Mentoring Consultant

Surrey and Sussex Strategic Health Authority: Leadership coaching to aid service improvement initiatives

In March 2005, Surrey and Sussex Strategic Health Authority launched an innovative scheme, Leadership for Service Improvement (LSI), for senior leaders within the NHS in Surrey and Sussex. The LSI scheme forms part of wider efforts to support the modernisation agenda in the NHS that aim to make services more accessible and efficient for patients. There is a large body of research that indicates a causal link between the quality of leadership and management skills and the quality of the patient experience. As a result of this evidence, the NHS has been investing in improving management and leadership skills throughout the organisation. The LSI scheme is just one example of this.

The design and launch

The scheme was launched in March 2005 by the Chief Executive of the Health Authority. The LSI scheme is designed to support service improvements within the 32 NHS Trusts in Surrey and Sussex, while also furthering the Health Authority's aim to enhance existing management and leadership development practices. The LSI is specifically not a development programme. Instead, it is a resource that is designed to support participating individuals with the delivery of a specific service improvement project. It links development to tangible action and, hopefully, results.

Each of the 32 NHS Trusts was asked to nominate up to three individuals (level 3 and 4 managers) to participate in the scheme. The chief executives of the Trusts were asked to participate in the nomination process to gain their support and commitment to the scheme. As a result, 90 participants (service improvement leads), including senior managers, chief executives and senior clinical staff, are taking part in the programme. Each participant chooses an improvement objective in line with his or her organisation's goals. 'It's all about improving the patient experience and improving access,' head of Leadership and Organisation Development Jonathan Harding said. 'We're not forcing what the project should be – it's important that participants are allowed to make a choice.'

Details of the scheme

The LSI scheme consists of a selection of different development resources:
- an online self-assessment tool that allows participants to reflect on their current practice. It also helps managers identify what skills they need to improve to deliver the project
- a development centre, provided by external consultants to assess participants' leadership style, capability and influence, as well as their service improvement capabilities
- a performance coach, selected and nominated by the service improvement lead, to offer formal support inputs and skills development, action learning sets and telephone support
- facilitated action learning sets of six to eight people, where service improvement leads peer review to look at progress, challenge practice and support individuals with the delivery of the service improvement project
- master classes to help managers learn from those who have led service improvement elsewhere, both inside and outside the NHS.

These developmental resources are focused on supporting participants to drive through real changes and improvements to services. Coaching forms a major element of the programme. Each individual chooses his or her own coach, usually a peer within the organisation to work with and coach him or her in developing and delivering the service improvement project.

Training the coaches

To prepare the coaches for their role, an external coaching consultancy was commissioned to run a series of performance workshops to develop the skills of the coaches. These two-day workshops are run for about 15 participants and cover introductory coach theory, models and techniques. During the workshop, coaches practise the skills and techniques by co-coaching each other. Following on from the workshop, coaches take part in two action learning set events over the next six months. These are again facilitated by the external coaching company and provide an opportunity for the coaches to talk about their experiences and any issues that have arisen and to explore how they should be tackled. The coaches can also contact the external coaching company for ongoing support during the lifespan of the projects.

Evaluation

Baseline data connected to each service improvement project was collected at the beginning of the projects for use in establishing the impact of the LSI scheme. Although those in the

Leadership and Organisational Development team know that it is going to be difficult to establish a correlation between the scheme and service improvements because of the numerous other variables that may affect results, they still believe it is possible to gain views about whether changes in performance can be attributed to the LSI scheme.

Feedback from participants about the coaching has been very positive. Some examples of comments include: 'Some of the most useful training I've had in the last few years – I will be able to apply it in many different parts of my work', 'Created confidence in my coaching ability,' and 'Gave me an opportunity to explore and test out my applied skills.' People who arrived feeling fairly cynical have left reporting that they have felt inspired. Participants have found out a lot about themselves through the development centres, and the coaching (along with other resources in the scheme) has helped them understand what they need to do to improve their leadership skills. To identify future improvements the organisers have asked the whole population of coaches and coachees for feedback on the scheme and what has been helpful/unhelpful.

The external coaching company is evaluating the impact of the coaching workshops by gathering information about how the coaches have helped participants deliver the service improvement projects. They are keen to develop a body of evidence about the impact of coaching and to try to make the link between coaches, coachees' performance and service improvements. They are also looking at the impact of the coaching workshops on improving coaches' skills and abilities by trying to gain expressive stories from them about the results they have seen from using their newly developed coaching skills.

A public relations company is helping the Health Authority to construct participants' stories about how the scheme has helped them develop both as leaders and in delivering service improvements. They aim to have around eight to ten stories to demonstrate the positive results of the scheme. The NHS leadership centre also intends to evaluate the coaching element of the scheme. All the evaluation results will be published and lessons learned will be incorporated into the ongoing design of management and leadership development practices.

Lessons learned about introducing coaching as part of the LSI scheme

For Surrey and Sussex Strategic Health Authority the challenge has been to identify not just what works in coaching and leadership development but also how to link this to addressing issues around improving services and financial performance. They do, however, believe that coaching is a cost-effective element of the programme. Jonathan Harding says:

> *Not only is coaching more effective than course-based learning, it's also cheaper. The authority will invest £150,000 in developing the coaching system, which will train 90 coaches and include 90 staff for them to coach.*

The LSI scheme has been running at the same time as a major review of the structure of Trusts in the Surrey and Sussex. As a result of this experience, Jonathan says:

> *I'd recommend trying to introduce coaching or leadership development programmes in a period of more stability.*

Another piece of advice Jonathan offers concerns setting expectations at the outset. He explains:

> *The board is looking for hard evidence of the impact of the scheme (at Kirkpatrick level 4) and this is difficult to establish. Having clear conversations upfront about what you're trying to do, the limits to evaluation activities and what data can realistically be gathered will help to position and manage people's expectations.*

Other challenges faced include people committing to the programme but then finding it difficult to attend or to spend sufficient time on it because of time pressures and other work priorities. This has resulted in an additional coaching workshop having to be organised to accommodate those who, at the last minute, could not attend the original workshops. Jonathan also advises:

> *Never underestimate the fact that development is often not valued or prioritised as much as other business activities ... When people attend the workshops they are very engaged, but afterwards they can struggle to create the space to think about how they manage and lead their people.*

One positive lesson has been the value of linking leadership development and coaching to pressing issues in the organisation. This has built support for the scheme and assisted its credibility. Jonathan Harding says:

> *Our approach has been developed and designed taking into account feedback from managers across the organisation. We've identified what will work locally in management and leadership development by taking into account some of the pressing issues within our management community – namely, the need to improve services and achieve financial balance.*

Information provided by Jonathan Harding, Head of Leadership and Organisation Development

Tate Museums: Gradually introducing coaching to the organisation

When the current learning and development (L&D) manager joined Tate 18 months ago, there was a selection of good core training programmes in place, but he quickly realised that in some instances staff would be sent on courses without a great deal of thought about how they could be supported in applying the learning back in the workplace.

As part of his new role, the L&D manager produced a learning and development strategy for Tate. The cornerstone of this strategy focused on creating a shift towards managers taking responsibility for facilitating the learning and development of their team members. Employees would also be encouraged to play a more active role in identifying their own development needs linked to their jobs and career aims. The L&D manager had experienced coaching in previous jobs and firmly believed that it would help to make this shift happen. As a result, Tate has pursued the development of managers' coaching skills using a solution-focused approach (looking towards the future by concentrating on solutions, not problems, and what is working rather than what is not).

The coaching programme for managers at Tate

The coaching programme was introduced at Tate in a gradual and low-key manner. The coaching programme was advertised on the company intranet and individuals were encouraged to take part if it was appropriate to their development needs. Take-up was slow at the beginning, particularly at senior levels, but the introduction of a new performance management system that emphasised a coaching style of management altered this. Managers' roles and responsibilities changed as part of this new system, and they realised that they needed support in developing new skills. So the coaching programme is becoming increasingly popular.

Each coaching programme has nine participants and is run as a two-day off-site programme facilitated by an external coach and the L&D manager. Taking part is via self-nomination signed off by the line manager. Participants have to fill in a learning needs questionnaire to make sure that it is the most appropriate form of development for them.

During the programme, a variety of topics are covered, including how coaching differs from management/counselling/mentoring, the role of a manager as coach, the GROW (Goal, Reality, Options, and Way forward) model, and coaching techniques such as quality listening, open questioning and providing constructive feedback. The solution-focused coaching approach is introduced as the framework for coaching at Tate. Quite quickly, the group start practising their skills in group exercises. Participants are asked to come to the programme with some issues that they would like to receive coaching on. Management issues tend to be the common themes, or challenges staff are experiencing at work. Participants work in threes – one person acts as coach, one person receives coaching, and the third acts as an observer. The observers are given a feedback checklist to assess the coach's coaching skills and are asked to use this to provide specific feedback. The observers are also expected to practise their own coaching skills when giving feedback to the 'coach'. Another exercise they use is 'three-minute coaching' to illustrate how coaching on a problem or issue can be quick and powerful.

The two-day programme is followed by a confidential one-to-one session with the external coach. This allows participants to discuss issues that arise during the programme, as well as giving them an opportunity to receive coaching themselves (and it allows them to see the coaching approach in action again). A further half-day session for the whole group is organised by the L&D manager. During this session, they share and celebrate individual successes with coaching, identify areas that individuals need to continue developing and work on some of these as a group. The concept of using coaching informally at work is also introduced to help individual and group problem-solving. To date, about 80 people have attended the programme over the course of one year.

Other coaching initiatives at Tate

Alongside the coaching programme for managers, other forms of coaching are used for development within Tate. The L&D manager regularly undertakes 'corridor coaching' with people who approach him for advice on problems they face, but because he has limited time, if the person requires regular or in-depth coaching because the issues are more deep-seated or long-term, he talks to him or her about seeing an external coach for a few sessions. Sometimes the L&D manager sees an opportunity where external coaching could help, but other times people

CASE STUDY continued

come to him and specifically ask to see a coach. When choosing coaches to work with Tate, the L&D manager considers the coach's personality, the coaching style and the business experience. He has a preference for coaches who are familiar with a solution-focused approach because this helps reinforce a common language in the organisation. Ideally, coaches will also be trained to use psychometric tools and techniques (eg Myers-Briggs) to help tease out issues and build the coaching relationship.

When matching individuals to coaches, the L&D manager considers the individual's needs and personality and tries to find a coach who he or she can work with, but who will also challenge him or her. The L&D manager suggests a coach to the individual and they meet each other without any commitment, to see if they think they can work together. The individual makes the final decision about which coach he or she works with, because he or she has to feel that the chemistry is right.

Coaching is not always the answer. Tate continues to use a range of training courses and development programmes and also offers mentoring to staff via the Arts in Business mentoring network. However, the L&D manager believes that coaching is a particularly strong form of development because it specifically targets an individual's needs and is a continuous and supportive developmental process. The difficulty of transfer of learning back to the workplace is removed. Overall, he believes that coaching is a less intimidating form of development. It builds confidence and is generally more productive for the individual.

What has been the impact of coaching? Has it been successful?

The L&D manager firmly believes that coaching has had an impact. Several managers have reported noticing improvements in the management style of their direct reports – eg celebrating successes with their teams as a way of improving motivation. And team members are also noticing differences in their managers, saying 'I've noticed the change in 'A' – he used to tell me what to do and now he asks me what we should do.'

Coaching is certainly becoming more common in the organisation, and one director commented recently that it had provided members of her team with a common language. More and more people understand the benefits coaching can bring and managers who have not attended the programme realise that there is a tranche of skills that they are lacking and need to develop.

However, the L&D Manager feels it is very difficult to quantify the difference because Tate has not yet undertaken a formal evaluation, although there are plenty of stories around of how the coaching approach has worked for teams and individuals. At the end of the coaching programme, the facilitators seek feedback about the design of the programme and ask how helpful participants have found it in developing their coaching skills. About a month later, participants are also given a level 2 evaluation questionnaire to assess what they have learned and applied from the programme. Participants' feedback was used recently for a flyer for the intranet, quoting positive comments from people who have been on the course.

Senior management buy-in

Four of Tate's directors have attended the coaching programme. As the programme is starting to have an impact and, as results are seen, other directors are becoming more interested.

At the end of last year, the L&D manager suggested coaching techniques to get people talking and discussing issues and ideas throughout a strategy/planning day for the directors and department heads at Tate. As a result, the Head of Policy and Planning said that the quality of submissions was markedly improved. He feels this is a tangible piece of evidence demonstrating how coaching techniques can be used to improve the productivity of day-to-day activities, and hopes that he can build buy-in for coaching at senior levels by demonstrating how coaching can be used with positive effects.

Lessons learned about use of coaching at Tate

Some people were leaving the programme thinking 'What next?' and had no clear view of how to continue using coaching in practice. The L&D manager realises that it is important for people to understand that coaching can be used in a variety of informal and formal situations in the workplace, and that managers are supported in using their coaching skills back at work.

The L&D Manager feels that senior team buy-in is ultimately essential to the successful embedding of coaching within an organisation and he has been working hard with directors to help them understand the link between coaching and performance and hence the value to the organisation longer-term. At first a gradual approach to the introduction of coaching seemed appropriate, focusing on regularly reporting results and progress with coaching to the senior team. As time goes on he hopes that word will spread and they will actually see the changes in people themselves.

A few people have left Tate after receiving coaching. It seems to have helped these individuals focus on what was really important to them and how their careers should develop. Tate does not view this negatively – if people leave on a positive note feeling that the organisation has helped them to work out their next career steps, they will talk positively about their time there. The L&D manager feels that coaching provides an important opportunity for line managers to have honest discussions with employees about their careers and means that Tate is acting as a responsible employer.

The future of coaching at Tate

Tate wishes to continue building coaching capability within the organisation, by creating a network of coaches (HR advisers and some high-potential managers trained as internal coaches) alongside continuing to develop managers' coaching skills. Other plans include encouraging support networks to buddy up existing coaches with managers attending the coaching programme. It is hoped that this will ensure the transfer of learning back to the workplace and will provide them with sources of support and advice.

The Tate's view is that it is essential to join up initiatives in the organisation so that people can see how they all fit together. In the future, links between coaching and the managers' objectives (via the performance management system) will be made more explicit, as well as ensuring that coaching activities are fully aligned with Tate's strategic goals. Aligning coaching in this way will ensure that it is not seen as an isolated initiative unrelated to the organisation's goals, and will help to build its credibility.

Information provided by Colin Coombs, Learning and Development Manager

Developing a coaching culture at The Children's Society

The Children's Society is a national charity in England, employing approximately 800 employees. It aims to support disadvantaged children and young people, including those who are disabled, refugees, at risk on the streets, or in trouble with the law

The Children's Society increasingly has to deal with the dynamics of a rapidly changing world, and as a result has recognised a need to strengthen local accountability and develop managers who are capable of growing the business. To enable these goals to be met, a new leadership style and culture is being developed to move away from a command-and-control leadership style and towards a model of collective leadership. The charity believes coaching can help change and embed a new culture within the organisation by empowering people at the grassroots to take responsibility and develop accountability.

The Children's Society has no formal strategy for its coaching activities, but coaching does form part of its emerging approach to management development. The Society's management team aspires to develop a coaching culture, and a series of initiatives has been undertaken to introduce coaching to the organisation:

- six-month coaching contracts for senior managers with external coaches
- a series of coaching skills workshops for managers to build up internal coaching capability
- formal, external training for some HR professionals to become internal coaches
- coaching by internal and external coaches to support key individuals taking part in a development programme
- workshops on 'performance and development coaching' for middle and senior managers to develop their coaching approach and style
- plans to introduce action-learning-style peer-coaching groups, which will encourage mutual support and progress for people in dealing with 'live' issues.

To date, the coaching activities have been received well, but the learning and development manager feels that demonstrating tangible results will be critical to their ongoing success.

Interestingly, one of the main barriers to coaching is understood to be the dominant 'training culture', in which employees assume they must attend a training course to be able to do something. Instead, the Children's Society sees itself on a journey towards a model of work-based self-managed learning, its employees being offered a wider variety of ways to learn.

The Children's Society's plans for developing an internal and external coaching network all sit within its aspirations for changing the leadership style/culture and meeting its business goals. Developing a coaching culture is understood to be an important element in achieving its organisational strategy.

Information provided by Michael White, Learning and Development Manager (Central Region)

United Utilities: Developing a network of internal executive coaches to support culture change

Four years ago, a large culture change programme began at United Utilities (UU) as a result of the new Chief Executive's belief that the company needed to develop more of a 'can do' cul ture where people were less risk-averse. So a culture change programme, called U Can, was introduced, in which all employees participated over a 12–18-month period. The programme involved a two-day workshop focused on developing interpersonal skills and helping people to work together more effectively in the business.

Coaching at United Utilities developed as a direct result of the U Can programme. Coaching skills were identified as being critical to sustaining the culture change and to improving people development skills in the business. Traditionally, UU used external executive coaches to deliver coaching in the organisation, but given the size of the coaching population (the company wants to make coaching available to all managers), this was going to be an approach that would be expensive and difficult to manage. So instead, they decided to train internal executive coaches to deliver the coaching services within UU.

To date, 63 people are active as executive coaches – these have included managers, directors and HR professionals. Selection of coaches for the programme was done by publicising plans to train a body of internal executive coaches and asking for volunteers to apply. The volunteers attended a one-day development centre where their coaching skills and potential, as well as their commitment and interest in coaching, were assessed. Those with the greatest levels of skill and commitment were chosen to go forward for the coaching programme.

Internal executive coach training

United Utilities work with an external coaching company to deliver the coach training. When selecting the coaching provider, they assessed the extent to which the companies could support them on a number of business objectives associated with the culture change programme. These included:
- bringing the culture change values to life
- supporting UU in developing a coaching culture
- developing a high-performance organisation
- using coaching to support lasting behaviour change.

The coach-training programme at UU lasts for about nine months and involves a series of input modules. Before the course, each participant has to identify a coaching 'guinea pig' who they can practise their new coaching skills on – they are called their 'pet clients' and are generally a colleague, rather than somebody in their direct team. The programme starts with a two-day course delivered by an internal trainer at UU and an external consultant. It comprises a variety of input sessions on topics such as models of coaching, principles of coaching, listening skills, and how to support behaviour change. Alongside these sessions, participants work in threes to practise the coaching skills and techniques they have been discussing.

Following the two-day course, participants have a period of six to eight weeks in which to practise their coaching skills with their pet client. After this, they have three separate input days where they review their learning, are introduced to new coaching models, techniques and ideas, and practise their skills. There is also an opportunity for them to raise issues they have been facing and to receive some coaching and advice on how to manage them. Each input day is separated by about six weeks, during which the coaches practise their new skills. The programme is designed to constantly increase the skills levels of coaches over the course of several months while allowing them to continually practise their skills. A critical part of the design of the programme is its capacity to react to the needs of coaches in a spontaneous way. In each follow-up day, participants take part in an interactive session to discuss and review their development over the last few weeks (what their strengths are, what issues they have faced, etc). The programme generally takes nine months to complete and at the end the participants are accredited as an internal coach within the business.

After the programme, the external coaching company runs external supervision days for the internal coaches so that they can share learning and receive independent advice and coaching on difficult situations they experience. It is a minimum requirement to attend two supervision days every six months. United Utilities are now looking at how to support ongoing continuing professional development and supervision for their coaches in the long term, preferably involving a mixture of internal and external resource. This would mean that trends and common themes arising during coaching could be monitored, but also allay concerns about confidentiality.

Matching coaches and coachees

Before internal coaches participate in the training, they are required to discuss with their manager the time commitment required. If managers are not supportive, the individuals are not taken on the course. Each coach has a maximum of two or three clients at one time. Given that the average coaching relationship lasts for five or six sessions, with people meeting about once every six to eight weeks, the majority of coaches have not reported finding it too much of a burden. However, a few have reported finding it hard to make time for their coaching relationships because of the other demands on their time.

Matching of coaches and coachees has been an evolving process. Initially, the matching approach that United Utilities adopted was considered too cumbersome and time-consuming for the coachees. Coaches produced a personal profile of information about their background and their approach to coaching. When individuals requested coaching, they were given a few coach profiles and were asked to look through them and call them for an initial discussion. They were then expected to choose which coach they wanted to work with.

This process had only limited success because it required a great deal of administrative time and effort and the clients reported feeling uncomfortable assessing the prospective coaches in this manner. Following this feedback, they have reverted to a simpler method by which clients are matched to coaches by a central resource team, based on the needs of the coachees. It is, however, made clear to the client that if the match doesn't work, he or she can ask to see another coach. The matching process has become much more organic as time has gone by. Coaches have started to take on clients themselves or pass people through the coach network to other coaches with more appropriate skills or background. The simplified process now seems to work well. The eventual aim is to have available an online client coach matching arrangement through the company's intranet.

Evaluating the impact of coaching

United Utilities have made a huge investment in coaching and are still working to find workable ways to quantify the results. There is, however, plenty of anecdotal evidence about the positive impact of coaching. One of the ways the company evaluates the success of the coaching programme is to ask coaches who have completed the training a series of questions via a survey. Questions include:

- What difference has coaching made to you?
- Can you give me an example of what you have done differently as a result of the coaching programme?
- What feedback have you had from colleagues about how you have changed?
- How valuable has the coaching programme been to you?
- How valuable is coaching to the business?
- What else would you like to get out of the coaching programme?
- Can you rate your skill sets/competencies/confidence?

Similarly, the clients of the coaches are asked a similar series of questions to assess the impact of the internal executive coaching on their performance and behaviour.

But despite all the positive feedback, UU want to be able to measure the business benefit of coaching. As Roger Williams states:

> *While we have had a lot of good feedback, how do you turn that into cash?*

Unexpected spin-offs from coaching

UU has noticed some successful spin-offs from the coaching programme and from having the internal coaching resource within the business. They have realised they can use this internal resource for wider initiatives and have used the internal coaches to help with the ongoing implementation of the change programmes. The internal coaches are helping to lead development programmes to train managers as coaches and are also contributing to initiatives focusing on developing high-performing teams. UU has also provided further training for some of the internal executive coaches to give them more in-depth group facilitation skills – these individuals are now used as team coaches. These coaches also support the senior management team by facilitating meetings. The flexibility and transferability of coaching skills for use in other initiatives in the organisation is considered to be an extremely helpful and unexpected outcome of the coaching programme.

Other types of coaching at UU

External executive coaches are still used across UU for senior executives and in other instances when it is deemed appropriate. It is not seen as an either/or decision. Internal coaches are still relatively inexperienced, compared to many external coaches. And the business is also conscious that internal coaches are taking on the coaching part of their role on top of their day jobs, so external coaches can help to relieve the demands on their time. Another issue that has arisen is people thinking that coaching should be part of the role of line managers.

CASE STUDY continued

Using internal coaches is seen to complement coaching by managers and is believed to help particularly when the coach can bring specialist skills to the issues.

Learning lessons and moving forward

UU wants to get to a position where coaching is seen as a critical skill within the business. A few short taster sessions have been run at leadership conferences to introduce coaching to that group. Demand for these taster sessions is continuing, and the feedback has been positive. The company is now organising them as one-off breakfast or lunchtime sessions for the people who were unable to attend during the conferences.

The working relationship with the external coaching firm has worked extremely well and is felt to be a real partnership. This is considered to be extremely important to the success of the programme. Using and talking about coaching in the context of other initiatives (management, leadership, high-potential teams) has been helpful in preventing it from being seen as something separate from HR and the business.

Information provided by Roger Williams, Project Manager

References

ALEXANDER, G. (2001) Chapter 12, in West L. and Milan M. (eds) *The Reflecting Glass: Professional coaching for leadership development*, Basingstoke, Palgrave Macmillan; pp145–56.

AQUILINA, E. (2005) An internal model of coaching – a single-site case study, *International Journal of Mentoring and Coaching*, Vol.3, No.1; pp 92–111; or www.emccouncil.org.

ARGYRIS, C. (1994) *On Organisational Learning*. Oxford, Blackwell.

ASSAY, T. P. and LAMBERT, M. J. (1999) The empirical case for the common factors in therapy: quantitative findings, referenced in Sills (2003) Towards the coaching relationship, *Training Magazine*, February.

BALDWIN, T. and FORD, J. (1988) Transfer of training: a review and directions for future research, *Personnel Psychology*, 41, 63–105.

BEAM PINES INC. (2005) Trends in external and internal coaching, internal report, New York.

BEE, F. and BEE, R. (2003) *Learning Needs Analysis and Evaluation*, 2nd edition, London, CIPD.

BELENKY, M., CLINCHY, B. M., GOLDBERGER, N. R. and TARULE, J. M. (1986) *Women's Ways of Knowing*, New York, Basic Books.

BERGLAS, S. (2002) The very real dangers of executive coaching, *Harvard Business Review*, June.

BIGELOW, B. (1938) Building an effective training program for field salesmen, *Personnel*, 14: 142–50.

BRAMLEY, P. (2004) *Evaluating Training*, 2nd edition, London, CIPD.

BURDETT, J. (1998) Forty things every manager should know about coaching, *Journal of Management Development*, 17 (2); 142–52.

CAPLAN, J. (2003) *Coaching for the Future: How smart companies use coaching and mentoring*, London, CIPD.

CARTER, A. (2001) *Executive Coaching: Inspiring performance at work*, Report 379, Brighton, Institute for Employment Studies.

CASSIDY, S. (2004) Learning styles: an overview of theories, models and measures, *Educational Psychology*, Vol.24, No.4, August; 419–44.

CAVANAGH and GRANT, A. M. (2006) Coaching psychology and the scientist-practitioner model in LANE and CORRIE (2006).

CLARKE, G. (2000) Case study, in LANE (2000), London, CIPD.

CLARKE, M., BAILEY, C. and BRISTOW, M. (2003) *Innovations in NHS Senior Leader Development*, Cranfield University School of Management.

CIPD (2004) *Training and development 2004*, Survey Report, London, CIPD [Download from: www.cipd.co.uk/surveys]

CIPD (2005) *Training and development 2005*, Survey Report, London, CIPD. [Download from: www.cipd.co.uk/surveys]

CIPD (2005a) *Managing external coaches: practical tips for HR. [online]*. Tool. London, CIPD.

[CIPD members only can download, at: http://www.cipd.co.uk/subjects/lrnanddev/coachmntor/_manextcoach.htm?IsSrchRes=1]

CIPD (2006) *Learning and development 2006*, Survey Report, London, CIPD. [Download from: www.cipd.co.uk/surveys]

COLONE, C. (2005) Calculating the Return on the Investment in Executive Coaching for a Corporate Staff Function in a Large Global Financial Services Company, MA project. PDF/Middlesex University.

CLUTTERBUCK, D. and MEGGINSON, D. (2005) *Making Coaching Work: Creating a coaching culture*, London, CIPD.

DAWDY, G. N. (2004) Executive coaching: a comparative design exploring the perceived effectiveness of coaching and methods, in *School of Education*, Capella University.

DE HAAN, E. and BURGER, Y. (2005) *Coaching with Colleagues*, Basingstoke, Palgrave Macmillan.

DINGMAN, M. E. (2004) The effects of executive coaching on job-related attitudes, in *School of Leadership Development*, Regent University; p.140.

DOWNEY, M. (1999) *Effective Coaching*, London, Orion Business.

EATON, J. and BROWN, D. (2002) Coaching for a Change with Vodafone, *Career Development International*, 7 (5); 284–7.

ELLINGER, A. and BOSTROM, R. (1998) Managerial coaching behaviours in learning organisations, *Journal of Management Development*, 18 (9).

Engineers Employers Federation (EEF) and CIPD (2004) *Maximising Employee Potential And Business Performance: the role of high-performance working*, London, CIPD.

FELDMAN , D. C. (2005) Executive coaching: a review and agenda for future research, *Journal of Management*, 31; 829–48.

FRISCH, M. H. (2001) The emerging role of the internal coach, *Consulting Psychology Journal: Practice and Research*, 53 (4); 240–50.

GEBER, B. (1992) From manager into coach, *Training*, 29 (3); 25–31.

GRAHAM, S., WEDMAN, J. F. and GARVIN-KESTER, B. (1993) Manager coaching skills: development and application, *Performance Improvement Quarterly*, 6 (1); 2–13.

GRANT, A. M. (2004) Keeping up with the cheese! Research as a foundation for professional coaching of the future. Proceedings of the First ICF Coaching Research Symposium, November 12, 2003. Mooresville, International Coach Federation.

GRANT, A. M. and ZACKON, R. (2004) Executive, workplace and life coaching: Findings from a large-scale survey of the International Coach Federation, *International Journal of Evidence-Based Coaching and Mentoring*, 2 (2); 1–15.

GRECO, J. (2001) Hey, coach! *Journal of Business Strategy*, March/April.

HALL, D. T., OTAZO, K. L. and HOLLENBECK, G. P. (1999) Behind closed doors: what really happens in executive coaching, *Organizational Dynamics*, 28; 39–53.

HARDINGHAM, A. (2004) *The Coach's Coach: Personal development for personal developers*, London, CIPD.

HAY, J. (1995) *Transformational Mentoring*, London, Sherwood Publishing.

HERNEZ-BROOME, G. (2004) Impact of coaching following a leadership development program: coaching is key to continued development, in Second ICF Coaching Research Symposium, Quebec City, Quebec, Canada, International Coach Federation.

HONEY, P. and MUMFORD, A. (1992) *The Manual of Learning Styles*, Maidenhead, Peter Honey Publications.

HORNER, C. (2002) Executive coaching: the leadership development tool of the future? MBA, dissertation, Imperial College of Science, Technology and Medicine.

JARVIS, J. (2004) *Coaching and Buying Coaching Services. A guide*, London, CIPD. [Download from: www.cipd.co.uk/guides]

KAMPA, S. and WHITE, R. P. (2002) The effectiveness of executive coaching: what we know and what we still need to know, in LOWMAN, R. L. (ed.) (2002) *The California School of Organizational Studies: Handbook of organizational consulting psychology: A comprehensive guide to theory, skills, and techniques*, San Francisco, CA, USA, Jossey Bass.

KEEP, E. and WESTWOOD, A. (2003) *Can the UK Learn to Manage?*, London, The Work Foundation.

KENTON, B. and MOODY, D. (2001) *What Makes Coaching a Success?*, Roffey Park.

KIDD, S. (2000) Case study, in LANE (2000) London, CIPD.

KILBURG, R. (1996) Towards a conceptual understanding and definition of executive coaching, *Consulting Psychology Journal*, 48 (2); 134–44.

KILBURG, R. (1997) Coaching and executive character: core problems and basic approaches, *Consulting Psychology Journal: Practice and Research*, 49 (4); 281–99.

KILBURG, R. (2001) Facilitating intervention adherence in executive coaching: a model and methods, *Consulting Psychology Journal: Practice and Research*, Vol.53, No.4; 203–13.

KIRKPATRICK, D. L. (1967) Evaluation of training, in CRAIG, R. L. and BITTEL, L. R. (eds) *Training and Evaluation Handbook*, New York, McGraw-Hill.

KOLB, D. A. (1999) *The Kolb Learning Styles Inventory, Version 3*, Boston, Hay Group.

KUBICEK, M. (2002) Is coaching being abused?, *Training Magazine*, May; 12–14.

LANDALE, A. (2004) Sales training bags the results for Cleanaway, *Industrial and Commercial Training*, 36; 216–8 (213).

LANE, D. (1994) *Human resource management in small and medium businesses*, London, CIPD.

LANE, D., PURI, A., CLEVERLY, P., WYLIE, R. and RAJAN, A. (2000) *Employability: Bridging the gap between rhetoric and reality* [Second report: employees' perspective], London, Professional Development Foundation/CIPD.

LANE, D. and CORRIE, S. (2006) *The modern Scientist-Practitioner: a guide to practice in psychology*, London, Routledge.

LASKE, O. E. (2004) Can evidence-based coaching increase ROI?, *International Journal of Evidence-Based Coaching and Mentoring*, 2 (2); 41–53.

LOCKE, E. A. and LATHAM, G. P. (2002) Building a practically useful theory of goal-setting and task motivation. A 35-year odyssey, *American Psychologist*, 57 (9); 705–17.

LUDEMAN, K. and ERLANDSON, E. (2004) Coaching the alpha male, *Harvard Business Review*, 82 (5); 58.

LUTHANS, F. and PETERSON, S. J. (2003) 360-degree feedback with systematic coaching: empirical analysis suggests a winning combination, *Human Resource Management*, 42 (3); 243–56.

McGOVERN, J., LINDEMANN, M., VEGARA, M., MURPHY, S., BARKER, L. and WARRENFELTZ, W. (2001) Maximising the impact of executive coaching: behaviour change, organisational outcomes and return on investment, *Manchester Review*, Vol.6, No.1; 3–11.

MASCIARELLI, J. (1999) Less lonely at the top, *Management Review*, April.

MAYO, A. (2004) *Creating a learning and development strategy*, London, CIPD.

OLIVERO, G., BANE, K. and KOPELMAN, R. E. (1997) Executive coaching as a transfer of training tool: effects on productivity in a public agency, *Public Personnel Management*, 26 (4); 461–9.

PALMER, G. (2003) Developing performance. Report Commissioned by Cable & Wireless Plc, Aquarius Executive Coaching Ltd, July 2004.

PARSLOE, E. (1995) *Coaching, Mentoring and Assessing: A practical guide to developing competence*, London, Kogan Page.

PARSLOE, E. (1999) *The Manager as Coach and Mentor*, London, CIPD.

PHILIPS (*http://www.roiinstitute.net/websites/ROIInstitute/ROIInstitute/*). [Accessed13th March 2005]

PIRIE, P. (2004) How do companies evaluate their executive coaches, in *Organisational Psychology*, London, Birbeck College; 78.

PURCELL, J., KINNIE, N., HUTCHINSON, S. and SWART, J. (2003) *Understanding the People and Performance Link: Unlocking the black box*, London, CIPD.

REYNOLDS, J. (2004) *Helping People Learn*, London, CIPD.

REYNOLDS, J., CALEY, L. and MASON, R. (2002) *How Do People Learn?*, London, CIPD.

RICH, G. A. (1998) Selling and sales management in action: the constructs of sales coaching: supervisory feedback, role modelling and trust, *Journal of Personal Selling and Sales Management*, 18 (1); 53 –63.

SANGHERA, S. (2004) I went in for coaching, but couldn't stay the course, *Financial Times*, Monday July 5, London edition; 8.

SAPORITO, T. J. (1996) Business-linked executive development: coaching senior executives, *Consulting Psychology Journal: Practice and Research*, 48 (2); 96–103.

SHERMAN, S. and FREAS, A. (2004) The wild west of executive coaching, *Harvard Business Review*, 82, 82.

SMITHER, J. W., LONDON, M., FLAUTT, R., VARGAS, Y. and KUCINE, I. (2003) Can working with an executive coach improve multisource feedback ratings over time? A quasi-experimental field study, *Personnel Psychology*, 56 (1); 23.

SPARROW, J. and ARNOTT, J. (2004) *The Coaching Study 2004*, University of Central England.

STARR, J. (2003) *The Coaching Manual*, London, Pearson Education.

STERMAN, J. D. (2002) All models are wrong: reflections on becoming a systems scientist, *System Dynamics Review*, 18(4); 501–31

THACH, E. C. (2002) The impact of executive coaching and 360 feedback on leadership effectiveness, *Leadership and Organization Development Journal*, 23 (4); 205–14(10).

TOBIAS, L. L. (1996) Coaching executives, *Consulting Psychology Journal: Practice and Research*, 48 (2); 87–95.

VENTRONE, R. (2005) Trends in external and internal coaching. Internal Report, New York, BeamPines Inc.

VINNICOMBE, S. and SINGH, V. (2003) Women-only management training: an essential part of women's leadership development, *Journal of Change Management*, 3 (4); 294–306.

WABC (forthcoming) go to: www.wabccoaches.com

WAGEMAN, R. (2001) How leaders foster self-managing team effectiveness: Design choices versus hands-on coaching, *Organisation Science*, 12 (5); 559–77.

WALES, S. (2003) Why coaching?, *Journal of Change Management*, Vol.3, No.3, February; 275–82 .

WASYLYSHYN, K. M. (2003) Executive coaching: an outcome study, *Consulting Psychology Journal: Practice and Research*, 55 (2); 94–106.

WEST, L. and MILAN, M. (2001) *The Reflecting Glass: Professional coaching for leadership development*, Palgrave.

WHITMORE, J. (1996) *Coaching for Performance*. 2nd edition, London, Nicholas Brearley.

WOOLNOUGH, H., DAVIDSON, M. and FIELDEN, S. (2004) Challenging perceptions: leadership, career development and mentoring pilot programme for female mental health nurses in NHS Trusts. Final Report, N.M.A.L. Centre, Editor.

THE WORK FOUNDATION (2003) Coaching and Mentoring, *Managing Best Practice*, October, Report 111.

Index

Membership has its rewards

Join us online today as an Affiliate member and get immediate access to our member services. As a member you'll also be entitled to special discounts on our range of courses, conferences, books and training resources.

To find out more, visit www.cipd.co.uk/affiliate or call us on 020 8612 6208.

Also from CIPD Publishing . . .

Making Coaching Work:
Creating a coaching culture

David Clutterbuck and David Megginson

Coaching can help you improve your employee retention levels, succession planning and organisational creativity. But it only works in a culture that is supportive: where managers, coaches and coachees all trust each other and are working together.

Even the best-managed coaching programme, with the very best coaches, will fail if the real world where the coaching takes place doesn't support it.

Spending money on coaching without first ensuring that the groundwork has been done is a fast-track to failure. Make sure your training and development budget delivers more by creating a coaching culture.

Order your copy now online at www.cipd.co.uk/bookstore or call us on 0870 800 3366

David Clutterbuck is one of Europe's most prolific and well-known management writers and thinkers, with over 40 books to his name, including *Managing Work–Life Balance* and *Learning Alliances*. His *Everyone Needs a Mentor* is now the classic book on the subject, and he is recognised as the UK's leading expert on mentoring. He is co-founder of the European Mentoring and Coaching Council, and is Visiting Professor at Sheffield Hallam University.

David Megginson is Professor of HRD at Sheffield Hallam University and a co-founder of the European Mentoring and Coaching Council. He is on both the Membership and Education Committees of the CIPD and the CPD Working Group and has written a number of books with the CIPD.

Published 2005	1 84398 074 6	Paperback	224 Pages

The Chartered Institute of Personnel and Development is the leading publisher of books and reports for personnel and training professionals, students and all those concerned with the effective management and development of people at work.

The Coach's Coach

Personal development for personal developers

Alison Hardingham
with Mike Brearley, Adrian Moorhouse and Brendan Venter

Being a coach is a tricky job, so whether you are an experienced coach or just starting out; a specialist consultant or a coaching manager, this book will help you become better and enjoy coaching more. It will help you to help the people you are coaching improve their performance – which, after all, is why you became a coach in the first place.

Alison Hardingham is a successful business coach and offers advice, techniques and examples drawn from experience of coaching people in all kinds of organisations and with the contributions of three phenomenally successful sports people: Mike Brearley, Adrian Moorhouse and Brendan Venter, you will be on track to being 'coach of the year'.

Mike Brearly is one of England's best known and most successful cricket captain; **Adrian Moorhouse** broke the world record in breast stroke five times and won an Olympic gold medal; and **Brendan Venter** was a member of the Springboks, South African Rugby Team, and subsequently played and coached at London Irish.

Order your copy now by visiting us online at www.cipd.co.uk/bookstore or call us on 0870 800 3366

Alison Hardingham is a business psychologist with more than twenty years' experience of coaching individuals and teams. She is a successful author and conference speaker.

2004	1 84398 075 4	Paperback	216 pages

The Chartered Institute of Personnel and Development is the leading publisher of books and reports for personnel and training professionals, students, and for all those concerned with the effective management and development of people at work.

Also from CIPD Publishing . . .

Everyone Needs a Mentor:

Fostering talent in your organisation

4th Edition

David Clutterbuck

Mentoring is the most cost-efficient and sustainable method of fostering and developing talent within your organisation.

Mentoring can be used to:
- stretch talented employees to perform even better by exposure to high performing colleagues;
- ensure that experience is passed and kept within your organisation; and
- power your diversity programme by supporting employees from groups that are under-represented in your organisation by having them talk with others who have overcome similar barriers.

It is the ultimate win-win business tool. The employee gets a helping hand to fast-track their career and the mentor gets the satisfaction of helping others develop, while the organisation gains from improved performance and employee retention.

This text explains what mentoring is and how it differs from coaching. It shows you how to make the business case for mentoring and then how to set up, run and maintain your own mentoring programme – everything from selecting and matching mentors and mentees to measuring the results.

Order your copy now online at www.cipd.co.uk/bookstore or call us on 0870 800 3366

David Clutterbuck is one of Europe's most prolific and well-known management writers and thinkers. He has written more than 40 books, including *Managing Work–Life Balance* and *Learning Alliances*. *Everyone Needs a Mentor* is now the classic book on the subject and he is recognised as the UK's leading expert on mentoring and co-founder of the European Mentoring and Coaching Council. He is Visiting Professor at Sheffield Hallam University.

| Published 2004 | 1 84398 054 1 | Paperback | 200 pages |

The Chartered Institute of Personnel and Development is the leading publisher of books and reports for personnel and training professionals, students and all those concerned with the effective management and development of people at work.

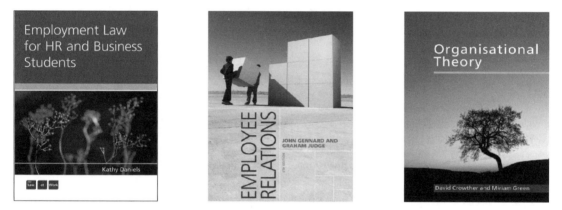